PRAISE FROM READERS OF *TALES OF A FEMALE NOMAD*

"I wonder if you realize how important your book is to women all over the world. Never before in history have women been able to travel the world without the safety of either a group or an escort. You have taught us that it can be done." —*Carol Smoots, 48, Oakton, Virginia*

"In an age when we hear so much about why we should mistrust each other and expect the worst from strangers, it was refreshing to hear about the adventures of someone who refuses to lose faith in the basic humanity that is common to us all....I hope your book and your life inspire more of us to trust and accept and learn about each other."
—*Katherine Almy, 37, Arcata, California*

"I think your book will inspire women all over the world to see their true selves, listen to their inner voices, and strive to fulfill their souls. I think it will help men to understand women better."
—*Karine Bakhoum Riffaud, 38, New York, New York*

"I'm hooked and you tipped the scale! At the age of 60 I'm ready to roll."
—*Ann Hoar Floyd, a very young 60, Edgartown, Massachusetts*

"What a wonderful gift you have given the world, women in particular....
Your book may top my list of all-time favorites."
—*Barbara K. Rothschild, 57, Columbia, Missouri*

"You are living my dream...Thanks for all the tips on how to do it. I have finally decided to quit 'waiting' and just go for it. I sent in my application to the Peace Corp yesterday." —*Pat Cegan, 58, Orlando, Florida*

"I'm 15...and I have to tell you that I loved your book....It made me want to go out and...meet people and learn why they do the things they do and why America isn't the only place in the world....You did what so many women dream of doing, but you didn't dream, you did it."
—*Rachel Brainerd, 15, Ann Arbor, Michigan*

"I don't know where to begin. I just inhaled your book. I could not read it enough." —*Sharon Blumberg, 43, Hammond, Indiana*

"Since my divorce, I've been incredibly lonely and somehow absolutely unable to strike out and begin building the new life I envisaged....*and then your book!* In an instant I remembered how wonderful and exciting life can be, how safe it is to open up to new people, to smile back, to initiate conversations....I would so love to give you a big hug, to feed you my favourite 'wild chicken' dish, and talk through the night over many pots of tea."

—*Jenny Chadwick, Narrabundah, ACT, Australia*

"It is very inspiring to read that life is still full of changes and surprises when you're at an age when that is not supposed to happen anymore."

—*Johanna "Joke" Sperling, 42, Chevy Chase, Maryland*

"Your book came to me at a crucial time in my life. After four years of trying to be a traditional family doctor, I have decided to try to find work in an African country to help in whatever way I can. I know that the experience of living and working with another culture is one that will nourish my own soul's development, as is so well illustrated by your book. Thank you for inspiring me."

—*Yamini Goswami, 36, Monsey, New York*

"Recently, I've felt a stirring in my soul, a restlessness, and a thirst for new experiences. Your book called out to me. I had to buy it. In it were all the things I've dreamed of."

—*Anupama Chathampally, 32, City of Lake Worth, Florida*

"I have just finished reading your book, and I feel like I have found a new friend....Reading it interfered with my trial preparation (lawyer) and my term paper (master's degree) but that is as it should be....I am sending your book to my mother. There is no higher compliment."

—*Mary J. Maudsley, 57, Linwood, New Jersey*

"I was just diagnosed with breast cancer....You have no idea how much reading your book has helped me. Thank you for taking me far away and helping me cope with my situation." —*Patricia Arvin, 55, Placerville, California*

"I know that everyone that e-mails you must say the same thing, and I hate to be ubiquitous, but, hey, you're inspiring....Thank you for following your heart and spreading your words of trust and love. You have helped change this world for the better."

—*Elijah Shannon Malloy, 33, New York, New York*

TALES OF A
FEMALE NOMAD

RITA GOLDEN GELMAN

Living at Large in the World

THREE RIVERS PRESS
NEW YORK

For Jan, Mitch, and Melissa, with love.

And in loving memory of

my parents, Frances and Albert Golden.

Copyright © 2001 by Rita Golden Gelman

Published by Three Rivers Press, New York, New York.

Member of the Crown Publishing Group, a division of Random House, Inc.

www.randomhouse.com

THREE RIVERS PRESS and the Tugboat design are registered trademarks of
Random House, Inc.

Originally published in hardcover by Crown Publishers in 2001

Printed in the United States of America

Design by Lauren Dong

Library of Congress Cataloging-in-Publication Data
Gelman, Rita Golden.
Tales of a female nomad : living at large in the world / Rita Golden Gelman.—1st ed.
1. Gelman, Rita Golden—Journeys.   2. Voyages and travels.   I. Title.
G465.G443   2001
910.4—dc21   00-064529

ISBN 0-609-80954-7

10 9 8 7

CONTENTS

Indonesia

United States

Indonesia

Canada/United States

New Zealand

Thailand

United States

PREFACE

I am a modern-day nomad. I have no permanent address, no possessions except the ones I carry, and I rarely know where I'll be six months from now. I move through the world without a plan, guided by instinct, connecting through trust, and constantly watching for serendipitous opportunities.

People are my passion. Unlike a traditional nomad, when I go somewhere, I settle in with the locals long enough to share the minutes of their days, to know the seasons of their lives, and to be trusted with their secrets. I have lived with people in thatched huts, slept in their gilded palaces, and worshipped with them at godly ceremonies and dens of black magic. I have also cooked with women on fires all over the world.

I've been living and loving my nomadic existence since the day in 1986 when, at the age of forty-eight, on the verge of a divorce, I looked around and thought: There has to be more than one way to do life.

There is.

Mexico

CHAPTER ONE

THE BEGINNING

1985.

I am living someone else's life. It's a good life, filled with elegant restaurants, interesting people, and events like the Academy Awards and the Grammies. My husband of twenty-four years and I dine with celebrities, we see the latest movies before the rest of the world, and we're invited to all the book parties in Los Angeles.

Because of his job as an editorial consultant to some top magazines, we've been able to create a life that is privileged and glamorous. But now that I'm there, I realize that I don't like feeling privileged and I'm uncomfortable with glamour. I am living in a designer world that has been designed for someone I no longer am.

I prefer Goodwill to Neiman Marcus, Hondas to Mercedes, and soup kitchens to charity banquets. My house is too big; my garden, too trim; my friends, too white and American.

I first realized something was missing about five years ago when a woman wearing a floor-length muumuu and sandals sat next to me on an airplane. She told me she was in the business of booking sailing tours for captains around the world and was returning from the Mediterranean, the Adriatic, and the Gulf of Mexico. As she was telling me about her trip, tears began streaming down my cheeks.

"I'm sorry," I said, embarrassed. "I don't know where that came from." I wiped my eyes.

But I did know. I was crying for my lost spirit. As the woman spoke, I remembered that once I'd dreamed of sailing around the world, of paddling down the Amazon, of sitting around a fire with tribal people and sharing their food and their lives. I had loved the person who had those dreams. She was daring and idealistic . . . and gone. My husband had no interest in boats or tribal cultures.

"If I were to take a sailing trip," I said to the woman, "there are three things that I would want: a salty old captain who has tales to tell and philosophy to spout, a crew that likes to sing, and a place that is rich in experiences. I hate lying around on beaches."

She didn't even have to think. "Go sail on the *Tigris* in the Galápagos Islands."

Three months later, I boarded the *Tigris* without my husband, toured the spectacular volcanic islands, interacted with sea lions and blue-footed boobies, snorkeled the tropical waters, and touched the magic of otherness. I was never the same again.

When I returned from the Galápagos, that long-dormant fire of adventure had been rekindled and the glamour of my life turned gray. The gourmet dinners, the exclusive press screenings, the concerts, the parties, and the evenings at the theater suddenly felt like empty substitutes for discovery, for learning, for penetrating the unknown.

I knew that I couldn't run around the world adventuring, not if I wanted to stay married, which I did. But after the Galápagos trip, I needed something more in my life. I came up with a compromise. I would go to graduate school in anthropology and get my adventure from books.

The timing was right. My two kids no longer needed a full-time mom. Mitch was in his freshman year at Berkeley, and Jan was about to graduate from high school.

I had a fairly successful career as a writer of children's books. I enjoyed the wild and imaginative leaps into fantasy and the visits to schools and the modest recognition, mostly among first- and second-grade teachers; but I happily put my work on hold and plunged into academics.

I spent the next four years at UCLA, reading ethnographies, studying with anthropologists who had lived in exotic cultures, watching films, listening to lectures. By 1985, I am finished with most of the course work for the Ph.D., and I'm ready to choose a place and a topic for my dissertation research. Although my husband puts up with the hours I have to study, I doubt he would join me or endorse the idea of my doing fieldwork for a year in some far corner of the developing world. So I plan to do my thesis among the urban tribes of Los Angeles.

Meanwhile, our marriage is floundering. Over the years, our divergent interests and our personality differences have pushed us deeper into opposite corners. I'm basically laid back and sometimes careless. I tend to excuse my own mistakes as well as other people's; and from time to time I find it necessary to adjust my ethics to the situation at hand. He is a perfectionist, reliable, honest, and prompt. He sets high standards for himself and has high expectations of others. More and more we find ourselves in minor skirmishes. The bell keeps ringing and we come out bickering.

Finally, after yet another squabble that escalates, I suggest that we take a break from each other for a couple of weeks. I need time alone, I tell him, to figure out what's wrong with the marriage and how we can fix it. When I come back, I say, I'd like us to try some marriage counseling. He agrees to a break and counseling but adds that two weeks is not enough. He suggests two months in which we are both free to see other people.

His response surprises and frightens me. Eight weeks of independence is very different from a two-week break to clear our heads. And I hadn't even thought about dating. I'm not sure I can be with another man after twenty-four years of marriage; I don't really want to. But I accept his suggestion. When he leaves the room, the tears roll down my cheeks. As in so many of our conversations these days, we are talking different languages, and I realize that once I introduced the idea of a break, I could not control his reaction.

If the break had been for two weeks, I probably would have checked into a hotel near Los Angeles. But two months is too long for a hotel. I decide to go to Mexico. It's a place I've always wanted to go and my husband hasn't.

By the time I leave, we both fear that this is more than "a break."

I walk weak-kneed down the steps of the plane into hot Mexico City. My eyes are red, my nose is stuffed, and I feel as though my head is filled with lead weights. I am more frightened than I have ever been. I've initiated something that has already taken off in a direction I never intended.

I slip my arms into my backpack and follow the signs out of the terminal. In spite of my heavy head, I warm to the musical sound of Spanish all around me. I've loved the language from the first day I entered Mrs. James's Spanish 1, as a sophomore in Bassick High School in Bridgeport, Connecticut.

When I step outside, I am greeted by five young men waving brochures. The hotel I decide on looks decent, the price is right, and I don't have to pay for a cab. I'll only be there for two nights anyway. In two days I begin a Spanish language course in Cuernavaca; the school has arranged for me to stay with a family. It's the only plan I've made for the two months.

It is seven-thirty at night when I check into the hotel, which gives me plenty of time to clean up and find a restaurant for dinner. As I salivate for Mexican food, I realize that I have never, in my forty-seven years, had dinner alone in a restaurant. When I was young, I had plenty of friends to share meals with. I married at twenty-three, and then I had a husband. I have never eaten out by myself . . . and I don't feel like beginning tonight.

I use the phone in my room to call for room service.

"Discúlpeme, Señora. No hay comida en el hotel." My high school Spanish registers the words. There's no food in the hotel.

When I think about going out, an advance video runs through my head: I am sitting at a table trying to look content. The restaurant is filled with smiling, chatting people. I am the only one alone. They are staring, pitying me, wondering where I'm from and why I have no companion.

I sit on the bed and think about having to choose a place, get there, eat the meal while pretending to be happy, and then return to the hotel. How do I pick a place? Do I take a cab or walk? Is the neighborhood safe?

I can't do it. I'd rather not eat.

So I shower, put on my nightshirt, and curl up with the guidebook. Tomorrow I will go to the market. I plot the route to the central market on buses, and then I turn out the light, hungry and disoriented, as though I am not connected to the body lying in the bed. Who is this person in this strange hotel, alone for the first time in her life? Why am I here? What have I done? I feel as though I'm in a play, following a script that was written by a stranger. Part of me is scared; but there is another part, deep inside, that is excited at the idea that I am about to enter the unknown.

As a child, I loved the unknown. Every summer my parents, my brother, Pepper the dog, and I went on a one-week vacation in the car. My father would drive and my mother would sit next to him, a map on her lap. Every once in a while, when my mother said, "Turn right," my father would get a funny look on his face and turn left. Within minutes we would be lost. Then we'd have to knock on a farmhouse door (when it happened, we were always in farm country) to ask directions. Sometimes we'd be invited to see the newborn calves. Or watch the cows being milked. Often we'd get to throw a handful of grain to the chickens. Lost meant adventure, and I loved it. It's been years since I've been lost, and I can't remember the last time I stepped into the unknown.

I am out on the street at six-thirty in the morning. The day is sunny, the Spanish language sings its musical sounds all around me, and cars whiz through the city ahead of the morning rush hour. Early mornings have a special energy that I like. I decide to walk the couple of miles to the market and get something to eat on the way.

Entering the market through a side entrance, I am immediately surrounded by *piñatas:* Mickey Mouse, Goofy, Donald Duck, and an assortment of animals and aliens dressed in their colorful papier-mâché skins. They are standing on the floor and hanging over my head, hundreds of donkeys and dinosaurs, cats and dragons, boys and girls, hogs and bugs. All the colors of the rainbow are swirling in front of me, swinging to the *salsa* music that is blasting out of unseen speakers. I am swinging too. The brassy, percussive rhythm of the Caribbean is contagious.

Then I am out of *piñatas* and into avocados, shades of green and brown in massive piles on flowered oilcloth. Then mounds of sweet smelling mangos fight for my attention with the pineapples. There are booths of papayas, red, yellow, and green; bananas, big and small, thin and fat; dozens of varieties of peppers and *chiles* fresh and dried and mounded in cubicles; *tomatillos, jícama,* carrots, tomatoes, and bunches of green leaves. For a while, *cilantro* dominates the air, until I pass a table full of oregano. Seconds later, I stop next to a table covered with yellow squash blossoms and wonder what they taste like.

There are children in the booths, babies swinging in tiny hammocks, nine-year-olds wooing customers, "Señora, buy my watermelon. Good taste. Sweet."

The music streaming through the fruits and vegetables is a whiney, unrequited love song that I know from the Mexican radio stations in Los Angeles. It's called *ranchero* music. Though the music is sad, my body is light. My fears of the night before have turned into excitement.

I pass through mountains of green and red and brown and rust-colored pastes, three feet high, the essence of *mole* sauces, redolent of cloves and garlic, oregano and cinnamon. Nothing is wrapped in plastic or sealed in containers. It is all out there to be smelled and seen and tasted and bought. I am surrounded by the colors, the smells, the sounds of a culture that lives life full out.

In meats, fifty little butcher shops compete for the shoppers' business.

There are brains and stomachs and kidneys and tongues, feet and tails and intestines. Butchers are slapping and smashing meat on huge wooden blocks, beating red blobs into tenderness. They are scissoring and chopping up yellow chickens that have been fed marigolds so their skin and flesh are gold. Heads here, feet there. Innards sorted.

The butchers are mincing beef and hacking pork, sharpening knives and chopping slabs. Cleaving, slapping, scissoring, beating. It's a spectacular percussion band, with its own peculiar instruments.

The shoppers, thick in the aisles, are carrying string and plastic and cloth bags full of newspaper-wrapped packages of their purchases. I walk among them, enjoying the touch of our bodies.

I wriggle through the crowd to peer into waist-high vats of thick white cream and barrels of white ground-corn dough called *masa*. I cannot stop smiling at the explosion of joy I have felt since I passed under the canopy of *piñatas*. It's exciting to be exploring a world I know nothing about, discovering new smells, and moving through a scene where I am a barely noticed minority of one, swallowed up by the crowd.

I follow my nose to the eating area of the market. Sausages are frying, soups are bubbling, *chiles* are toasting. I sit at a picnic table and eat and smile, surrounded by Spanish-speaking women. I bite into my *quesadilla* stuffed with stretchy Oaxaca cheese and strips of sweet, green *chiles*.

"*Muy sabrosa.*" Delicious, I say to the woman sitting on my right. She asks me where I am from. I answer some simple questions and ask her name. When our conversation runs out of words, I move to another table and try a *sopa de flor de calabaza,* squash blossom soup with garlic and onion, zucchini, corn kernels, green leaves, and bright yellow squash blossoms . . . with strips of sweet *chiles* on top. The blend of flavors, the texture of the different vegetables, the thickness of the broth are like the Mexican people, filled with spice and spirit.

Then, at about twelve o'clock, after nearly five hours in the market, I head off to the anthropology museum. I have never been big on museums or churches or most tourist attractions. As I wander through, I am thinking that I want to move into the enclosed tableaux, to live with these people, to celebrate with them, to cook and eat with the families. I want to experience their lives, not look at them through glass.

Many of the exhibits represent cultures that no longer exist; but there are plenty of living, breathing indigenous people in Mexico today. How I wish I could live amongst them.

Then it hits me for the first time . . . during these two months, I do not need anyone's permission to do what I want to do. I am free to make my own decisions, follow my whims, and take whatever risks I choose. For me, these two months are not about dating or being with other men; they are about doing the things that I can't do with my husband. I decide, while looking at a Zapotec family behind glass, that for some part of this Mexican journey, I will live in a Zapotec village.

By five o'clock I am thinking about dinner, and yesterday's fear is back. It is not a fear of people; I loved being in the market, surrounded by people. Nor am I afraid that someone will hurt me or rob me; I'm not a worrier. What I am feeling is a deep psychological fear with its roots in adolescence: a fear of being *seen* alone. Alone means unpopular. Alone means that you have no friends. Alone means that you are an outsider. In the context of Mexico City, it makes no sense. But it is there, this vestigial fear, left over from my teenage years. Sitting alone at a table, where everyone can see me, is like shouting my inadequacy to the world.

I understand what I'm feeling and how foolish it is. But I still don't want to eat alone. I need to find a dinner companion, anyone, male, female, old, young, a family, a loner, a three-year-old. I've never been shy about talking to strangers. It doesn't matter whom I find; what I need is a human across the table.

I decide that it would be easiest, and safest, to look for a dinner mate in one of the better hotels. I study the guidebook and find my way to the most expensive hotel in the city, where I sit in a lounge chair by the pool and try to look as though I belong.

A family is sitting at the umbrella table next to my chair. "Where are you from?" I open. We talk: about Mexico City, about kids, about New York (where they are from and I used to be). An hour later, they gather up the kids and leave. They are a unit unto themselves; they don't need me.

A few lounges over, there is a man sitting alone. I am thinking that he will probably be joined by a wife full of shopping bags. What the hell. I can try. I smile at him, nod an opening, and we begin to talk. He's an engineer from Indianapolis, on business. Alone.

"I'm traveling by myself for two months," I say in answer to his question.

"Are you finding it difficult? I mean, what do you do about dinner?"

Yes. Yes. "Is that an invitation?" I ask. It wasn't, of course. "If it is I accept." I try not to sound as though I'm propositioning him.

He laughs and tells me that he is waiting to hear from a friend who usually calls in the morning. He suspects that their signals may have gotten mixed up. He'd be happy to have dinner with me, unless he hears from the friend. We make plans to meet.

I go back to my hotel, pleased with my ingenuity. I shower and get dressed. Then the phone rings. The friend has called; our dinner appointment is off. Back to zero. OK. I'll start again at a different hotel. It is 8:15 P.M.

I choose a hotel with three stars and take a taxi there. The lobby is small. No one is sitting in the stuffed chairs, so I stand near the wall opposite the reception counter and observe the activity. Nobody is hanging around this lobby. I stand with a silly smile on my face and watch people on their way out for dinner. The pace is brisk. There's no chance to make eye contact, which is a necessary part of picking people up. And no one lingers, so there's no opportunity to hook someone with a spontaneous comment. It is nearly nine o'clock.

I find myself watching the young woman who is checking in guests. She has a warm smile and expressive eyes. And her English is excellent. I wait until there is no one in line.

"I'm sorry to bother you. I know you're busy, but I'm here alone and I wonder if you could recommend a restaurant where I wouldn't feel uncomfortable eating by myself."

"Hmmmm. Let me think about that for a few minutes. I'll get back to you."

Good, I feel less alone already.

She continues checking in the guests and I retreat to my post near the wall. A line grows in front of her. It keeps getting longer. A half hour goes by. I am feeling more and more uncomfortable standing there. Just as I decide that she has forgotten about me, she calls me over.

"Excuse me," she says to the man at the front of the line. "I'll be just a minute. This woman asked me to recommend a restaurant where she could eat alone, and I promised I'd get back to her."

He smiles and looks at me. "An Englishman never lets a lady eat alone. I'm John and this is Lionel. We'd be delighted if you would join us for dinner."

I look at the woman and then at the men. "Thank you," I smile to all of them.

John directs the taxi driver to a small restaurant in Zona Rosa, the elegant part of the city. The *tequila* comes in a shot glass along with a small spicy tomato juice, and we begin our meal, all of us, with *ceviche* cocktails, raw fish "cooked" in a marinade of lime juice with diced peppers, tomatoes, *chiles*, green onions, and *cilantro*. Even before the main courses arrive, they buy me a wilting rose from the old lady who is selling them from table to table.

My chicken *mole* is fabulous. The three of us drink two bottles of wine and laugh and talk a lot. Lionel is John's boss, recently arrived from London. He's about seventy years old, fit and funny. John, who is a few years younger than I, is tall and slim. He has a little twist in his nose and brown hair that flops over his forehead. They are both wearing suits and ties. John has been in Mexico for six months, traveling in back country, negotiating and doing deals and being propositioned by all the eligible young women in the villages he visits. He mentions only the propositions, not what he did about them.

The men are vague about their mission in Mexico. As the *mariachi* band plays my requests, I have visions of drugs and Mafia and spies. Then Lionel lets slip something about guns. I ask and the answer is evasive. I leave it alone.

I tell them my story, including my apprehension and fear that my marriage may be over. I can feel the tears in my eyes as I talk. They say nothing except, "Have another glass of wine."

We walk back to their hotel, singing songs from the fifties, holding hands like old friends, me in the middle. The streets are empty and our voices are loud. It is half past two; most of Mexico City is sleeping. John and I deliver Lionel to his room. Then we walk down the corridor and around the corner. Suddenly he stops and puts his hands on my shoulders.

"Rita," he says, "I think you want to cry."

He opens the door to his room and locks it behind us. Then he puts his arms around me and I cry.

The next morning, I am confused as I walk back to my hotel. Who was that woman who just spent the night with a stranger? Two days ago I could never have done it. In twenty-four years, it has never happened. Is it possible that leaving the country has turned me into someone else?

I try to look at myself from another dimension, detached and nonjudgmental. This person is not wife, mother, daughter, writer, anthropology student, L.A. sophisticate. She is, of course, all of these things; but alone, without the attachments, she is a woman in limbo, whose identity has been buried in her roles. Away from those roles and alone, she is someone she doesn't know.

Clearly, my job over the next two months is not only to think about the state of my marriage and to discover new worlds, but also to uncover the person inside my skin.

I collect my things and check out of the hotel. They are expecting me today at the Spanish school in Cuernavaca.

The city bus is crowded. People are pushing. I have switched my backpack onto my stomach so that I can see it, and I am clutching my shoulder bag around the bottom. I've been warned about the dangers of city buses, but I like getting the feel of a city by riding the buses.

Five minutes into the bus ride, approximately thirty-six hours into my adventure, the bus lurches and a couple of teenagers standing next to me are thrown against my side. I fall to the floor. One of the teenagers helps me up. I don't even know that my wallet has been taken until I'm at the terminal looking for money to pay for the bus ticket to Cuernavaca.

Luckily, I'm wearing a thigh belt where I put most of my money, my traveler's checks, and my passport. I've lost about $25 in cash, $150 in traveler's checks, and a Visa card. I rush to a phone and try to call the American Express office in Mexico City to report the stolen traveler's checks. The line is busy. I try about ten times over the next week, and the line is always busy. (Months later, when I return to the States, I call them and they honor my loss.)

The money is negligible. The worst part is having to call my husband to cancel the credit card, which is in his name. The call is awkward and I feel like the stereotype of a helpless wife.

The school has made arrangements for me to stay with a young couple and their baby; I'm their first foreign guest. Pili is twenty-one, slim with long black hair, sparkling eyes, and a bouncy personality. Raul, her husband, is strikingly handsome. His eyes are deep and dark, his shoulders are broad, and his smile is real. But there is something weighing him down. I can see it when I look into his eyes. Perhaps it's the responsibility of a wife and a one-year-old baby at the age of twenty-two.

Neither Pili nor Raul speaks English, so I'm forced to communicate in Spanish, which is the reason the school houses its students in homes. I am amazed at how much I remember.

The classes are one on one and I'm flying through the lessons. It feels great. I've never studied a language in context; it makes so much more sense than sitting in the U.S. with a book. Here, everything and everyone around you is a classroom.

Then, one week into my visit, I wake up with a rash on my chest. I decide it's nothing. I'm in a new environment, new foods, new water, new everything. I ignore it. The next day the rash is all over my body. And two days later, it turns into something that feels and looks like a stage-three sunburn. Every inch of my body is bright red. Wherever I touch, it hurts. I also hurt when I wash, sit, and put on clothes.

I leave the house that morning clutching the little pamphlet that the school has given me; instead of going to school, I go to the recommended doctor a few blocks from my house. I say nothing to Pili and Raul. I'm hoping it's nothing, so it doesn't make sense to worry them.

"It's *varicela*," the doctor says. "The whole family must come in immediately to get gamma globulin injections."

I have no idea what *varicela* is, but I am humiliated. I have just arrived and I have brought disease. When I tell Pili, in my halting Spanish, that they all have to get gamma globulin shots, she is skeptical. She looks at my red arms and chest. "That is not *varicela*," she tells me and then brings over her dictionary.

Varicela, it turns out, is chicken pox. She's right. I know what chicken pox looks like and this isn't it. She calls another doctor, who agrees to come to the house the next day. I go to bed early and wake up in pain—my back hurts and so does my scalp. My ears and my eyelids and the bottoms of my feet are the color of tomatoes. My entire body feels as though it has been dipped in boiling water. And, I have a fever.

It is frightening to be so sick in a place where I don't know anyone. And my Spanish is not good enough to ask all the questions I have. I keep asking myself if it is safe to be treated by doctors trained in Mexico; I have no idea about the quality of the medical schools here.

Before the doctor arrives, I sit with a dictionary and prepare a list of possible causes. I am terrified that those village women who propositioned John, have given him, and me, a disease. I'm embarrassed to mention it to the doctor, so I bury it in the middle of my list.

> *varicela*
> *food reaction*
> *water reaction*
> *cat allergy*

venereal disease
reaction to Aralen, the malaria pills I've taken twice
hives
some tropical virus
a skin disease

The doctor examines me in my room. I hand him the piece of paper. "It is not chicken pox," he tells me. He looks at the rest of the list without commenting. "I don't know what it is. I will have to consult my colleagues."

When he leaves, Pili says, "My father is a doctor. He gets back from vacation tomorrow. I'll call him."

Pili's father doesn't venture a diagnosis either. He sends me off the next day to the top dermatologist in Cuernavaca. By the time I get to his office, my skin has changed again. It is not hurting anymore. Now it is peeling, and when I take off my shirt in the office, thousands of tiny flakes of dead skin fall off onto his floor. I am snowing.

"It is a reaction to something," he says. "But I have no way of knowing what. It is not chicken pox or a virus or venereal disease. It is probably a response to the malaria medicine. Stop taking it." He prescribes prednizone, a steroid. I ask if my illness is contagious. He says no.

As I ride home in a taxi, I am trying to decide what to do. "Probably" is not very reassuring. I cannot, will not, go back to Los Angeles to my family doctor. I'm not even going to call my husband. This is my trip, my freedom, my problem.

I feel very alone. Not only have I never had such a strange illness, I've never gone through *anything* on my own. I decide that if I don't get a confirmation of the diagnosis, I will go to Miami, where I have a friend who is a doctor.

I walk in the door and Pili greets me. Doctor number two has called. He and his colleagues are calling my condition Stevens Johnson syndrome, a reaction to medication, probably the malaria prophylaxis, Aralen, although none of the literature discusses this side effect. He too prescribes prednizone. OK. There's consensus. I decide to stay.

My condition gets worse. The fever brings on hallucinations and my vision becomes blurred. My legs blister so badly that when I stand still, the pressure and pain are intolerable. I have to sit on the shower floor while I bathe and brush my teeth because when I stand still for more than a few seconds the blisters feel as if they are going to explode.

Midway through this ordeal, I begin to see the illness as some kind of

Herculean challenge that I must endure in order to become a new woman. I have also convinced myself that I am not in serious danger. (Months later, when I see my doctor in L.A., he tells me that Stevens Johnson syndrome is, in fact, extremely rare and dangerous. He has seen it twice, and both times he hospitalized his patient. The danger is infection; people die from it. He also tells me that the illness can do permanent damage to the patient's eyesight.)

After two weeks, I still cannot stand still. I have to sit with my legs up to reduce the pain. Occasionally I go for walks, pushing the baby in the stroller. One day I go to the bank and discover that there is a line. I jog in place like a runner at a traffic light.

Every inch of my body is peeling. The more delicate parts of me flake onto the floor. Even my nipples and my ear lobes are peeling. The skin on my fingers peels off, like the skin of a snake, intact. And my legs are still blistered. I have turned into one of those hideous pictures in a medical book.

Then, as I lie in bed one night, burning up and in pain, I get the first spiritual message of my life: in shedding my skin, I am being reborn. I am symbolically peeling away the person I have become and releasing the woman who has been trapped inside all these years. Soon this new me will be going out into the world on a journey of self-discovery.

The next night Pili and the baby go to bed at nine o'clock and I sit with Raul, my feet up on the coffee table, until two in the morning. Until now we have never had a conversation in depth. We have talked about food, about school, about his baby, and my illness; but language has always prevented our conversation from going beyond the superficial.

Tonight is different. We talk with dictionaries on our laps, and we share an extraordinary conversational intimacy. We are not an old American and a young Mexican. Nor are we man and woman in any sexual sense. There is certainly a mother-son component to our discussion; but it is more than that. We are friends, sharing feelings.

We begin when I tell him my revelation about rebirth. Like most Mexicans, he is Catholic, but he has never thought much about what he believes. We talk about souls, inner selves, the basic nature of human beings. He asks me about my marriage and I tell him, with tears in my eyes, that I don't know if my husband will want to stay married when I return, and that I am both afraid and challenged by the thought of being alone in the world. Raul confides in me his fears for his own marriage. Ever since his son was born, Raul has been noticing other women, wanting them, fearing his fantasies. We talk on and on, much of the time with tears in our eyes. Somewhere in the middle of our talk, I realize that I am comfortable speaking Spanish.

Slowly, I heal. My fever disappears; my blisters dry up; my skin is renewed. From beginning to end takes less than three weeks. When I am well enough to go back to school, I have no patience for the classroom. I no longer want to study. I am ready to move out into the unknown, to experience life with a new sensibility, to embark on my journey of inner and outer discovery.

On the Sunday morning before I leave, Raul, Pili, the baby, and I pile into the car and drive off for a farewell tour of Cuernavaca. The first stop on our tour is to buy *chicharrón,* fried pigskin that's been boiled for hours in a vat of lard, left to dry, and then boiled again. You can buy thin, non-fatty pieces, or the fattier middle part, or you can look around for pieces that have a little meat attached. Raul buys a huge bagful and I reach in for a hunk.

I've been a health-food nut for years. I can't remember when I last had bacon in my house, even though I love that crispy smoky meat surrounded by mushy fat. I banished it years ago when I became concerned about what went into my kids' bodies. But now, it is my body, and my host can't wait for me to taste this Mexican treat. Neither can I.

I crunch through the tasty, crisp cells that have puffed up into a light airy snack; it's wonderful. I reach into the bag for another piece, feeling exhilarated when I bite through sections of fat.

I feel no guilt as I demolish some long-cherished no-fat rules along with the *chicharrón.* I'm not sure why I am guilt-free. Perhaps it is the setting; rules tend to reduce their grip when you cross borders. Perhaps it is the *chicharrón,* crunchy, light, and bacony; it's easy to put aside guilt in the enthusiasm and taste of the moment. But more likely, the joy I feel at this guilt-free moment is a sign that I really have peeled away the old and begun the process of self-discovery.

As I reach into the bag for my third piece, Raul informs me that *"el domingo sin chicharrón no es domingo."* Sunday without *chicharrón* is not Sunday. With *chicharrón,* he affirms his place in a stable world.

My experience of *chicharrón* is a different kind of affirmation. It sug-gests that I have let go of the old and given myself permission to move on.

CHAPTER TWO

IN A ZAPOTEC VILLAGE

Pili and Raul drive me to the bus stop. There are six other backpackers headed to Oaxaca. A man from Denmark, and three women, one from the U.S and two from Germany, are sharing information about places to stay in Oaxaca. I join them and am immediately included in the conversation.

There is also a young couple off to the side by themselves, speaking Spanish.

This is my first encounter with "the travelers' network." It's made up of young people, mostly Europeans, who are on the road long-term, from a few months to several years. They travel cheaply, stay in backpacker places, and are nearly always looking to meet other travelers. During my Central American travels, I meet and hang out with dozens of backpackers, forming quick and easy friendships and sometimes going off together for weeks at a time.

Once I discover the travelers' network, I have no more problems about eating dinner alone. In fact, I'm almost never alone, unless I choose to be. My mistake in Mexico City was looking for companionship in the better hotels.

Hotels are the domains of tourists on short-term vacations. They see the sights, eat in the best restaurants, and sun by the pool. In backpacker places, people are more relaxed, more frugal, and friendlier. They travel as much to meet other travelers as they do to see the world. Many of them are traveling without companions . . . and no one really wants to eat dinner alone.

The typical backpacker is unmarried, educated, but not yet on the career track. Among the backpackers, there are always a lot of young Europeans who work for a year or two at home, save their money, then travel until it runs out. Canadians and Australians are also backpack travelers; so are Israelis, taking a year off after serving in the army, and New Zealanders on their great "OE," overseas experience. There are Americans as well; but the Americans are usually on a tighter schedule, and I find them less friendly, at least to me.

I also discover on the backpack trail that the age barriers we live with in the United States are not shared by the rest of the world. I am forty-seven; they are mostly under thirty. And it doesn't matter to anybody. I love the energy of the young, and they accept me without hesitation. The variations in age add spice and depth to the conversations.

From time to time I meet other women my age who are backpacking, but I rarely meet men over forty who are traveling alone. Older men, it seems, are not as courageous as women; all those years of being responsible have diminished their capacity for adventure.

When the bus to Oaxaca makes a snack stop, I sit down with the Spanish-speaking couple, Miguel and Ana. They're from Medellín, Colombia; he's a lawyer, just out of school. With his jeans, long hair, and soft features, he looks about sixteen. He's also a musician, carrying a guitar and trying to decide whether to go into his father's law firm or work toward a career in music. Ana, his fiancée, is a teacher and spectacularly beautiful—dark sparkling eyes, and straight, shoulder-length black hair. She thinks Miguel should go into music, at least until they have children three years from now. If he hasn't made it by then, she says, he can join the firm. But he owes it to himself to follow his dream, not his father's. They're a nice couple.

When we get to Oaxaca, my busmates and I check into a hostel. I serve as a translator for Miguel and Ana so they too can be a part of the group. My Spanish is far from perfect, it isn't even good; but I feel so pleased that I can communicate. I'm really happy I took the time to study and practice in Cuernavaca. Already it has opened a door to people and a story I would never have known.

We are all put into the same dorm room. As soon as our beds are chosen and our things are stored, we wander the streets together. By the time we go to dinner, we are old friends. Friendship happens quickly on the road.

I learn that the American woman is taking a six-month break between undergraduate and graduate school; she's studying psychology. The German women are college professors on a four-month trip. And the Danish man is a mechanic; he's been traveling for eight months. No one is over thirty. The seven of us wander together, split up for a while, and meet again for dinner. Then we all go to a bar to hear Miguel play and sing.

As I listen to the music, I look at myself, sitting there confident and comfortable with five interesting people, all of whom know my name. I have come far in the few weeks since I stepped off the plane, afraid of being alone. I can't wait to find out what's ahead. Then I hear my name, as Miguel dedicates a song to *"Señora Rita, la escritora de los estados unidos."*

After four days with my new friends, I decide to act on the resolution I made in the anthropology museum. I am going to leave the group and try to find a Zapotec village where I can settle in long enough to connect with the people and get a feel of their way of life.

I know nothing about the communities in this area. I haven't read a single book about Zapotec culture; nor have I studied any Zapotec language. If I were a scholar, I'd have spent a year learning all I could about the people I am about to visit. Instead, I know only that Oaxaca is surrounded by Zapotec villages, and that I have spent the last four years studying anthropology and yearning to live in other cultures. I'm really not interested in "studying" anybody. I just want to slip into another way of life, not as a tourist, not as an academic, but, as much as possible, as a part of the community.

I look at a map and blindly choose a village about forty miles north of Oaxaca. There is a road that goes to the village, but no one can tell me when or where to get a bus, so I start out walking. If a bus comes along, I'll stop it. If there isn't one, I'll hitch. I have never hitchhiked before, but this seems like a good time to start.

The sun is blistering hot; the road is hilly; and the fields on both sides, as far as I can see, are brown and withered. I'm wearing sneakers, a baseball cap, and jeans; and I'm carrying a small backpack and a bottle of water.

After only fifteen minutes, I'm dripping in sweat. Not a single car has passed. Finally, after about forty-five minutes, a car approaches. Relief, I think. I stick out my arm with my thumb up, a move I've seen millions of times from the inside of my car. It's not an easy gesture. Feels a lot like begging. The car whizzes by me. Then two more pass. Then two trucks.

Now I feel even more self-conscious. Who would've thought five drivers could ignore a forty-seven-year-old woman trudging along in the hot sun? I wonder what they're thinking as they speed by. Aren't they even a little bit curious?

A part of me wants to go back to Oaxaca and join my friends; it's so much easier being part of a group. But I have dreamed for years of living in another culture where I am the only outsider. I want to know what I will do and how I will go about connecting with the people. I have read dozens of ethnographies over the last four years, vicariously living in the shoes of the anthropologists, sharing their experiences. Now I want to do it on my own.

So I keep sticking out my arm, thumb up. Two more cars go by. After a while, I'm not embarrassed any more; I'm just hot and desperate.

I've been walking for more than an hour when a white rusted pickup stops. I tell the driver the name of the village where I'm going, and he motions for me to get in the back with three turkeys in a cage and about ten cases of beer and Coca-Cola. I toss my backpack in, but I can't get my body in; the truck is too high. I can't even get my foot into a position where I can swing the other foot over the back. The driver waits. Finally he motions me into the front seat.

We talk in Spanish amid rumbles and rattles and a muffler with a hole in it. Where am I from, where am I going, and why?

"I'm writing a book about life in Mexico for American children," I lie. "I'd like to include a chapter about a Zapotec village. I'm hoping that I can stay in the village for a month."

The driver is intrigued when he hears that I want to live in this village. He tells me that I have to talk to the *alcalde,* the mayor. After about an hour, we rattle into a village, the center of which has two stores in what used to be living rooms. The driver stops the truck in front of a group of men and talks to them. It is twelve noon. Five men, beer bottles in hand, greet me.

"*Buenos días,*" I say. "Please, may I speak to the head of your village."

One of them approaches. "*Hola, Señora.* I am very sorry. The head of our village is in Mexico City. He will be back the day after tomorrow. Please come back then."

Shit.

I tell them that I would like to stay in the village for a month and that I will return in three days. "Oh, yes," they tell me. "The *alcalde* will be here then."

"Do you think he will give me permission to stay?"

The men shrug at each other. One speaks. "If he can find a place for you to live." Then they all start to talk in Zapotec, presumably about places where I could live. I don't understand a word.

"I would be very happy if you would tell the mayor about me."

"Por supuesto, Señora." Of course.

The thought of turning around and going back to Oaxaca doesn't appeal to me. But no one has suggested I can stay, even for one night.

I buy a cold Coke. "Can I walk around a little before I leave?"

"Por favor," they say. Please.

None of the men walks with me as I walk up the gravelly paths and down. It is a village built on hills. The up part isn't too bad, but I keep slipping on the down.

There are women in the village, but none of them greets me when I pass by, smiling and nodding. In fact, they run. Every once in a while I catch someone looking out a window or peering from behind a tree.

There are children playing. As soon as they see me, they take off, like a flock of birds. It is clear that I am not welcome. I feel like a disease that must be kept at a distance. I walk around the village for about ten minutes. Then I go back to Oaxaca.

Turns out there is a bus that goes back and forth to Oaxaca. I find out by accident. As I'm walking, it just appears and stops. No one in the village bothered to tell me.

When I arrive three days later, the same men are standing in the same place. This time it is ten in the morning. They are all, once again, holding beer bottles.

"Buenos días, Señora," they call as I walk toward them.

The head of the village welcomes me. "We are pleased that you wish to visit us for a month. José has a room for you in his yard."

José is a small, muscular man with a mustache and wavy black hair. His wife will take good care of me, he says. The small house where I will be living is very safe, he tells me as we walk. It is made of concrete and there is a strong lock on a heavy metal door. I wonder why his first words are about security.

He tells me that he would like to give me the house for nothing, but it is the dry season and he has no money. He asks me for seven dollars a day for the room and food. It will help him feed his family. I'm sure it's a fortune to him, and I'm also sure that everyone in the village thinks that he's ripping me off. I don't try to bargain.

My house is a one-room concrete shed about forty feet behind the house where José, his wife, and his three children live. It is clean except for a big black mass of something in one corner of the ceiling. The bed, a piece of foam rubber on a board, turns out to be firm and comfortable. The only openings in the room are the door and a two-foot by one-foot barred window above the door.

Margarita, José's wife, arrives with coffee, trailed by three children under four. The children don't speak Spanish; their mother speaks just enough to get by. (The language they speak is Zapotec.) I ask her to sit while I drink. She is twenty years old. She was born in this village and she has been to Oaxaca only once when her mother was in the hospital there.

When I finish the coffee, I ask about a toilet. She walks with me out the gate, across a dry, rocky field, and down a little hill to the cracked riverbed. The toilet. There are a couple of trees to squat behind, but I am wider than both of them. The rest of the foliage is mostly low and practically leafless. I decide to hold it in for a while longer.

I have brought no dresses or skirts, only pants, pants that I will have to lower below my knees in order to pee, and even then, walking away with dry feet and pants is pretty unlikely. All the women I've seen are wearing skirts. They just have to hike them up a bit and they can pee unobserved. They probably don't wear underpants.

"Each morning," says Margarita in broken Spanish as we walk back to the house, "I will bring you a pail of water to wash with." Then she drops me off at my cement block and goes back to her house. I decide to go for a walk.

The village is almost totally vertical, steep ups and equally steep downs. There is only one car-size road that goes from the main road to the square. The rest of the village is for walking. As I walk down each gravel- and rock-filled hill, I place my feet on the ground carefully, slowly, making sure I have secure footing before I lift my other foot. I am halfway down one of the hills when a man walks by. No, he runs by. And so does everyone else. The villagers point themselves downhill and sort of fall, letting gravity take them down. Their legs paddle beneath their moving torsos and keep them standing upright. If the gravel or rocks slip under their feet, it doesn't matter, because they don't wait to be secure, they're already on to the next bit of rock and gravel. For the whole time I live here I try to walk the hills the way they do. I succeed on the lesser hills and on the steep ones that are mostly grassy. But on the rocky ones, I continue to go down inch by inch, securing each foot as it touches the ground.

The first children I see are playing marbles. Two are squatting, getting ready to shoot. Four others are standing and watching. I am more than ten yards away when I'm spotted. Someone squeals and shouts something. I don't understand what he says, but suddenly the game stops and they run in all directions. Only one boy stays long enough to gather up the marbles. Then he disappears like the others. As I walk on, little heads peek at me from behind bushes.

The women are not any friendlier. Some rush into the nearest house until I pass. Some hide, like the children, behind a tree or bush. No one returns my smile or my *"Buenos días."* Only the men in the plaza talk to me, and most of them are drunk most of the time. It is the dry season, they tell me, as they touch my arm, my shoulder, my neck. Their work is farming and they cannot farm, so they drink.

I return to my cell and study Spanish. Margarita comes with lunch: two hard-boiled eggs, two pieces of white bread, and coffee. She places the tray on a small table in front of my house and leaves. During the month that I live there, she never sits with me; nor am I ever invited into her house to eat with her family. Meals for me are always solitary. I feel like an object to be served, never a friend.

For four days I continue to disperse crowds of children. When I stand at a distance and try to watch them playing soccer, they stop the game. Except for Margarita and a raving old woman, not a single woman talks to me. I continue to smile at them all, but my smile is getting weaker and phonier. I have read that there are many cultures that consider blue eyes witchy. Not only are my eyes blue, but my hair is blond (they all have dark hair) and my skin is pale (theirs is a rich light brown). One day I put on sunglasses to hide my blue eyes, but no one else is wearing them and I feel as though I am putting even more of a wall between us.

The men, on the other hand, gather round me whenever I come near them, usually trapping me in the middle. They ask questions, they tell me stories, and they touch me. After the second day, I avoid the plaza hangout of the drunk male population.

Usually I spend my days wandering around with a notebook, pretending I have something to do. Every once in a while I take notes or draw a diagram. Sometimes I sit and read. With no one to talk to and nothing to do, I am bored and lonely.

My meals are always the same. A hard-boiled egg, a slice of white bread, and coffee for breakfast. Two hard-boiled eggs and two slices of white bread with coffee for lunch. And a cup of stew with beans and a few bits of chicken and more white bread for dinner.

My concrete house is cool, and I like it, even though I have to share it with hundreds, no thousands, of daddy-long-leg spiders—the breathing blob in the corner of the ceiling. They are very discreet. When they are a black blob, they are sleeping. When they wake up, they seem to have places to go. I know they live there, but they don't bother me and I don't bother them.

Going to "the toilet" is just as I expected. I walk to the dry riverbed and take down my pants. Then I get into position facing uphill and leaning forward, feet wide apart, behind sticking up so that the squirt will go downhill and not onto my shoes or pants. I carry a little piece of toilet paper and bury it when I'm finished. I try not to think about the audience that I'm sure is out there. Fortunately, they are discreet enough not to laugh out loud.

When I wander through the village, none of the women talks to me. After four days, the only woman I have had a conversation with is Margarita, and she treats me as though she's my maid. I'm not sure what I expected, but this wasn't it. I keep reminding myself that I have vowed to spend a month here. But there's another little voice that tells me I'm free to leave whenever I choose.

Then, on day five, a young woman and her three-year-old child stop me on the top of a hill. She is wearing the traditional dress of the village: a full skirt of heavy woven fabric, a sash around her waist, and a handwoven blouse.

"Hello, my name is Juanita. Where are you from?"

I introduce myself and tell her I'm from Los Angeles.

She doesn't say anything for several seconds. During the silence, her eyes fill with tears. Then she can't stop talking. Her Spanish is excellent, unlike Margarita's.

Juanita is a twenty-year-old widow, an elementary school teacher. Her husband, Roberto, went to the United States two years ago and got work washing dishes and busing in a Greek restaurant in Santa Monica, California. I have actually eaten in the restaurant. For one year he sent her money every month. Then, a few months ago, she got a telegram. There had been a fire in the kitchen and he was dead from smoke inhalation. They sent him home in a box. Shortly after that, the restaurant owner sent Juanita one hundred dollars. In the accompanying note, he promised to send more, but she never heard from him again.

Now *my* eyes fill with tears and I tentatively put my arm around her and tell her how sorry I am. She snuggles into my shoulder and I hug her.

(Two weeks later another young man from the village returns from Los Angeles in a pine box. He'd been shot on the street. I go to the funeral.)

"Would you like a cup of coffee?" Juanita asks that first day as we stand on the hill. I can't believe it. I'm actually being invited into someone's home!

She takes me into her two-room house. It is simple and clean and nicely furnished. She'd bought the furniture to surprise Roberto. He never saw it. As we are drinking our coffee, Juanita studies me, one of those head-to-toe perusals.

"Would you do me a favor?" she asks.

Uh oh, I think. She's going to ask for money.

But she surprises me. "Will you try on my clothes?"

She opens a trunk and takes out a skirt that matches the ones all the women are wearing. It is woven with thick cotton threads into a heavy striped fabric. I step into it.

"Hold this end," she says as she starts to wind a five-inch-thick sash around my waist. I grow fatter and fatter as she winds.

She goes around four or five times, then secures the end with a safety pin. I am already feeling like a hippopotamus when she takes a huge woven blouse out of the trunk and puts it over my head. My width has doubled. I am dressed in a bottom layer of khaki pants and a T-shirt, then the thick blanket-layer of skirt, a mile of sash, and a tentlike blouse. Juanita is finished. She steps back, turns me around, and exclaims, "You look beautiful! I will lend you these clothes while you are in my village."

I walk toward the door, wondering whether my expanse will fit through. Two women are passing by as I emerge. They look at me and smile and nod their heads. Then they giggle. And so do the other women I meet. Suddenly, I am not so strange. My eyes, my hair, my skin are the same; but now I am wearing the traditional clothes of the village. They are willing to accept me.

From that point on, I am one of them. Each morning I go to Juanita's house, greeting women by name when we pass on the path. Juanita always checks me out when I walk in. Sometimes she removes my waist scarf and does it up again. Wrapping a mile-long scarf around your waist alone is not that easy and I don't do it very well.

During my second visit I write a letter to the restaurant owner who sent Juanita the money. I introduce myself as a journalist from L.A. and ask about the additional money he promised. I describe José's child and wife and say that I hope he will send her more money. I tell him that I will stop by when I return to Los Angeles. (When I visit the restaurant several months later, I am told that it has changed ownership. I don't know if Juanita received any response to my letter.)

On the third day Juanita gives me my first lesson in the Zapotec language. Soon I can say good morning, how are you, and how many children do you have. And I can answer the same questions and a few more. Now the mothers begin to talk to me. The children show me their favorite marbles and let me scrunch down and watch them shoot. Some of the kids point to things like trees and houses and tell me the words in Zapotec. And they take my hand and bring me to their soccer games.

And, not least of all, with my skirt on, I can pee without mooning the world. (I do not wear underpants.)

One morning, about three weeks into my visit, Margarita tells me that there is going to be a festival in our yard. The whole neighborhood is coming. She and José have been in charge of the neighborhood church organization (Catholic) for the past year and there is about to be a change of leadership, which means a big party.

I go with her to buy the turkey, to a part of the village where I've never been. She climbs over a fence into a pen. The turkeys are running loose. One after another, Margarita picks up a turkey's leg and pokes and pinches while the turkey squawks. Finally she finds a nice fat bird. We carry it home alive.

That night our yard fills with people and preparations. Men are fixing the fireplace, carrying in chairs and tables, setting up speakers on the roof, and drinking. Women are bringing utensils and food and getting ready for tomorrow's cooking.

Once the speakers are in place, they blast with the joys of romance and the whines of unrequited love. The same songs play over and over again.

I try to be useful, but no one wants my help. All evening and long into the night, the preparations go on. Finally I say good night and go to bed. I study Zapotec for a few minutes and turn out the light. The people noise diminishes, though the speakers are still going at full volume; and finally, there is nothing but music.

I fall asleep for maybe half an hour. Then I'm jolted awake by a woman's scream. I sit up and listen. I hear a slap, then more, and screams, and a man swearing. It is happening just outside my room. I move the chair to the opening above the door and climb up. It is dark inside so I am able to look without being seen. José is beating Margarita, slapping her, punching her. She is crying. He doesn't stop. I am watching and shaking.

I continue to watch from my blind, knowing that I will interfere if I think she is in danger. After four years of anthropological training, which teaches that we must not project our own values onto another culture, that professionally we must remain in the nonjudgmental role of "participant-observer," I realize that, in this situation at least, I am more an individual than I am a professional. If I have to, I will step in.

Fortunately, he stops before she is in serious trouble. I'm sure this isn't the first time he has beaten her and I'm just as sure it isn't the last. I also suspect that in this small village, wife beating is common. And no one else's business but the husband's.

I am unable to sleep. All night my mind replays the beating, and I cry.

The next morning Margarita brings my breakfast. Her eyes, both of them, are black. Margarita knows I have seen her shame. She tells me she is afraid of her husband, but she cannot leave. "Where would I go? How would I feed the children?" she asks.

I give her a hug, but I say nothing. This village, this marriage, this life are her destiny.

In the early afternoon, the women begin arriving and the cooking begins. The turkey is killed, dipped in boiling water to loosen the feathers, and plucked. Then the bird is chopped up. Body parts, head, feet, and innards are boiled in a giant terracotta pot with garlic and onions and salt. When the turkey is cooked, it is taken out of the broth.

I position myself in the middle of the action, helping to remove parts from the pot, washing utensils as they are used, stirring, and copying what everyone else is doing. I am thrilled to be working with the women. I love the bonding that takes place in the kitchen, even when the kitchen is in the yard. It is no different here than it is in a Thanksgiving kitchen in New England. Women working together, talking, laughing, telling secrets. Some of the most meaningful and touching moments of my years as a nomad will happen over cookfires.

Huge pots are sending out the smells of turkey and cloves and cinnamon and herbs. Everyone is busy. When I can find a space to stand, I chop or slice or peel something. The women smile at my participation, surprised that I am able to peel an onion or cut up a garlic. If I ask what I can do, I get no answer; it's OK to step in on my own, but they are not going to give me an assignment.

Finally, one of the women takes the stems of oregano from a little girl who is stripping off the leaves. Understanding my need to be needed, the woman dismisses the girl and hands me a stem. The child sulks off; I have stolen her job. But I am happy as I pull off tiny leaf after tiny leaf and put them into a bowl. Meanwhile, the *mole* ingredients are getting toasted and blended and sautéed. Three different kinds of *chiles,* charred and chopped, are tossed into a blender with mounds of grilled tomatoes. There are peanuts and almonds and sesame seeds, chocolate and raisins and onions and garlic, oregano, cloves, *mole* paste, and, I suspect, a whole lot more that I miss.

This is the first time since I arrived that I have seen a group of women together. Unlike the men, they do not congregate in the village square.

As the women cook, they talk in Zapotec and laugh. I can tell from their laughter and their eyes and their hands that they are talking about their men, making fun of them. I make faces as though I understand too; and then they talk about me, mimicking my tentative walk on the hills and my pronunciation of their words. From time to time someone reaches over to pat me, a gesture that says, we're only kidding. And I know they are. We are laughing together. Another barrier has fallen over turkey *mole.*

In the early evening the guests arrive. There are speeches and reports and loud, loud music from the speakers. Then the live band arrives. The trumpets and bugles and trombones are so far off-key that they sound like a parody of a bad brass band. But the accordion carries the tune and everyone starts to dance.

At first I'm flattered at my popularity. The men are standing in line to dance with me. But when it becomes clear that they are all drunk and that they can't stop touching me, I am nervous. The women see what is happening, and they move in. Soon I am surrounded by four women, then five, holding hands, dancing around me in a circle. I dance in the middle. From time to time one of the women joins me in the middle, taking my hands and swinging to the music. All night I dance protected by women. The men can't get through.

Finally, the party is over. The band goes home and the tapes blare again from the roof speakers. The guests leave and I go to bed.

About an hour later I'm jolted awake by a knock on my door. I don't answer. The knock turns into pounding.

"Rita, open the door!" I recognize José's voice. More pounding. "I know you are there! Let me in!"

I am huddled in bed, shaking. More pounding. "Rita! Open the door!"

I lie there praying that my cement fortress, with its heavy metal door, holds up. After about ten minutes, he leaves.

I lie awake all night, curled up with my pillow, waiting in terror for the next knock and the call. For the first time I realize that traveling alone is more than occasionally feeling lonely; it can also be dangerous. Especially for a woman.

Naïve as it sounds, when I decided to travel alone, I didn't even think about the dangers. I have never been a worrier, I enjoy the adrenaline surge that comes with taking risks, and I have a tendency to trust people. On some level I must be instinctively sensitive to danger. And lucky. I have never been mugged or cheated or hurt in any way. Interestingly, the lock on my door was not there at my insistence; it was something José, or perhaps the community, knew I might need. People tend to look after their guests.

In the morning, José apologizes. "I had too much to drink. I wouldn't have hurt you. I just wanted to talk."

In the safety and sobriety of daylight, I look at my host and wonder if I would have been raped if he'd had a key. But strangely, I feel neither fear nor anger; I feel pity. José is a small man with a tired, hung-over look in his eyes. Like the other men in the village, the drought and the dry season have stolen his living. There is no off-season work. These men have been stripped of their pride, robbed of their manhood. There is nothing left to do but drink . . . and lash out at the world around them.

Oaxaca, a little more than an hour away, is a city filled with tourists who have cash in their pockets. My entrepreneurial soul can think of all sorts of items the village people could make and sell: carved wooden things, corn husk dolls, weavings, beaded jewelry. But neither the men nor the women have developed any skills. How easy it would be to create a village industry. What a waste.

Four days before I am to leave, Diego, Roberto's nineteen-year-old brother, comes to talk to me. A week earlier, he walked with me to the cracked fields that will soon be plowed, and he told me about the beans and *chiles* and corn that will fill the fields in a few months. I like Diego. He's one of the few men in the village I can talk to, and I've never seen him drunk.

Now he laughs and informs me that I can't leave the village until I have climbed the mountain. He points to something looming in the sky about a mile away.

"Every person in the village climbs the mountain at least once. You have to do it before you leave," he says and offers to guide me up.

I have never climbed a mountain, not even when I was younger and stronger. But I have taken off a lot of weight on Margarita's three hard-boiled eggs and a cup of stew a day, and I've been walking up and down hills for nearly a month. I accept the challenge.

"Take lunch and water," he says. "I'll pick you up at eight tomorrow morning."

We go up and down two little mountains before we get to the big one. By the time we arrive at the "real" mountain, my legs are hurting.

We walk through trees, over rocks, up gravelly slopes. Most of the route is steep; I move slowly. Like the rabbit in his race with the tortoise, Diego plays, climbs trees, leans against rocks, and feigns boredom. I'm in agony, but I refuse to quit. Everyone in the village knows we are doing this climb. Unlike the tortoise, I keep stopping to rest.

After five hours, I reach the point where I am going from tree to tree, struggling to breathe. My legs feel like logs. My muscles are aching. I only have to get to that tree, I tell myself. And when I'm there, I hold onto the tree and pick the next one. And so it is from tree to tree that I finally get to the top and collapse. Diego cannot believe that a three-hour climb has taken seven hours.

When we reach the peak, I stretch out on my back, thinking that it would not be a bad place to spend the rest of my life. Diego comes close, sits at my side, and informs me of the ritual of the mountain: once a couple has reached the top, they must have sex.

I laugh.

"No problem," says Diego, probably relieved.

We start off for home an hour later. It is dark long before we get to the bottom. Diego never even considered carrying a flashlight. The hike had never taken him until dark. Before we are down we hear voices and see lights. José has organized a search party.

For two days I cannot walk. I joke with Margarita that I will probably never walk again. There is a strange look on her face. I think she believes me.

When it is time for me to leave the village, women, children, and men walk with me to the road. Two little boys give me marbles. There are tears as I hug Margarita and Juanita and the children. Everyone waves as the bus disappears.

When I get to Oaxaca, I go to a real hotel where I get a private room with a tub, hot water, and a toilet. I soak for hours, sleep all afternoon, and stare at a ceiling without any pulsating black masses. *This* is the definition of luxury.

While I soak in the tub, I think about my village experience. I walked into a foreign world where people were afraid of me, and I walked out with hugs and waves and even a few tears. Initially, I thought I could connect with a smile; but it wasn't enough. I needed a teacher. Juanita's lesson would serve me well for the rest of my life: Connection requires participation. In this setting, clothes and language were the passwords to acceptance.

But the most touching and meaningful lesson of all was the intensity of *sisterhood.* Even now, sixteen years later, I can feel the warmth and strength of those women as they danced around me and with me, the affinity I felt, the bonding that occurred, the strength they projected as they held hands to protect me from their men.

The next day I call my husband to tell him I'm coming home. Our two-month separation is over. We have not had a conversation since day two, when I reported my Visa card missing.

"Hi," I say. "How are you?"

"Not very good," he says. "Except to go to work, I haven't been out of the house since you left. I need another two months." He explains why, but my head is spinning and I can barely hear him.

When our conversation is over, I lean against the window of a curio shop. Cars are honking. *Mariachis* in red-and-gold costumes are playing guitar and singing. And I am frightened. My two weeks have turned into four months; my break has become a lengthy separation. I had no idea when I started this in motion that it would spin so far out of my control.

It is clear that at the moment, my husband and I are in two different realities. He is home, answering questions about our separation and confronting his fears and loneliness on a daily basis, while I have barely thought about the world I left behind. I am suddenly afraid of the unintended consequences of my leaving. As I unfold the map to decide where I'll go for the next two months, my hands are shaking.

CHAPTER THREE

LETTING GO IN
PALENQUE AND L.A.

T he day after the phone call, I move onto the backpacker trail, mixing with the travelers who are on and off the buses and in and out of the hostels. At first I run from place to place, from group to group. I am afraid to stop moving, afraid to be alone, afraid that these next two months are the beginning of a lifetime of loneliness. I want very much to talk, but I cannot share my pain; it is too new and my companions too young.

Finally, after a little more than a week, I cannot run anymore. I don't even know what I'm running from. When I think about it, I feel good about myself. During the last two months I have discovered parts of me I didn't know were there: the part that can embrace strangers and enrich my life through knowing them, the part that enjoys making independent decisions, and the part that adores living spontaneously. Until the phone call, I hoped to be bringing this new me into a marriage that could benefit from rejuvenation. But now I fear that my personal development is going to be guiding me instead through a different stage in life, that of a divorced woman.

Once I slow down, I feel better. I tour Chiapas with an American woman for two weeks. I wander in the mountains with two Danish men, part of the time on horseback. I hang out in Playa del Carmen, with a mixed group of Europeans. After a while the anxiety diminishes.

"Go to Palenque."

It's a refrain I've been hearing for weeks. "Palenque's amazing." Everybody says it. And then they talk about the art and architecture of the ancient Mayan civilization that flourished there in the seventh and eighth centuries and the extraordinary spiritual presence that still lingers. A month after I leave Oaxaca, I'm on my way.

But first I detour through Mérida to buy a hammock. Hammock buying in Mérida is not the same as hammock buying at Hammacher Schlemmer. There are many choices to be made: cotton or nylon, white or multicolored. How many strings per inch, how wide, how long, how strong? I am overwhelmed. It's like choosing leather in Florence or silver jewelry in Taxco. When confronted with overkill, I always have trouble making decisions. I walk around for more than an hour, from one hammock seller to another. Finally, I choose white cotton, the biggest, the most tightly woven, the best. Then I board the bus to Palenque.

The guy across the aisle with the huge beard and bushy brown hair is in his mid-thirties. He looks like the "Nature Boy" in Nat King Cole's song that was popular when I was a teenager. That song still slips into my psyche now and then, especially when I'm walking in the woods or along a river. It tells about a "strange enchanted boy" who wanders the world. And here, in the middle of Mexico, that boy/man is sitting across the aisle from me. His name is Wolfgang and he's from Germany. He is exotically attractive, and he's on his way to Palenque.

Wolfgang is an engineer. He's been on the road for nearly a year. I love his wildly exploding head of hair, his very blue eyes peering out from under the hair, and the massive beard that hides his lower face. He's been told that the place to stay in Palenque is the campgrounds near the ruins. I join him.

The campgrounds border the jungle. When we check in, we're told there is only one platform left. We go have a look. A platform, it turns out, is a wooden floor, a thatched roof, and posts for tying up hammocks and holding up the roof. Ropes swing from the beams for hanging food or backpacks. If we want to stay at the camp, Wolfgang and I will have to share a platform. It's not a problem. I've been sleeping in dorms, sharing rooms, and making instant friends for more than a month now. At first I struggled with modesty, but I knew I had to get rid of it if I was going to travel this route. I've almost succeeded.

I hang my hammock. It's huge.

Wolfgang explains that the best way to sleep in a hammock is diagonally, so your body is level.

"Watch," he says and wiggles his body into a diagonal position.

I sit on my hammock, feet on the floor, and reach for the far end of the netting so that I can twist myself into position. I end up on the floor, laughing.

Wolfgang swings himself out of his hammock and helps me up. Then he holds my hammock as I get in, talks me into the right position, and gives me a push. It's delicious. When the hammock stops swinging, I pull on a rope that is not too far from my shoulders; and I rock myself like a baby, thinking that if my marriage is over, I will rent an apartment somewhere and sleep in a hammock forever.

The next morning I wake up to the sound of a lion roaring in the jungle.

"What was that?" I ask quietly, not wanting to alert some wild beast to my location. Wolfgang is sitting on the floor writing in his journal.

"Don't worry," he says. "It's just a howler monkey. They're not really fierce. There's something about their throats and the configuration of their jaws that makes them sound like lions."

They sound close, but they're not. The roar travels for miles every morning as howlers call out a claim to their jungle territory.

I slip out of my hammock and get dressed, modestly turning my back to Wolfgang as I slip out of my nightshirt and into my bra. It's the only option in our open-air, unwalled platform. Oops. There are two guys walking down the hill in front of me. The backpackers' trail is not for the modest.

Heavy morning mist, the melodic songs of unseen birds, and a powerful sense of moving back through time accompany us as we walk through what was once a lush tropical jungle surrounding an ancient Mayan city. Neither of us speaks. I breathe deeply, trying to hyperventilate myself into a hypnotic state. I am about to reenter the seventh century, when Palenque was a thriving city nestled into the foothills of the mountains that surround us.

Instinctively, we both know this is a solitary experience. Without speaking, we separate. I sit on a rock, staring across the plaza toward the Temple of the Inscriptions, imagining it as it once was, radiating red in the rays of the tropical sun. Squinting, I can see the Mayans moving gracefully through the plaza and climbing the steps of the temple, their bronze skin glowing, their exquisite blue-feather headdresses adding color and character to the scene. In the plaza women are carrying baskets of fresh fruit on their heads, standing around in groups, talking, laughing. They are real people, I can feel them, sense their spirits in this place that still holds their secrets. I close my eyes.

I wake up two hours later feeling as though I have visited another world. I join the stream of visitors climbing the sixty-nine nearly vertical steps of the temple. At the top, I sit, exhausted from the climb, and once again I imagine the city filled with ancient Mayan people whose brilliant achievements in sculpture and architecture, math and calendars and hieroglyphics have fascinated the modern world.

Every once in a while I peer down the steps and my heart begins to pound. I am terrified at the prospect of going down. There is no railing and the angle is sharp. I wait until all the climbers have descended and I begin. I realize immediately that I cannot face out; my whole body shakes and I feel as though I am about to fall. I turn around and face into the steps, and, like a toddler, I go down the steps on my hands and knees and feet, from the first to the sixty-nineth step.

When I am on solid ground again, I wander from structure to structure, fascinated by the stucco sculptures and the sophisticated architecture. What could have happened to these extraordinary people and their culture?

Along the way I meet Wolfgang and we walk back to the campgrounds together. It's startling to enter the compound. There is laughter and noise coming from the picnic benches. Nearly everyone staying in the camp is gathered there. It turns out that across the road and over the hill is a cattle farm; and when the rain is right (it was last night), psychedelic mushrooms grow in the cow dung and people make omelets and tea in the camp.

I have never tried anything psychedelic, but I've always wanted to. Would I be wrapped up in colors, attacked by sounds, filled with insights about worlds I don't even know exist?

Wolfgang isn't interested, but he promises to stay with me in case I have "a bad trip." I have always promised myself that if I ever tried LSD or mushrooms, I would have someone I trusted at my side.

True, I just met Wolfgang; but he is a gentle man. I know I can trust him. One of the most valuable tools I have honed in the last months is a sense of whom I can trust and whom I cannot.

Fred, an American my age whom I instinctively do not trust, seems to be in charge of the mushroom events. He offers me a cup of tea. I accept. He's put sugar in it, but the brew is bitter. I look around at the assembled crowd. There's a glaze over their eyes, all of them. I'm the last one in. In minutes, my head begins to float. I am euphoric, smiling, swaying, silent.

I remember very little about the next twelve hours. Every inch of my body from my bubbly head to my floating feet is leaping, flying, soaring.

The world is filled with colors and music. There is nothing between my inner self and the outer world. We are one.

Wolfgang doesn't leave my side. When the sun goes down, we go back to our platform; he puts his arm around me as we walk. When we arrive at the platform, I fantasize climbing into his hammock and burying my head and hands in his beard; but it is a fantasy that stays inside my head as he helps me gently into my hammock. I close my eyes and float through the night.

A couple of days later, ten of us pile into the back of a pickup for a trip to the spectacular Agua Azul Park, where turquoise water crashes down rocky cliffs, caresses massive boulders, and slides sinuously over silky stones.

A group of us wander off the trail to a waterfall that is cascading down forty feet of cliff. The final vestiges of my modesty are tossed off with my clothes as we all run into the falls, the warm and powerful water pounding our heads and shoulders and pouring down our bodies. We laugh and squeal and dance in the sun and the sparkling falls. I am not sure who this woman is, but she is certainly not the me of four months ago.

That night I lie in my hammock, swinging gently and thinking about the last five days. I have buried my fears, abandoned self-consciousness, and allowed myself to slide into sensation. I like the person I have become. I am even feeling positive and optimistic about the marriage. Surely these new experiences will enable me to bring something different and exciting into our relationship. In less than a week, I will be in Los Angeles.

Before I board the plane in Mexico City, I call my husband.

"I may have to go to a meeting," he says. "If I'm not there, take the Super Shuttle."

A four-foot-long sign with bright red letters is stretched between two giggly little girls in braids: *Bienvenidos Papi.*

Two uniformed men, holding placards high above the heads of the crowd in front of them, are looking for their passengers.

A clutch of people speaking Mandarin are calling to an old man arriving in a wheelchair. His face is glowing and smiling with recognition.

A shriek pierces the air and a twentyish woman swings her lithe body under the rope and gallops to greet the young shrieking woman who is walking behind me.

A couple in front of me cannot stop kissing and touching.

It's a scene I usually love, families and friends hugging and calling and chattering in different languages, nearly everyone smiling. But this time my heart is pounding and my eyes are tearing. No one is there for me.

I call the Super Shuttle.

Forty-five minutes later, I fumble with the key, my fingers barely able to hold it. The house is the same as it was when I left four months earlier; nothing has changed. Except now it feels cold and empty. And it is screaming at me: I'm not yours anymore.

Actually, it never was. I feel nothing for this place, this building. I never did make it "mine." Nine years ago we moved to L.A. from Manhattan, a family of four (Mitch was fourteen and Jan was thirteen) and a dog. Most of our New York furniture was threadbare, so we brought only a few pieces.

We bought the house and all its garish furniture from the previous owners, who needed money in a hurry. I was thrilled that with no effort or shopping on my part, the rooms were filled. There were, and still are, "smoky" gold-spattered mirrors; a white-and-gold fake French bedroom set; a hideous carpet in the family room with an orange, red, yellow, and green print; velvet curtains; a white furry love seat; and more. None of it my taste. I figured we'd decorate when we had the time and money, but we never got around to it. Decorating has never been my thing. As long as lamps light, couches sit, and beds sleep, I'm happy.

So when I walk into the house that has been my family's for nine years, it does not cuddle me. I feel only emptiness, abandonment, alienation.

My husband arrives a few hours later and announces that he has decided to end the marriage. He has already talked to a lawyer.

I have been preparing for this moment for four months, but I cannot stop the tears. The Pollyanna part of me that believes anything can be fixed if you really want to fix it is devastated; the tears are for the fact that I'm not even going to have a chance to try . . . and for the lost dreams of a young couple in love.

But the realistic part of me knows that I cannot continue to live as we were. In the last months I have been a woman who has felt joy, shared laughter, explored other worlds, and rediscovered a hidden me. I will not, cannot, bury her again. I too hire a lawyer.

I do not want alimony; I have always had an aversion to dependency in either direction. And I do not want *things,* not even the things that are mine, like books and paintings and records and clothes. I have always dreamed of owning nothing but the stuff I could carry on my back. Now that I am answering only to myself, I can make that happen. I shed my skin in Mexico; now I am shedding the material trappings of my life.

My husband and I work out a dollar figure for our joint possessions. When we are finished, I do not own a book, a towel, a chair, or a spoon.

Fortunately, I do have a source of income. As a writer of children's books, I know I can sell most of what I write. But it's not reliable income, and it isn't that much; not enough to support myself in the U.S. If I stay here, I will have to get an apartment and a regular job in order to survive.

I don't want an apartment, and I have even less interest in a job. What I want is to do more of what I was doing in Mexico: discover the world and interact with the people in it.

I can write fiction for kids wherever I am and send the manuscripts to my agent in New York. If I live in developing countries, I don't have to make very much money.

I sit down with some loose figures. Let's say my expenses are $10 a day for food and lodging; that's $3,650 a year. Double it for plane fares and entertainment and miscellaneous expenses: $7,300. Then double it again for health insurance (around $3,000 a year through the writers' union) and luxuries and amenities like a bookkeeper and gifts and taxes: $14,600. Not very scientific, but it'll do. If I stay in developing countries, I can live nicely on $15,000 a year! *Very* nicely.

Happily, three of my books—*More Spaghetti, I Say!*, *Why Can't I Fly?* and *The Biggest Sandwich Ever*—are doing well. My annual royalties from them and other already written books will probably be around $12,000. One new book a year will bring in at least $3,000 more. I should be in great shape.

For the five months it takes us to do the legal stuff, I feel like a lost child. I live in the tiny (eight-foot by eleven-foot) office that I've been renting in Venice, California, for a number of years. I join a gym so I can shower. And I eat every meal out, in restaurants and fast-food places, constantly aware that I am alone in the place where I live, which is even harder than being alone in a place where you don't know anyone. There is no "travelers' network" for me in Los Angeles.

The kids are not around either. Mitch is in Singapore, studying for a year on a Rotary International Fellowship. And Jan is finishing up school at the University of Colorado in Boulder. We talk often and write at least once a week, but basically we are all going through this divorce separately.

Most of the time I am not interested in talking to people or going out.

Or even joining friends—the ones who are left. Most of my nine-
social life in Los Angeles was with couples that we knew through my husband's work. When I return from Mexico, I never hear from any of them
again.

Divorcing also marks the end of the "glamorous" events in my life. I am
no longer connected to the world I was in. The strings have been cut and I'm
floating, looking on from outside as an observer instead of a participant.

As an observer, I am particularly interested in watching women, married, divorced, single. So many of them are trapped in lives they think they
must live, in roles they have come to resent, with little joy and no laughter.
They've "settled." They've compromised. They've learned to adjust.

Among the divorced, many are bitter, coloring their lives with resent-
ment; others live only to meet the man who will complete them.

I have no intention of adjusting, and I am not looking to define myself
by the man I am with. The new me is feeling rebellious, looking for excitement, bursting with energy to explore. There is no way that I am going to
sit around feeling sorry for myself, thinking that the only way I can enjoy
life is with a man.

With no possessions, no home, and no precedent, I am free to design a
life that fits me. Best of all, I have tasted the life I want. My Mexican adventure opened me up. I want more. During my four months away, I met interesting people, I was never bored, and I laughed more than I had in years.
I resolve to continue exploring the world, ignoring the *they* who define
how people should live.

"I'm going back to Central America," I tell anyone who asks. The more
I say it, the more I like how it sounds.

Before I leave, I do a couple of responsible things. I set up an invest-
ment account so when the house sells, the money will have somewhere to
go. And I arrange to get my own credit card, which I've never had before.

Then I hire a bookkeeper and forward my mail to her. I also open a
joint checking account with her so she can pay my bills and deposit my
royalty checks. I pay her by the hour and trust her to keep accurate records.

I do not ask for permission to live this new life, not from my kids, not
from my parents, and not from my friends, many of whom are convinced
that I'm avoiding the real world.

I'm not interested in hearing lectures from people who seem to know
better than I how I should live my life. I already know that single women
of my age are not supposed to wander aimlessly around the world, hanging out with backpackers. They vacation in places where they can meet

men, like on Caribbean cruises and European tours. And they stay in hotels that are "safe." Unattached women rarely embrace their freedom. And about-to-be-divorced women like me do not renounce their possessions. Everyone has advice for me; but I'm not listening.

One of my friends buys me a drink before I leave. Taking off like that, she says, is not psychologically healthy. "You've got to deal with it. You can't run away."

But I'm not running away. I'm running toward . . . toward adventure, toward discovery, toward diversity. And while I was in Mexico I discovered something intriguing: Once I leave the U.S., I am not bound by the rules of my culture. And when I am a foreigner in another country, I am exempt from the local rules. This extraordinary situation means that there are no rules in my life. I am free to live by the standards and ideals and rules I create for myself.

Guatemala

Chapter Four

Learning How

For the first time in my life I am not worrying about how my behavior might reflect upon my family. My parents are a continent away in Connecticut, my husband is no longer my husband, and my kids are busy building independent lives. It's a heady place to be for a woman who has always lived her roles appropriately and played the game by the rules. *I can do whatever I want to do!*

And what I want to do is move through other worlds, learn what it is that makes us all human, and interact with people who are different from me.

I decide to begin my new life in Guatemala. This time I leave with hope and excitement instead of tears. Mexico has shown me that the world is peopled with fascinating varieties of human beings. And I am convinced that most of them are just as eager to meet me as I am to meet them.

I pack everything I own: two pairs of pants, one skirt, four T-shirts. A sweater. Underwear. A bathing suit. Toothpaste, toothbrush, deodorant, sunblock, insect repellant, sneakers, and four plastic bags. I put in my Spanish dictionary, the Lonely Planet guide to Guatemala, a novel to read and trade, a Swiss Army knife, and a sleeping bag. And finally, I pack two empty spiral notebooks, some ballpoint pens, and the smallest secondhand manual typewriter I can find. I've given everything else away.

A friend gives me a threadbare (as requested) face towel that can fit in a small space and wash and dry easily.

I've decided to go to the colonial town of Antigua, a popular stopover on the backpacker trail. But this time I'm not plugging into the backpacker network; I'm planning to settle in and become part of the expatriot community, which is made up, I'm told, mostly of Americans.

On the plane, I am overwhelmed with doubt for the first time since I made my decision to live an alternative life. Images of being alone and friendless rush into my head. Do I really believe what I've been telling myself about what makes me happy? Maybe there are fundamental reasons why people don't go off permanently adventuring.

During the five-hour flight, I struggle to convince myself that I have made the right decision; and then, as the plane nears Guatemala City, the pilot announces that the airport is backed up because of bad weather. We will have to circle for half an hour. A bad sign, I think, feeling uncharacteristically superstitious.

And then I look out the window. The plane is surrounded by rainbows, bright, sparkling, full-color rainbows against a sky full of clouds. Four, five, maybe six rainbows are arcing on all sides of us.

We circle out of the rainbows and fly around, and then they are back, these spectacular symbols of joy and harmony and peace. What a fabulous sign that my new convenant with life is the right decision.

Tucked into a valley forty-five kilometers from Guatemala City, Antigua is a charming colonial town surrounded by three volcanoes. The streets are cobblestone; the houses and public buildings, colonial; and the central plaza, with its fountains, shade trees, and wooden benches is designed for people watching.

Within a few hours of my arrival in Antigua, I sign up for Spanish classes and move in with a family recommended by the school. The family, who are instructed to speak only Spanish to me, consists of two teenage children and a couple in their early forties. When I am introduced, the kids smile politely, but they do not talk to me. Elena, the mother, asks me a few questions, tells me that dinner is at seven o'clock, and returns to her housework. My room has a bed, a chest, and a desk.

I unpack and dig out an address. When I was in Los Angeles, a friend told me about a Frenchwoman, Brigitte, who is working to set up a day house for street kids in Guatemala City. She and her staff live in Antigua. I'm hoping she'll let me be a part of the project. One of the things I missed most in my L.A. life was a hands-on, face-to-face involvement in helping people. As a teenager in Connecticut, a college student in Massachusetts, and a young mother in New York, I spent many hours volunteering in orphanages, mental institutions, city beaches, public schools. Somehow, I never got it together to volunteer in L.A.

When Brigitte hears I'm a writer, she welcomes me warmly. She has been looking for someone to help her write a proposal in search of additional funding. I join the team: Brigitte, the Frenchwoman, who has already raised enough money to buy a house in the central part of Guatemala City; Amy, a British woman who has been working with Brigitte for several years. And Gary, a seventeen-year-old American who recently signed on; he's a hard worker, bright, and probably a runaway.

The day I make contact with Brigitte, she is taking some people to see the scene in the central city, kids sniffing glue hidden in paper bags, kids sleeping in the gutter, other kids begging. They are the homeless, the rejected, the castaways. Brigitte's idea is to give them a place they can go during the day, with a toilet, a shower, a place to sit, and some lunch. I am looking forward to working with the kids and ecstatic to be a part of the project. This is it; this is what I've been needing and wanting. Even before I begin, I feel fulfilled.

My first assignment is to write the proposal. I'd rather be wandering the streets talking to kids, but I take the job seriously. After nearly two weeks of intense writing, the proposal is finished. Brigitte is pleased with my work and she invites me to join the team in the city. The house is nearly ready, but it needs scrubbing and painting and patching.

I don't see much of Brigitte during the days of "housework"; she is off being political and soliciting support from the local officials. But her energy infuses all of us as we sweep and wash and fill in cracks in the walls.

And as we work, we talk and sing and share our life stories. Each day I feel closer to Amy and Gary. Often we eat together; and at night we sit around talking. I cannot believe how lucky I am to be a part of this project. It's a perfect fit. I walk around smiling. Brigitte comments one day that my walk has a new bounce.

Somewhere toward the end of the spackling and scrubbing, I make a quick trip to the United States for a family event. I am radiating with joy as I tell everyone that I have found the meaning of life and it's in giving and sharing and hands-on helping. I am bursting with enthusiasm; and I haven't even begun working with the street kids.

When the house is ready, Brigitte plans an open house for city officials, local donors, and an assortment of invited guests, mostly Guatemalans. I buy a simple blue dress, a pair of silver earrings, and black leather sandals. I am heart-pounding excited to be a part of it all.

I arrive at Brigitte's house in Antigua ten minutes before we are to leave for the city. Gary and Amy are in the living room.

"Rita, I have to talk to you," says Amy, taking me aside. There is something about her eyes that tells me this is not going to be good news.

"Brigitte has decided that there are too many gringos involved in this project. She feels the local officials will be put off if they see so many foreigners. She does not want you to attend the open house."

I am disappointed, but I understand. It's probably true that this invited crowd of Guatemalan officials and moneyed society people would be more receptive if there were more Guatemalans than gringos in the group. Brigitte has recently hired two local women.

"OK," I say. "I can wait until tomorrow." The next day the doors will open for the kids. "I'm much more interested in the kids than the officials anyway. What time are we leaving in the morning?"

"I haven't finished," says Amy. "Brigitte doesn't want you on the project at all. I'm sorry."

I cannot believe what I am hearing. This can't be happening. Just like that, I have been discarded. No apology. No thank you. No effort to be gentle. The tears well up in my eyes and I feel as though I am going to faint. I turn and walk home in a daze. That is the last I ever see of Amy or Brigitte or Gary.

The minute I enter my room, I begin to sob. I cannot stop. I do not come out of my room for dinner. Or breakfast. Or lunch.

My hostess is worried. She knocks on my door and I tell her I'm OK. I am not feeling well and want to rest. No, I don't want to eat, thank you.

Actually, I am not OK. I have been working on this project for more than two months. It has filled every minute of my time in Guatemala. It has also filled my psyche. I love Brigitte and Amy and Gary; and the project has given new meaning to my life. I also know how good I am with kids. They haven't even seen that part of me. I am devastated.

When I recover enough to reflect on what happened, I see Brigitte's side of it. There is something about a preponderance of foreigners that reeks of colonialism and sends out a message of superiority. Of course it is better to have a staff of Guatemalans. I do understand. But her way of telling me, and her timing, were painfully insensitive. Over the next years I will meet other people whose lives are devoted to great causes but whose sensitivity to individuals, including their families, is defective. I applaud their work and their commitment, but after my Brigitte experience, I am wary of their friendship.

When I am ready to join the world again, I decide to rent an apartment for six months. I check out the bulletin boards in the center of town and put a deposit on a great two-bedroom place. Doña Lina, the owner, a wealthy Guatemalan woman of Spanish extraction whose family has owned the house for generations, lives with her husband in the back part of the property; there is a central courtyard between us. Doña Lina is a small woman but she stands tall; her presence is a bit haughty. She promises me hot water and quiet.

I carry my bags over and move in. Now I need some friends. I'm going back to my initial plan of making friends in the ex-pat community. There are several dozen ex-Americans who own homes and businesses in Antigua. I haven't met them, but I know they are here; I've seen them congregating in Doña Luisa's restaurant for breakfast.

Doña Luisa's is two blocks from the main plaza. The restaurant is in the covered courtyard of an old colonial mansion. The day after I move into my own place, I arrive early at Doña Luisa's for breakfast and take a seat near the door, where everyone who comes in or out has to pass by my table. I want to be noticed.

I sit without a newspaper or a book and people-watch, nodding and smiling (a small smile accompanied by a short nod) at anyone who looks in my direction. The table for eight in the middle of the room is where the in-group sits. They arrive one by one and greet each other like old friends. I eat my scrambled eggs and toast and sip the wonderful, rich coffee and wonder if I will be sitting with them a week or so from now. That's my plan. Step number one is to get them to notice me, so I sit at my table for more than an hour with a friendly expression on my face.

The next day I take the same table and smile the same smile, this time with a hint of greater familiarity, justified by the fact that I'd seen them the day before and I know they saw me.

Day three I say, "Hi." And I get nods and Hi's back. By now they must be wondering who I am.

Finally, on the fourth day, a chunky fiftyish guy with a big black beard asks me where I'm from. I tell him Los Angeles and ask him how long he's been here. Years, he answers.

"How long are you in Antigua for?" he asks.

"I've just rented an apartment for six months, maybe a year." Then, with a little laugh, I ask, "Does that qualify me to join your table? I'd love to meet some of the locals."

"Sure," he says. And I'm in.

Most of the ex-pats in this group are Americans. One woman owns a successful art gallery on the main square, with fine paintings, assorted crafts, and books. Her taste is exquisite and the shop is thriving. The fellow with the beard collects, preserves, and sells butterflies to museums and anyone else who wants a framed, glassed-in butterfly collection.

I am invited to visit the greenhouse of a retired doctor and his wife. The glass house is hot, the smell is earthy, and dozens of exquisite orchids fill the tables and hang from beams. Their daughter, an adult, is also living in town; she is coming off of a broken marriage and has been living in Antigua for nearly a year with her son. She and I become friends.

They are all living well. Some of them have cooks, cleaners, drivers, and women who do laundry. The staff-people are "servants," which is one of those words one doesn't use in the U.S. any more. Here in Guatemala, I am told, the servants are happy to have the jobs, even though the salaries are small. The ex-pats are living in luxury on next to nothing.

Over the next months, I have an occasional dinner in an ex-pat home; and at least twice a week, I join the flexible group in Doña Luisa's for breakfast.

The ex-pat lives are very much in order. They pay someone to go to immigration in the city to renew their visas, they take a monthly deworming pill, not even bothering to check to see if they need it, and they entertain elegantly, their servants cooking and cleaning up after the party.

Many ex-pats have their own cars, their own clubs, their own pools. And most of them are aggressively anticommunist. I avoid conversations about Nicaragua and the Sandinistas.

One Saturday I meet an ex-pat from Guatemala City when he buys a handwoven fabric from María, a young indigenous woman who sells weavings on the street. María is gorgeous and one of the best sellers in town. The long shiny braid, the flirty dark eyes, the hint of a great body under her boxy *huipil* blouse, and her fearlessness in the face of foreigners are the keys to her success. Every day I stop by her spot near Doña Luisa's and we talk.

That Saturday morning when I come to say hello, she is holding out a beautiful red, yellow, and black weaving to an American man. He is looking for a tablecloth. I help her by taking one end.

"It's good quality," I tell him. "María comes from a family of weavers. Five sisters and their mother. Their work is the best."

I hold María's baby, Diana, while she negotiates a price. When they are finished, buyer and seller are both smiling.

María invites me to Diana's first birthday party. Her family lives in San Antonio Aguas Calientes, a village in the hills about fifteen kilometers out of town. I have been there three times to share celebrations. I am honored by their invitations.

"Can I come early and help?"

"Sure," says María. And she quickly disappears into a hard sell with a couple who are walking toward her.

"A cup of coffee?" the man says to me as he slips the tablecloth into his backpack. Why not?

Eric is in his early forties, a Warren Beatty look-alike with a southern drawl. He lives in Guatemala City, but he's spending the weekend at one of the better hotels in Antigua. We have coffee in his hotel. After coffee, he invites me to join him on a trip to Chichicastenango the next day.

At eight the next morning Eric arrives in a light blue Mercedes. I don't like riding in expensive cars, especially when I am going to be driving through places where people can't afford bicycles. But I have no choice.

We drive along a twisty, dusty, mostly dirt road. The day is windy and dust is flying around us like a plague of locusts. I keep hoping that dust will cover the car, nick its sleek exterior, and hide its identity; but that Mercedes symbol proudly precedes us wherever we go. The dust seems to slide off the car as if the finish has been done in ScotchGuard.

Above the road on both sides of us are terraced fields of beans and corn. The women working in the fields look like paintings, each wearing nearly identical splashes of color. Like the women from many indigenous villages in Guatemala, the Chichi women wear matching *huipiles,* blouses made from rectangular weavings with openings for the head and the arms. You can know a woman's village by the *huipil* she wears. The Chichi *huipiles* are decorated with brilliantly colored flowers.

Chichicastenango sits in a valley; its buildings are whitewashed adobe; its streets, cobblestone; its roofs, red tile. The steps of Santo Tomás church, which is the focus of the plaza, are filled with women selling flowers and lighting incense. Eric buys me a lily, paying nearly as much for one as the seller was asking for the whole bunch. The village smells of sweet wood, burning in the cooking stalls, of incense from the religious ceremony that is taking place on the church steps. The streets and alleys are a huge palette of oranges, bananas, melons, papayas, and flowers in every imaginable color.

Eric and I wander in and out of the fruits and vegetables, along a passageway of weavings, down alleys of leather and woodcrafts. I buy some candles and a wrought iron candle holder. Eric buys a wool blanket for himself and a floppy hat for me. Then we wander over to the Mayan Inn for a lunch of grilled meats, cheese, black beans, *salsa*, and fried plantains. Eric is easy to be with, relaxed, bright, comfortable with himself. It's a great day; I like this man.

In the car going home we talk about ourselves. He tells me that he plans to live the rest of his life in Guatemala. He lives in a big house in the outskirts of Guatemala City, surrounded by a tall fence. He has a pool, a maid, and a Mercedes. He says he's discovered paradise.

He has been here for three years without ever going back to the United States. "And I never will," he says.

"How can you be so sure?" I ask, surprised at the conviction in his voice.

He looks at me with a smile on his lips but not in his eyes, "I am wanted for bank robbery in Texas."

The following Sunday is my forty-ninth birthday. It will be the first time in my life that I've been away from family on my birthday. There are no cards in the mail, no gifts, no one to give me a birthday hug or take me out to dinner. I feel empty and sad. I don't want to be alone on my birthday.

I think about telling some of my ex-pat friends, but they've only known me a few months. Besides, I am spending less time with them and more with María and her family these days. It is not a surprise that I feel more comfortable with the indigenous community; the privileged life of the ex-pats feels lofty and too exclusive for me, though they are quite willing to include me in their world. When I am with them, I find myself recreating a persona that is reminiscent of the me I no longer want to be.

I decide that on my birthday, I will invite María and her large family to my apartment for hot dogs and beans; but I do not tell them that it is my birthday. Fifteen people show up, twelve kids and three moms. When they arrive, I see Doña Lina, my landlady, peering across the yard at us, disapprovingly.

I have bought a small gift for each guest. No one has a clue what the party is all about . . . but we eat and sing (not "Happy Birthday"). And they open presents. When they leave, María reminds me of her daughter's birthday party on Wednesday.

As soon as the gang walks out the door, my landlady knocks. She is not happy with my having filled her house with indigenous people, but she doesn't say so. Instead, she asks me how I know them and if I have ever been to their home. She offers a gratuitous warning, "Be careful. They think nothing of stealing."

Then she invites me for lunch on Tuesday, two days from now. This is the first gesture of friendship she has proffered, and it is a significant one. She tells me she would like me to meet some of her friends. Until now, our relationship has consisted of polite greetings and the exchange of rent money. I'm hoping the luncheon will be the beginning of a new relationship. She will be the first friend I have in the Spanish (white) population of Antigua.

The invitation is for *doce* (twelve) *y media,* except I hear *dos* (two) *y media* and I show up two hours late. By the time I get there, lunch is over and her friends have gone home. I apologize profusely, explaining my mistake. But the significance of the invitation, the embarrassment in front of her friends, and the rudeness I demonstrated in not showing up ruin any possible relationship. She no longer talks to me when she sees me in the yard or on the street. I am disappointed. I'd been hoping a relationship with her and her friends would give me an insight into the Spanish population; but it isn't to be.

The next day is Diana's party. María's village is a short bus ride into the hills. I arrive with a birthday book for Diana (she is one) and a bottle of bubbles for the other kids. As I walk toward the small adobe structure, I can hear the clapping of *tortillas.* It's the sound of villages in Central America, someone clapping a *tortilla* into its round, pancake shape before it goes on the grill. I've been hearing the sound for months. Now I'm about to do it.

María's mom patiently demonstrates. We are sitting in the cookhouse, which has a dirt floor, open walls, and a tile roof. In one corner there is a wood fire heating a pot of beans with bits of meat, and throwing its flame and sparks whenever the wood is turned. A second wood fire is being fed and getting hot for the *comal,* a rectangular steel griddle that will cook the *tortillas.*

We are sitting at a slab table pulling off blobs from a huge pile of *masa* dough and rounding them into balls between the palms of our hands. *Masa* is made from corn; it's halfway between cornmeal and corn flour, finely ground and mixed with ground lime and water.

Mamá puts the ball of *masa* into the center of one palm. Then, using a rhythmic clapping motion, she turns her hands, *clap, clap, clap, clap, clap,* in opposite directions; then back, *clap, clap, clap, clap, clap, clap.* The dough grows rounder and flatter until finally, *clap, clap,* you have a *tortilla* around ten inches across. Each new *tortilla* gets put onto a growing pile of *tortillas* waiting to be cooked. There are three of us slapping and twisting in the tiny, smoky hut filled with the sweet smells of burning wood and bubbling beans. And soon, the *tortillas* are flipped onto the *comal,* and the smell of toasting *tortillas* dominates the room.

As the younger kids and a couple of the men string streamers around the lower tree limbs and chase bubbles around the yard, and four women clap and cook in the hut, two of the sisters are attached to their backstrap weavings, working the threads into beautiful patterns. The loom is attached to a tree on one side and the other side is held in place by leather straps stretched around the backs of the weavers.

By the time the guests arrive, about twenty-five in all, there are three piles of cooked *tortillas,* each one about a foot and a half high. When the food is ready, Mamá hands each guest a *tortilla.* The *tortilla* is both a plate and a spoon as bits of it are torn off and used to pick up the beans that have been plopped in the center of the disc.

I am watching the guests line up for beans when I hear my name. Mamá is holding up a *tortilla* with raggedy edges and holes in the middle. She laughs.

"This one is Rita's."

Everyone, including me, joins her laughter. I collect my *tortilla* and she goes back to passing the others out until the next malformed *tortilla* appears.

"Rita!" she calls. "*Esta es tuya.*" This is yours. More laughter.

By the time she finishes, I have six *tortillas* in front of me. But more important than the *tortillas* is the sense we all have that I am becoming a part of them.

I study weaving with Mamá (after five hours of classes, my tablecloth is six inches long and two feet wide). I help María and some of the teenagers improve their selling-English. I play with the kids (María's daughter and her nieces and nephews).

I discover that the family, and many others in the village, have benefited from the Christian Children's Foundation. One of María's sisters is taking sewing lessons paid for by the foundation. She brings me a skirt she has made. A younger sister shows me letters from her sponsor. They are carefully pasted into an album with a *quetzal* bird on the cover, its long tailfeathers nearly hanging over the edge. Then she runs to show me some of the new clothes she's been able to buy. CCF is real, more than just an ad in a magazine.

One morning I arrive in the village to work on my weaving. Before I am down the steps of the bus, four teenagers are all over me.

"Tienes que acompañarnos a la playa." You have to come with us to the beach. *"No puedes decir no!"* You can't say no!

Several families have rented a bus for a weekend holiday at the beach. They want me to join them. I am honored by the invitation and excited by the prospect of spending three days on a family vacation.

A week later, the loaded bus picks me up in the plaza at seven in the morning. María has saved me a seat. Three hours out of Antigua we have our first flat tire. The second flat tire comes an hour later. We arrive at the beach community just before dark.

One of the men (there are four) goes off to find us a hotel room and the women spread colorful but threadbare "tablecloths" on the sidewalk. Some of us sit on the sidewalk, others sit on the curb, feet in the street, and we open up the food that was packed that morning. There are fourteen of us in the family group; we take up most of the sidewalk. Other tourists, forced to walk around us, make comments that I cannot translate, but I know what they are saying.

As we sit on the ground, cars blowing exhaust in our faces, we eat, tossing the papers and wrappings into the street. It is hard for me to throw garbage into the street; I can feel the years of conditioning pulling on my arm as I toss. I think about picking up our trash and finding a garbage pail; but I think again. I am a friend, not a teacher. If I pick up after them, I am making a judgment that says I know better than they. Even if I walk with my own garbage to a pail, I am making a statement.

I am an invited guest. I do as they do.

Before we are finished, two girls in braids and white embroidered blouses stained with dirt come by selling drinks in plastic bags. Everyone except me buys a drink. I don't like sweet, sugary drinks, so I'm carrying bottled water.

Sitting on the curb and spilling over into the street, we are taking up a parking space. Cars drive by looking for parking spaces and honk. No one moves. Then suddenly a car swoops in and nearly amputates five pairs of legs. We jump up, spilling things all over the street. The driver screams something unpleasant at us as he steps out of the car and crosses the street. No one in our group says anything. This is not a country where indigenous people confront the Hispanic population.

Finally José comes back from his hotel search. There are no rooms. His brother-in-law joins him and the search continues. We wait on the sidewalk. An hour later, the men come back. They have found a room . . . one room for fourteen of us.

After a walk on the beach and some splashing in the water, we go to our room. It has one double bed that sleeps five and floor space for six more. Three of us sleep in the hall outside the room.

I am in the hall when the procession begins in the middle of the night. Everyone is vomiting, the babies are crying, adults are dry-heaving. We all go to the beach, which is down a hall and out a door. The ocean tide is coming in. There are drunk noises coming from the bar next door. Under the full moon, thirteen of my family stand, vomiting.

I go into the bar and buy as many big bottles of water as I can carry. As the sun comes up, some of us are back in the vomit-smelling-room-for-fourteen. I decide to stay on the beach. I wrap my eyes in a sweatshirt and try to sleep. By nine, everyone is on the beach, the mothers washing clothes in the ocean, the children playing in the water, screeching with glee in the waves. That night, the room is quiet and the hall is cleaner.

We leave at noon the next day. There is only one flat tire on the way home, but there are no more spares. This time we sit for two hours on the side of the highway. Luckily, no one is selling drinks in plastic bags.

As I sit there in the hot sun, sweating and dirty, surrounded by the adults, holding one of the babies in my arms, and feeling as close as I have ever felt to people from another culture, I realize that I have left no space between me and them, no room for anthropological distance. I feel as though they are family. Their pain is my pain; their joy, my joy. And it feels right.

It is clear that I am far more a mother than I am an anthropologist. This odd and messy weekend has helped me to define what I want to do in my travels: I want to know many cultures . . . from the inside.

Meanwhile, back in Antigua, between weaving, touring, and breakfast-ing, I have completed a thirty-two-page children's book called *Stop Those Painters!* It's about two guys who can't control their urge to paint. They begin with walls and move on to chairs and stairs and toys and boys and teachers and cars and trucks and policemen and, finally, as they stand on the wings of a jet plane, they gleefully paint rainbows in the sky. It's my first book as a nomad, inspired by the colors and the rainbows of Guatemala. I send it off to New York.

A month later I hear from my agent. Scholastic wants the book. I will be able to live for five months on the three thousand dollars they will pay me. I decide to go to the States for a few weeks, to visit my kids and my parents.

Mitch has settled in Manhattan after his year in Singapore. I see him several times during my visit. It is wonderful to hear, face to face, his sto-ries of studying and playing in Singapore; of visiting China, where he took classes in Mandarin; of touring Asia with a softball team; and of visiting Bali. He is working as a journalist in New York, and I've never seen him so happy.

Jan is still in Colorado, working as a journalist on *The Vail Trail.* I call to make arrangements to visit her, but she tells me that she's coming to visit me in Guatemala. Great! I can't wait to introduce her to my world.

I spend a week with my mother and father in Connecticut. They are careful what they say to me about my new life. I know they would prefer to have their daughter married; I also know that they don't believe me when I say I'm very very happy. They know better; women are only happy if they have a husband. It's the way life should be. My mother tells me she recently sent a birthday gift to my ex-husband. She doesn't say it, but she is hoping for reconciliation.

My brother, who is three years younger than I, married and securely settled in a well-furnished home and his own successful business not too far from my parents, takes me to the airport shuttle when I leave.

"Not ready to return to the 'real world' yet, huh?"

When I tell him I *am* in a real world, it's just not *his* world, he smiles knowingly. "I give you another six months. You'll get it out of your system."

They do not understand that the more I live it, the more I want it.

But Jan seems to understand. She backpacked with her best friend for six months in Europe when she was a junior in college, and my life is her dream, though I'm sure she would configure it differently.

Two weeks after I return to Guatemala, she arrives. For one month, she plays with the babies, dines with the ex-pats, meets a whole crowd of back-packers, and crafts a young adult novel.

Together, Jan and I travel around Guatemala by bus, and we take a plane trip to Tikal, a Palenque-like Mayan ruins in northeast Guatemala near Belize. The best part of it all for me is getting to know Jan as an adult.

Three days after Jan leaves, while I'm still missing her and feeling an emptiness in my apartment, Henry sits down next to me on a park bench. An Australian agronomist, he has just arrived from Nicaragua, where he has been working for the last six months. He's fortyish, small, angular, and friendly. He's in Antigua to take a break from Nicaragua and to study Spanish.

He's come to the right place. There are so many language schools in town that some days I think every native in Antigua is teaching Spanish. Signs, fliers, posters, children, adults all promote schools and teachers.

Henry's plan is to study intensively for two months and then go back, overland, to Nicaragua. The Sandinista government has offered him a job advising cooperatives on agricultural matters.

I ask him about Nicaragua. The Reagan government has been telling Americans that the Sandinista government is a serious threat to the free world and that the Nicaraguan people are virtually prisoners of a commu-nist regime.

"It's a hard place to live," Henry says. "Mostly because of the U.S. embargo. Every one is hurting. There's no food in the markets, no medi-cines, no parts for machines. And no professionals . . . they all left with Somoza. The whole educated class moved to Florida."

As an agronomist, Henry has a skill to offer. Apparently, there are thou-sands of Henrys from all over the world who have come to Nicaragua to help out. Ever since I arrived in Guatemala, I've been listening to their sto-ries, so different from what I read in the U.S. newspapers.

I've been thinking about going down to see for myself, but I haven't wanted to make the trip alone. It's a long and possibly dangerous trip through Honduras. And I don't know how the Nicaraguans would treat an American. It is, after all, my country that is training and arming the Contras, who are dropping American bombs on the people. Henry would be a great escort. I am trying to decide if I can ask him to take me along when he says, "Can you recommend a place in Antigua where I can stay for a couple of months?"

Yesssss.

"I have a two-bedroom apartment," I tell him. "Why don't you stay with me? It won't cost you anything, and we can study Spanish together. I need to work on mine too." Then I explain the string. In exchange for a room, he has to take me to Nicaragua.

Henry can't believe his good luck. He likes the idea of a travel companion; and even more, he is thrilled to be able to live rent free. And I am excited to be pointing in a new direction. It's time for me to leave Guatemala and move on. I love making deals where everybody ends up happy.

Henry moves in; and one day we invite Doña Lina, my landlady, to join us for dinner. She is talking to me again. She was flattered that I took Jan to meet her. Until then, she hadn't even nodded hello since I missed that lunch in her house.

And she wasn't too happy at first about Henry moving in until I assured her that he was neither paying rent nor sleeping with me. His payback, I told her, is that he is going to be my escort-over-land to Nicaragua. Our dinner with her is friendly, and good Spanish practice for Henry and me.

Two days before Henry and I are due to leave, Doña Lina stops by to tell us that her nephew, who lives in El Salvador, is driving through town in his truck next week on his way home from Mexico. She thinks he might like our company.

We'd have to delay our trip for two days and detour through El Salvador, but we accept. Neither of us has ever been to El Salvador, and riding in our own private truck sounds like fun.

Antigua has been a good place for me. Filled with friends and "family," I have met the first challenges of my new life, and I'm more confident than ever that I will thrive.

Nicaragua

CHAPTER FIVE

THE END OF POLITICAL

INNOCENCE

A ndrés arrives around noon in a red truck with a twenty-foot trailer and a cabin big enough for the three of us. We begin our conversation with family. It's the universal opener. Andrés and his wife and two preschool children live in the capital city of San Salvador.

Half an hour into our trip, I ask about life in El Salvador.

"I will talk to you because we are inside my truck and no one can hear us," he says. "In El Salvador I never discuss politics. Even here in Guatemala I won't talk if I'm on the street. You never know who might be listening."

El Salvador has been involved in a civil war since 1979. Left-wing guerrillas in the mountains are trying to overthrow the government. Agents of the government "disappear" people who are suspected of being in sympathy with the guerrillas. In 1987, any country trying to fight off left-wing movements gets support from the United States, which is willing to overlook government-sponsored atrocities. The army of El Salvador is trained and supplied by the United States.

"Do you know about the *escuadrones de muerte?*" Andrés asks. The death squadrons, supported by the government of El Salvador. "They came for my brother two years ago. We haven't heard from him since. My brother was a student. He was critical of the government. One day my brother and four of his friends disappeared. We are afraid to ask what happened to him or they will come for us."

For the rest of the trip, Andrés tells us horror stories of disappearances and atrocities committed by the "democratic" government.

When we arrive in San Salvador, the capital city, he takes us to a *pupusería. Pupusas,* a spicy mix of pork, cheese, and sausage wrapped up in a corn *tortilla,* are to El Salvador what hot dogs used to be to the U.S., before fast food came along. You can buy *pupusas* everywhere, in the markets, on the streets, and in *pupuserías.*

"Now you will have your first taste of El Salvador," he laughs for the first time. "Without *pupusas,* El Salvador would not be El Salvador."

Andrés is relaxed as we drink our beers and enjoy the spicy delights of our *pupusas.* He plays a song on the juke box about *pupusas* and he sings along. We are halfway through our meal when three men sit down at a table next to us. They are young and good-looking, probably in their early twenties.

"Stop talking," whispers Andrés, not moving his lips. His breaths shorten and his hands begin to fidget. "Don't tell anyone you are going to Nicaragua," he adds.

Even without hearing us talk, our neighbors know that Henry and I are foreigners. One of the men asks us a question in Spanish.

"I am sorry," I lie. "I do not speak Spanish."

Another man asks in English, "Where are you from?"

"The United States," I say. Henry, who is from Australia, says nothing, hoping they will assume he is my husband. If these guys are part of the government or members of the *escuadrones de muerte,* my country is on their side.

"How long will you be in El Salvador?"

"Two weeks. I would like to stay longer but I am a teacher and I have to go back to the U.S.," I say, embellishing my lie. "El Salvador is a beautiful country. The people are very friendly and *pupusas* are delicious."

The more you lie, the easier it gets. The *pupusa* part is true.

Less than five minutes after the men arrive, Andrés says it is time to go. We have not finished our meal and my beer bottle is still half full. We leave.

"I do not trust those men," he says once we are driving again. His whole demeanor has changed. He does not say another word until he stops in front of a backpacker hotel and says good-bye. Now that we are in his country, he does not want to be seen with us. If we are on our way to Sandinista Nicaragua, we are the enemy of his government. And by association, he is subversive.

Early the next morning Henry and I walk through the streets of San Salvador, past corners where soldiers are hiding behind walls of sandbags, their guns poking through holes between the bags, pointing at the pedestrians. There is no eye contact between the soldiers and the people, no waves or smiles; one is the enforcer and everyone else a potential victim. I find myself wondering if I would be shot if I were suddenly to start running.

There were soldiers with guns in Antigua too, standing stiffly outside government buildings and banks. They were intimidating, but I was never afraid they were going to shoot me. I always felt that they were protecting something, like money or officials. Here in San Salvador, the guns are pointing at me, and I am frightened.

Henry and I leave on the first bus we can find to Honduras, another U.S.-friendly country. When we arrive at the Honduras border, each passenger is taken individually into a room where there are two armed soldiers. I am asked to stand across a table while two men turn the pages of an album filled with pictures of unwelcome foreigners. They look at the pictures and then at me. Up and down, page after page. It takes fifteen minutes to go through dozens of pictures. I am not in the album.

I have recently heard that there is a peace march, made up mostly of U.S. citizens, working its way through the countries of Central America and ending in Nicaragua. I have also heard that the Honduran government is planning to refuse entry to the marchers who are considered dangerous left-wingers, supporters of Nicaragua, supporters of peace. Presumably the marchers are also an embarrassment to the Reagan government, which is bombing Nicaragua. Who knows where the pictures in the album came from. Many of them look like passport photos. I wonder if they were supplied by the U.S. government.

When I leave the room, my passport is stamped and I am told I can go. I meet Henry outside and we walk down the road together. Neither one of us wants to do this alone.

"To Nicaragua?" we ask one of the uniformed, gun-toting Honduran soldiers.

He directs us to a bus that is already filled with people. It turns out that they are Nicaraguans on a chartered bus, returning from a shopping trip to San Salvador. The Honduran government won't permit Nicaraguans to step on their land. There is a soldier with a gun slung over his shoulder, sitting next to the bus driver, facing the passengers. In his hand are all of our passports wrapped up in a rubber band. We are told they will be returned when we arrive at the border.

In addition to people, the bus is stuffed with shopping bags, boxes, duffel bags, and suitcases battered and new, all filled with things that are hard to get in Nicaragua—things like toilet paper and toothpaste and deodorant, underwear, jeans, T-shirts, light bulbs, makeup, and toys. Contraband that will be sold on the black market in Managua.

During the trip, the soldier never smiles. He never interacts with anyone. He just sits there staring straight ahead, our passports in his hand. The gun is American made.

We get off the bus at the border of Nicaragua. Two soldiers accompany us until we have all crossed over into Nicaragua.

Borders are always a disappointment to me. Going from one country into another should be more than just walking down a road. The color should change. You should go from green to orange like you do on a map. At the very least you should be able to look off into the distance and see a line painted across the landscape. But the only line here is a ragged one of sweaty people carrying lots of bags.

There are no other people once we are in Nicaragua, just us bus passengers and Sandinista soldiers standing in the distance on top of the hills, staring off into the fields surrounding us. They are looking for Contras, the guerrilla army that has been trying to overthrow the revolutionary Sandinista government in what has become known down here as Ronald Reagan's war. The United States is training and supporting the Contras.

It is sweat-dripping hot. The women from my bus have towels or rags around their necks so they can soak up the sweat. I just drip, as though someone is wringing out clothes on my head. From time to time, I wipe the sweat with the bottom of my T-shirt.

"It's dangerous along this road," says one of the women. She points to the abandoned customs building where government officials used to check passports and luggage. The building is shot up with bullet holes, and the ground around it is littered with empty sardine cans, old plastic bags, torn wrappers, and some mangled pieces of metal. The reason the Sandinista government had to move the office away is that people were getting killed by Contras who were camped across the border in Honduras.

The government moved the people too—the ones who used to live in the disintegrating shacks along the side of the road, the ones who used to farm the fields that stretch into the distance. Too close. Too dangerous. Good fertile land that used to feed people has been abandoned.

After about a twenty-minute walk, everyone stops. We are to wait there for a ride to the new customs office. Some Sandinista soldiers join us, guns slung over their shoulders, smiles on their faces. They are kids in their teens. The people share snacks with them, and exchange greetings. The Nicaraguans from my bus do not think of these soldiers as the enemy; they are treated like family.

I share a bag of peanuts with two soldiers. When they ask me where I am from, I tell them, but I am nervous. The Contra bullets that are killing them are U.S. bullets fired from U.S. guns.

"No problem," says a baby-faced soldier who can't be more than sixteen. "It isn't the American people who are doing this to us. It is your government. You are welcome in Nicaragua. When you go home, tell your people we want peace."

After forty minutes of standing in the hot sun and fifteen minutes packed upright, like a giant bunch of asparagus, in the back of a pickup, we finally arrive at customs, a bunch of wooden shacks and rusty trailers. Henry and I are sent into different lines. When it is my turn to enter the first shack, the soldier inside asks me for my passport. Then he begins to fill out an entry card.

"What is your profession?"

"Writer."

The corners of his lips curl up into his mustache. "Me too. I'm a writer. I write poetry. What do you write?"

"Children's books."

"How nice. Do you have any with you?"

I look at the long line behind me as I fumble through my backpack. I pull out three books. He turns the pages of *Why Can't I Fly?* Then he looks up.

"I have a six-year-old daughter. May I take this home for her?"

I know that customs officials are always looking for bribes, but everyone has told me that Nicaragua is different. Besides, I am hoping to share my books in classrooms and neighborhoods all over the country. I don't want to give them to the first person I meet.

"I brought the books to share with the children of Nicaragua," I say. "And I haven't even met any yet."

"Okay. No problem. I understand. *Que le vaya bien.*" Have a good time.

And he passes me on to the other shacks and battered trailers for more questions and baggage inspection.

Twenty minutes later, I am walking along a dirt path that leads back to the main road, where Henry is waiting for me. As I walk, I watch a group of soldiers behind one of the trailers. They are playing a tape of break-dance music and two of them are dancing. Their guns are lying on the ground. I am so engrossed in this different breed of soldier that I don't notice the three boys and a girl approaching from behind.

"*Buenos tardes,*" say the four scruffy, barefoot kids. Good afternoon.

"*Cómo se llama usted?*" asks the biggest boy. What is your name?

When they hear my answer, they smile and nod to each other. Then the big one speaks again. "Would you read us a book?"

And there, late in the day, on a dusty path in front of the Nicaraguan customs office, I sit on the ground and read them a book.

A pickup and two buses later, we reach Managua. Henry, who will be living in government housing and working for the agricultural department, deposits me in the foreign-tourist part of town, and we say good-bye. I'm on my own.

I check into a motel: dark rooms, shared bathrooms, lumpy beds, and cheap (three dollars a night). The place I choose is the cheapest and most dilapidated among the hotels, but it has a common room, which seems like a good place to meet people. There are backpackers draped around the couches when I arrive.

"Hi," I say, introducing myself to the crowd. After we've been talking for a while, they invite me to go dancing with them—live music under the stars.

"Sure," I say. It's my new credo: Say yes to everything.

The parking lot turned into a dance floor is packed and sweaty. The crowd, all Nicaraguan except for the eight of us, is young and active and swinging to *salsa* and reggae and American rock. Hips are gyrating sensuously and the dancers are smiling, as reflections of mirrored balls and flashing lights whirl around their bodies.

When I first arrive, I am hoping to stand in the background and watch. Not a chance. There is an excess of single guys, and if you are close enough to watch, several hands and smiles greet you wordlessly at the beginning of every new dance.

"Where are you from?" asks Carlos, the young man I am dancing with. He looks about eighteen and he's wearing a Detroit Tigers T-shirt.

"What?" The music is loud.

"Where are you from?" he shouts.

"The United States," I shout back.

"How long have you been here?"

"I arrived three hours ago."

"Tomorrow," he yells at me, "I would like to take you to Xiloa!" A nearby lake with a beach.

Nicaraguans are not shy. Nearly all of the Nicaraguans I meet over the next eight months, especially the young ones, have an air of pride and confidence that comes from having made the revolution (in 1979) that got rid of the dictator, Somoza, and nearly all of the wealthy class, most of whom fled to the United States. Perhaps because I am an American, Nicaraguans are eager to invite me into their homes, to share their food, to show me that the revolution was a good thing. What I see and hear during my visit is very different from what I read in the U.S. newspapers about a people under siege by the Sandinista government. Up close, it is clear that the Sandinistas *are* the people.

"Sure," I say to Carlos's invitation. "I'd love to go to the beach."

The next day, Carlos, his little sister, an American woman from my hotel, and I take off at noon on a crowded bus where people are squashed together like those potato chips that come in a can, every body part fitting snugly into someone else's body.

We get off at a lake just a few miles outside of Managua. Carlos, his hair below his shoulders and his smiling brown eyes flecked with green, looks handsome in a navy T-shirt with the short sleeves rolled up to his shoulders. As we walk, teenage girls turn their heads. Carlos tells me he is a medical student in his second year.

"In the days of Somoza, I could never have thought about becoming a doctor. The university was for rich people. Now, even the poorest people can become doctors or whatever they want. Education is free."

As we approach the lake, we walk along a grassy slope that leads down toward the sand. The grass is spotted with picturesque pavilions, thatched roofs on poles with benches underneath—protection from the tropical sun. As we get closer to the water, we pass bars and restaurants with tables outside. It looks like an exclusive club, which it once was.

A pickup drives up and parks next to one of the pavilions. There are eight kids in the back and coolers and blankets and a skinny dog. And a radio playing Madonna. Four adults and two kids climb out of the cabin.

"That family would never have been here if Somoza were still president," says Carlos, pointing to the new arrivals. "Places like this were for the rich. Now they're for the people."

"Come on. Let's go in the water," says Carlos's sister, getting back to more important things. And we race across the burning sand to the cool water of the once off-limits lake.

Carlos does not fit the picture of the oppressed Nicaraguan I have read about in the U.S. papers. Like most of the young people I would meet in the eight months I live here, he is proud of his country and its revolution.

I spend the next days wandering, walking miles in the suffocating heat of the city or standing in line for hours to get onto buses where I can barely breathe. There are heads tucked under strangers' arms, waists into rear ends, legs and hands and feet intertwined. No one seems to be bothered by all this intimacy. In fact, it opens up communication. If you are holding hands with someone, conversation is almost inevitable.

After four days, I want to get out of Managua; it's hot, grimy, crowded, smelly, and I'm tired of squeezing onto buses. I want to see the rest of the country; but I don't want to do it alone. I'm sure there are plenty of visitors who want to escape Managua.

The next day I walk into Mirna's Pancakes for breakfast and ask a young woman if I can join her. After more than a year of traveling alone in Mexico and Guatemala, it has become easy for me to approach other tourists. Nearly every solitary traveler is happy to have company.

Jennifer is from Baltimore and she's as eager to get out of the city as I am; there is nothing to do here and the heat is unbearable. The hard part is figuring out how to get out. There are buses . . . but they are unreliable, overcrowded, and you have go where *they* want to go. There are also tours for foreigners; but they are expensive and carefully plotted to show you what the government wants you to see.

What we want is to share a car and driver and maybe find two more people to join us. We put up some signs in the motels and restaurants looking for people. "Leave a message in Hospedaje Santos for Rita or Jennifer." And we walk the streets, stopping every foreigner we see, asking if they want to join us or if they know any drivers with cars.

After two days, we get a lead on a driver. Marco, a cab driver, has taken this German couple around the country. He doesn't have a phone, and they don't know his address, but if we catch the Larreynaga bus and get off where the hospital used to be and then turn toward the water for two blocks (you cannot see the water, it is merely a direction), Marco's house is the third one on the right.

Sounds crazy, but we actually find the house and end up sitting with Marco's mother for two hours waiting for Marco, who will be home any minute. Doña Juana, Marco's mother, is a passionate Sandinista and she talks to us about what it was like during the revolution. There was fighting on her street and her house was used as a hospital. If there was no one else around, she was the doctor, removing shrapnel, cleaning wounds and stitching them up.

"Did you have any medical training?" I ask.

"No," she says. "Mothers know those things." She has five children and fifteen grandchildren.

While Jennifer and I wait for Marco, we meet eleven grandchildren, seven of them Marco's kids. Marco, his mother tells us, is thirty; he and his wife were fifteen and sixteen when their first child was born. Teresa is currently pregnant with number eight. I also discover that Doña Juana has several rooms that she rents out to international volunteers: political exiles, socialists, artists, adventurers, idealists from around the world. And she has a room for me if I want it. I do.

Finally, Marco drives his yellow taxi into the yard. Two of the doors are wired closed, the car has no grill, and he tells us later that only one headlight works. He'd been standing in line all day long to get a used carburetor. When he finally made it to the front of the line, they were out of carburetors. His car is a Chevy. Ever since the U.S. closed all trade to Nicaragua, no one can get parts.

Marco is swarthy, with a belly that hangs out over his pants and a shirt that is buttoned wrong. The seams of his sneakers are split. When he hears that we have been waiting for more than two hours, he bursts into an uproarious, contagious laugh that is hard to listen to without laughing along. Marco agrees to take us around the country for a week.

Jennifer and I go back to our motel, hoping to find two more people to join us. But two days later, on the morning we are due to leave, it's still just Jennifer and me. We are meeting Marco in front of the motel at 7:00 A.M. By 8:45 we have given up. He arrives at 9:00, with no apology; but we are so happy to see him that we say nothing.

We load our bags into the trunk and are about to get in the car when a tall, lanky guy with a British accent comes running down the street shouting. "Stop, wait, don't go!"

His name is Graham and he wants to join us.

"Hold on, I'll get my bags," he says, and he runs off.

Ten minutes later he's back with two monstrous duffel bags. Jennifer and I are each carrying a small book bag. We squeeze his bags into the trunk, wire it shut, and take off.

An hour later we arrive at a plaza in a small town. It's buzzing with people, and American rock music is coming out of loudspeakers. Graham, who hasn't said much during the hour we've been driving, asks Marco to take out one of the duffel bags. Except Marco doesn't understand; he doesn't speak English and Graham doesn't speak Spanish. Jennifer translates. Turns out her Spanish is near-perfect. From that point on, we address her as Translator. "Hey, Translator, come here," we call when we need her. She is Jennifer no more.

Marco takes the bag out, and Graham carries it to a crowded spot in the market. None of us has any idea why.

Then he unzips the bag, takes out four leather juggling balls filled with coffee beans, and begins to juggle. A crowd gathers, mostly mothers and children. Graham brings his audience into the act, tossing a ball to someone as he juggles and catching it when they throw it back. More and more kids shout to be included. Then, after five minutes of balls, he calls to me. I am standing next to his duffel.

"Rita, catch." And he throws me the juggling balls. One, two, three, four. "Toss me the bowling pins." And a juggler's assistant is born.

"Uno, dos, tres, cuatro," he counts, except his pronunciation is so bad that Marco, hysterical off to the side, mimics Juggler's sound.

Juggler, his name from then on, had been the headmaster of a school in Canada; and after that, he started a successful macadamia nut butter business in Hawaii. He made a lot of money in macadamia nut butter, but his dream was to travel around Central and South America, communicating with the people. He studied Spanish and failed miserably. He couldn't get the pronunciation. No matter how hard he tried, his Spanish sounded like British English.

So, four years ago, he took up a different form of communication... juggling. Unlike languages, juggling turned out to be a natural talent. By the time he caught up with us on the street in Managua, he'd entertained thousands of people throughout Central America, and he'd even done a stint in a circus.

Translator and I (now officially known as Writer) spend the next week as Juggler's assistants in plazas throughout the country. We fetch, we toss, we count, we carry. We make people happy. What a glorious experience. Juggler even teaches us to juggle three balls.

Over the next years, I will meet many street entertainers (called buskers), in airports, on street corners, in markets. And because of my brief stint as Juggler's assistant, I have a whole new respect and appreciation of the joy they bring to the world. Where once I hid in the back of the crowd, after Nicaragua, I move in close to the entertainers. I talk to them, buy them a drink, and share stories of buskers I have met (the international ones often know each other). All of the street entertainers love making people happy. So do I. From time to time I find myself wondering what it would take to become a clown. Maybe one day.

The climax of our whirlwind traveling show is Marco's idea. Late in the afternoon of our final day, our yellow taxi swings down a dirt road, and he stops the car outside a tan-colored stucco building.

"This," he announces, "is a home for deaf and dumb children."

Two Franciscan nuns in crisply ironed blue-and-white habits answer the bell and invite us in. Just inside the door, in a large entrance hall, ten girls, ages ten to sixteen, are sitting around a big table with huge piles of rice in front of them. They are picking out the bad grains.

Juggler grins and drops his bag. Translator and I open it up, toss him the balls, and he begins. At first the nuns and the girls are stunned. Then suddenly, the girls jump up and surround him with strange sounds and laughter. Kids of all ages pour out of classrooms to join us. They stand there mimicking Juggler's movements, like a mime chorus in a silent musical. And then Juggler brings them into his act by tossing the balls to them. There is magic in the room . . . and communication. Juggler can't speak a word of Spanish, but it doesn't matter, because his audience can't hear. Everyone, including the nuns, is glowing.

Juggler calls for the bowling pins, then the rings, then an assortment of objects, big and small, that he juggles together. Translator and I, his loyal assistants, toss him whatever he wants. Marco, meanwhile, pulls up a chair and sits near the door, bursting with pride.

The nuns interrupt the show briefly to give us drinks and Ritz crackers with a squiggle of honey. When we've finished the snacks, they won't let us go. Juggler performs some more and gives some juggling lessons to the kids. Finally, he signals that he is finished, and he hands out balloons to everyone.

Translator and I pack up his bag and carry it out the door, followed by the whole school. It is already dark when Juggler slips behind the yellow cab and siphons some gas from the tank. Then he calls for the bag that has never left the trunk. Marco unwires the trunk and Translator and I take out the bag. Juggler hides behind the car as he prepares for the final act.

"Get in and be ready to take off," he tells us. Marco jumps in behind the wheel and starts the car. Translator and I climb into the backseat and leave the front door open for Juggler's getaway. And then, in the dark, Juggler takes out a cigarette lighter and performs his grand finale: flaming torches.

When the flames go out, Juggler gathers the torches in his arms and jumps in next to Marco, who guns the engine. We screech off, shooting dust into the air and waving to our screaming and jumping audience.

When we get back to Managua, I move in with Doña Juana. Marco lives two houses down. We all share a big yard filled with cast-off car parts and used paint cans that occasionally become drums under the energetic banging of Marco's seven children from age one to age fourteen. Ramón, the oldest, will be drafted into the army when he is seventeen.

Marco and Teresa argue a lot about the war, the one that the U.S. is sponsoring. She wants to send Ramón to the United States instead of to the army. Marco, an ardent Sandinista, who is proud of the revolution that he fought in, asks, "Who will defend our country if not the youth?"

Teresa tells me, "All I can think about is Ramón in the mountains, cold and hungry, and in constant danger of being killed. I don't want my son to come back in a box."

After two months of living with Marco's family, I leave Nicaragua briefly for a visit with my parents and my kids. I also meet with Frank Sloan, an editor friend in New York. Over breakfast at the Grand Hyatt in New York City, to the live piano tunes of Strauss and Mozart, I tell Frank Nicaragua stories. He stops me midway through a story and asks if I'll write a book about my experiences.

I'm excited. What a great chance to present another perspective to American youth. I'll write it from the perspective of young people in Nicaragua.

A few days later I load up my book bag with a tape recorder, a pile of tapes, and a bunch of pens and notebooks. It's great to be going back to a place where I already have friends. Marco is meeting me at the airport.

As I walk outside the modern air terminal, I look for him. Thirty minutes later, I am still waiting.

Nicaraguan time is different from time in the United States; it's much more relaxed. *En punto,* on the dot, never is. A two o'clock appointment often means that you'll meet at three or four or five. "Later" can mean days. "I'll stop by tomorrow" can sometimes mean weeks. So I wait.

An airport bus comes by and the driver asks if I need a ride. I shake my head and wait some more. Another half hour goes by. The bus does three more swings before it stops again and the door opens.

"Come on," says the driver. "We'll take you to the Intercontinental Hotel." The hotel is closer to where I'm going than the airport is, so I climb in.

As we speed down the road toward the Intercontinental, the driver asks if I am here to work; he's used to picking up volunteers, mostly Europeans, who have come to help Nicaragua.

"I'm writing a book about young people in Nicaragua," I tell him.

"Oh," says the driver. "I have kids. Would you like to meet them?"

"Sure, why not?"

Nicaraguans are the friendliest people in the world. Sometimes, when I ask directions, people walk me to where I'm going. Strangers on the street invite me into their homes. Others just walk alongside me, wanting to talk. And now, a bus driver is taking me to meet his kids.

He swings off the highway and begins maneuvering his monster bus through narrow streets. He turns down dirt roads and winds around shack-like houses on what appears to be more a footpath than a road. As we move, we kick up swirls of dust in every direction. People rush out of their houses to stare. I feel as though I am on board a runaway bus in a TV cartoon. Then, finally, he stops and we get out.

I meet his kids and his wife, and I drink a *fresca* (tastes like Kool-Aid) while sitting in a rocking chair on a dirt floor.

"OK," he says half an hour later. "Now, where can I take you."

Ten minutes later, my private runaway bus pulls up in front of Doña Juana's house. The family, the neighbors, and everyone passing by swarm around us, as amazed as they are impressed by the giant bus that has delivered me.

Marco's yellow taxi is a few meters inside the gate. The hood is up and half the parts are on the ground. Marco is stretched out in a hammock.

"Rita, *hola. Cómo estas?*" he says, greeting me warmly, as though I am a wonderful surprise. Then he guffaws his endearing and boisterous laugh. No mention is made of our missed airport date.

I give him an angry look and walk inside to hug Doña Juana. He could have sent a message. For two days I refuse to talk to Marco. Then I forget about it. It isn't the first time he's been late; and it isn't the last time he stands me up. I know it isn't me; it's Marco. I learn to accept him as he is. It ought to be an advantage to share a yard and family with a cab and driver. No such luck.

As part of my research for the book, I decide to go to Quibuto, a village in the war zone that was attacked three months ago. But I don't want to go alone. Marco is unavailable. He's still working on his cab.

While I'm trying to figure out what to do, I meet a photographer from Spain who has a friend who has a car. It's a business deal. I pay expenses, he drives and takes pictures. And if there are some good photos, we'll try to sell them to my publisher.

The first day we drive to a town about two hundred miles from Managua and an hour's drive from Quibuto. We decide to save the drive to Quibuto for the morning. At 8:05 we arrive at the army post with our letter of permission. (It took days of standing in line to get the proper documents.) The soldiers study the letter.

"Your permissions are in order," we are told, "but foreign journalists can't drive the Quibuto road until after 10:00."

"Why is that?" asks the photographer.

"If the road has been mined overnight, the mines will be triggered by military vehicles or Nicaraguans before you get there. We don't want foreign journalists getting blown up."

For the first time since I came to Nicaragua, I'm scared. Mines that are planted at night by the Contras become part of the thousands of bumps in a dirt road during the day. We have been told to look for bumps as we drive; but it's the rainy season and the road is nothing but ruts and bumps and holes and rocks and tire tracks. There's not a chance we'd be able to tell the difference between a mine bump and an ordinary bump in the road. So we settle for trying to maneuver our low-slung car without scraping its bottom.

It is nearly 11:00 when we reach the turnoff to Quibuto. The road is blocked by more soldiers with guns slung over their shoulders. They inspect our permission letter and wave us on.

The photographer looks off into the tree-filled hills. "This kind of terrain is the perfect cover. There's no way you can tell if there are Contras in those trees or behind those hills."

One eight-inch-deep river and thousands of bumps later, we see the village. As we get closer, we notice a jumble of men, women, dogs, chickens, and kids about twenty yards from the road in an open field. We get out of the car and walk toward the crowd. There is a bright red mass of color in the center of the activity.

When we get closer, we realize that the red mass is a slaughtered steer that is being cut up for meat. The animal has been skinned, and the skin is spread out on the ground like a bloody leather blanket. The trunk of the steer, still warm, is resting on the skin. Only the head looks as if it was once alive. It is still attached to the carcass, the eyes staring out at the crowd. Off to one side is a giant, white misshapen ball, three times the size of a basketball. I ask what it is.

"The stomach," says a man. "It will be cleaned and the lining will be used to make rope." He shows me a braided rope made from stomach lining.

Two men are cutting off hunks of meat and sending them up to the porch of a house where they are being sold. Every eight days, we are told, they butcher two steers for the two thousand residents. In Managua, buying meat means standing in line with your plastic bowl, sometimes for five hours. In Quibuto, it means hanging around, gossiping, flirting, talking while the steers get chopped up. There's definitely an advantage to country living. If it weren't for the war.

A woman named Marisa comes over to talk to us. When we tell her why we are there, she takes us around to show us the damage the Contras did when they attacked three months ago. During the five-hour siege, they killed one man and destroyed fourteen houses and five public buildings, including the health center and a meeting hall. They shot up the school and blew up a brand-new truck that the community had just bought. They destroyed a food storage warehouse that had just been stocked. And they raided and machine-gunned the walls of the children's dining hall that had been inaugurated only a few days earlier, the project of a group of people from Spain that was to have provided milk and a balanced meal once a day for the children of the village.

As we wander around the village, Estela, a teacher, and her seven-year-old daughter, Geysel, join us. When Estela discovers that we are planning to be there for several days, she invites us to stay in her house. We accept.

The house is made of sticks and mud and corrugated metal sheets. The floor is dirt and, like the other homes in the village, there are no glass windows, only a wooden-hinged square that swings in and out. Nor is there electricity. A Contra attack blew up the power source for the whole village three years ago and it's never been fixed.

On the morning of the attack, Estela and her family were inside their house. They listened, terrified, to the shooting from the guns and the explosions from the hand grenades. They smelled the smoke from the burning buildings. And they heard the Contras screaming for Estela. Somehow the Contras had found out she was a teacher and they were trying to find her house.

While the family held each other in terror, the Contras searched other houses, asking for her. They eventually kidnapped eight villagers: a fifteen-year-old boy, his twelve-year-old sister, a teacher, and five others. All but the teacher eventually escaped. The teacher has never returned.

Later I meet a twelve-year-old girl and I ask her why she thinks the Contras are doing this?

"I don't know," she tells me. "I think the United States wants our land and our resources. It's the United States that gives the Contras their weapons, you know. But I really don't understand why they want to kidnap our children."

Back in Managua, everyone is getting ready for the First Communion of two of Doña Juana's granddaughters. Doña Juana is sewing the dresses. Her arthritis has been bothering her all month, and she wanted the tailor shop down the street to do the sewing, but their Singer sewing machines need parts. Doña Juana is awake until two in the morning finishing up the final stitching.

Before we go to church, Doña Juana and I cook for the party. We're making *gallo pinto,* the national dish of Nicaragua—beans and rice flavored with onions, salt, and pepper. It is to be my final meal with the family. My book research is completed. When the Communion party is over, I am flying back to the United States, via Costa Rica (there are no direct flights from Nicaragua to the U.S.).

I'm going to miss Doña Juana and her gang. The joy and pain of this family have become part of my life. Every few minutes, over onions and beans and rice, Doña Juana and I hug each other with tears in our eyes. I have never lived so closely with people whose emotions are so open and honest, whose hopes and fears are so freely expressed.

In spite of the difficulties of their lives, or possibly because of their problems, everyone in this family laughs hard, dances with abandon, and emotes with an exuberance that is contagious. I have learned from these people how to explode with laughter and dance with joy. The Nicaraguans, who have so little, have taught me so much.

When the onions are fried and the rice and beans are ready, Doña Juana and I go outside to sit on the porch until we have to leave for the church.

"Rita," she says to me, "you are educated. You have read many books and studied many things. May I ask you a question?"

"Of course," I respond.

And this grandmother, mother, and loyal Sandinista, who took bullets out of kids and celebrated with her neighbors when the revolution was won, who struggles every day in a Nicaragua that is without food and parts and necessities of life, looks at me with an enigmatic expression on her face and asks, "What is a Communist?"

My visit to Nicaragua marks the end forever of my political innocence, which was already seriously damaged by the Vietnam war. I write what I saw and heard. When the book *(Inside Nicaragua; Young People's Dreams and Fears)* is published, I worry that it will be seen as subversive; but instead, it is included in the American Library Association's list of Best Young Adult Books of 1988. For all my anger at the Reagan policies, I am thankful to be part of a country that honors freedom of the press. It is a theme that will be reinforced over and over again during the years I live in Indonesia.

For now, I am celebrating the freedom and independence of my chosen life. I would never have made it to Nicaragua if I'd had to ask permission to go.

Israel

CHAPTER SIX

ROOTS

Nicaragua was tough. The streets were too hot, the buses too crowded, and nothing worked. The trip to the war zone was psychologically wrenching, and saying good-bye to Doña Juana and Marco's kids was hard.

By the time I arrive at my son Mitch's apartment in New York, I'm drained. I plan to stay with him for a while. I know he's been worrying about me. As a journalist working the crime beat for New York *Newsday*, and frequently getting front-page bylines (I love seeing his name on page one), Mitch knows that gathering research material leads people to places that tourists don't go, places he'd prefer his mother stay out of. He also knows that, as I once did for him, he has to let me go.

As he talks about his concerns, I realize that he and I are experiencing a role reversal. To add to the image, I arrive with a bag of dirty laundry and a stack of stuff I ask him to store for me until I'm ready to take off again.

I fly to Colorado for a quick visit with my daughter, Jan, who is now the social and recreation editor of *The Vail Trail*. What a thrill to hang out with her as Vail socialites stop her on the street to give her news items, and headwaiters greet her by name and bring us complimentary drinks.

Jan is as concerned as Mitch about my Nicaraguan exploits (they've obviously talked about it); and she's also happy to see me safely back in the States. My next destination is Israel. There are bombs exploding in Israel, too, but they're not as concerned. Mitch has been there and Jan has heard stories. The unknown is scarier than the known.

I'm not sure what to expect in Israel. I grew up in a Jewish home where, during and after World War II, the importance of a Jewish homeland was a constant topic of conversation. The creation of Israel in 1948 assured world Jewry that there would always be a safe haven for Jews, and though we were not a religious family, fundraising for Israel was a major part of my childhood.

As an adult, my Jewishness is way down on my list of how I see myself. I am a woman, a mother, a writer, and now, a nomad. In the absence of anti-Semitism, the fact that I was born Jewish seems unimportant to me. But I wonder, nonetheless, if I will find a special bond with the Israelis, something stronger and deeper than I feel with people in other countries.

I am going to visit Israel as a traveling member of an international organization called Servas. I first discovered Servas in 1977 when a friend and I took Jan and her cousin, Susan, to Paris for a month and a half. We rented a big apartment on the Left Bank from friends of friends. It had five bedrooms and a giant living room with a library loft and a grand piano. The rental had been arranged long distance, and we gasped when we walked in. It was perfect.

The owner gave us a tour and then left on her vacation. Twenty minutes later, the telephone rang.

"Hi," said a young woman on the other end. "My friend and I are here from Denmark and we are members of Servas. May we stay with you?"

I had no idea what she was talking about, so I asked. Servas, she explained, is an international network of hosts and travelers who are committed to building peace and understanding by putting together people from different cultures. Its members are hosts who want to meet international travelers, and travelers who want to connect with the people of the country they are visiting. The family who owned our apartment were members, and their phone number—and ours—was in the host booklet of France.

The Danish couple were both seventeen. They stayed for a week. The day after they arrived, a pharmacist from Czechoslovakia called; then a couple, librarians from Montreal; then a Swedish couple who owned a farm. I just kept saying yes. Together we bought wine and cheese and bread, and there was always room for more. There were nights when five languages were spoken simultaneously around our table.

Jan and I vowed to become official Servas hosts as soon as we got back to L.A., but my husband wasn't interested. So Servas was shelved . . . until now, when I decide to visit Israel as a Servas traveler.

Servas and I are a good fit. Over the last two years I've learned that what I like most is to participate in people's lives, and that's what Servas is all about. I send for an application.

The essence of the application is the "Letter of Introduction":

> *Please describe yourself and your trip for your hosts ... include your background and previous travels, your involvement with other peace organizations and issues, your interests and hobbies, previous Servas experiences if any, and what you hope to learn on this trip and how it relates to Servas.*

I write my essay and go for an interview. When I pass the screening, the interviewer certifies me by stamping and numbering my application. Then he tells me that I must show each host the original application as soon as I arrive.

I pay forty-five dollars for a one-year membership and leave a fifteen-dollar deposit for a book listing more than three hundred host families in Israel, their names, ages, occupations, interests, the languages they speak, where they've lived, and where they've traveled. (In 2001, membership is sixty-five dollars and the host books require a twenty-five-dollar deposit.) The hosts indicate how many people they can take and how much advance notice they need. Some say NPNR, "no prior notice required." Others need two weeks.

I also discover that there are rules: a Servas visit lasts two nights, "allowing host and traveler time to begin a genuine exchange." The host usually offers breakfast and dinner to the guests. Guests are expected to spend time with their hosts and participate in their lives, help with the cooking and cleanup. Guests are also expected to be with the family in the evenings. None of which I knew when I was a substitute host in Paris ten years ago. No money is to be exchanged, but the literature emphasizes that Servas is not to be thought of as a free hotel; it's an opportunity for cultural exchange.

I had intended to study the Israel host book, plan an itinerary, and send off copies of my "letter of introduction" with requests to stay in various homes throughout the country ... before I left. Instead, I leave with no plans whatsoever. I've never much liked making long-distance plans; I'd rather do it there, wherever there may be. There's a list of backpacker places in the back of the Servas book.

I check into a youth hostel in Tel Aviv and plan my trip. Then I send off my letters with handwritten notes in the margin: "I'm planning to be in Israel for the next month and a half and am leaving myself a loose itinerary. Sometime in the beginning of December (or whenever), I'm hoping to be in your area. I shall call two days before, as you request. Looking forward to meeting you, Rita."

Three days after I mail the letters, I phone Sarah, an eighty-two-year-old woman who lives in the historic city of Sfat.

"Yes, yes," she says when I introduce myself on the phone. "I got your letter this morning. You will be my first Servas guest. When will you arrive?" All this in a crisp British accent.

I tell her I'm planning to be there around ten in the morning.

"That's no good," she says. "I go swimming at nine. You'll have to come at quarter to nine. You will swim with me."

She is brusque but welcoming.

When I say that I don't have a bathing suit, she says that she'll give me one.

It is exactly quarter to nine when I ring the doorbell. Chunky and erect, walking briskly with a cane, Sarah lets me in.

"Good, you're on time," she greets me and hands me a bag. "Here's your bathing suit, a cap, some goggles, and a towel. Let's go."

We get into her car and she talks nonstop in impeccable British English. "My family has been here for five generations," she tells me. "Over there, that's the Sephardic synagogue. Do you know who they are? The Sephardim are the people who came here from Spain and North Africa. It's very historic. We will go there this afternoon."

We arrive at the indoor pool. The bathing suit fits. So do the goggles and the cap.

After the swim, Sarah drives through town. "I'm going to drop you here so you can look at some of the galleries. Sfat is famous for its artists. Meet me back on this corner in two hours. I have some errands to do."

This is a woman who enjoys being in charge. She's a bit overwhelming, but I like her. I'm here to learn and she wants to teach. I take her to lunch.

That night we sit at her desk, which is covered with a huge jigsaw puzzle of a landscape in a dark forest. We work quietly, saying little, each of us trying pieces until we find ones that fit. After about fifteen minutes of comfortable silence, I ask about her British accent.

"I was born under the Turks and brought up under the British. Why don't you move here?"

The question takes me by surprise. I tell her that I don't want to live anywhere.

"You don't have to *live* here, just be *from* here," she says. "You can do exactly what you are doing. Your life doesn't have to change. When you're in Israel, you can stay with me."

"Who knows, maybe someday I will. For now, there's so much I want to see. Sarah, you must have seen a lot during your eighty-two years."

"My family owned a big hotel here in Sfat. When Menachem Begin was in the Irgun, fighting the British, he used to hide in our hotel. The British soldiers would come looking for him and the others, but we knew how to hide people. In those days that was an important skill. No one was ever found in our hotel . . . and they were always there, both the soldiers and the Irgun. Those British soldiers would go through every room, but they never found anybody." She laughs as she tells me about hidden passages and movable walls.

The next day we swim and lunch and puzzle and talk and laugh all over again.

"Listen," she says to me when I prepare to leave. "I don't know anything about Servas. My friend signed me up, and you're the first person I've had. But I don't care about two-day rules. You stay as long as you want."

I stay a third day and then move on to visit Ruth on a kibbutz.

Ruth is in her seventies. Her curly hair is dyed a light brown and she is full of energy. She takes me on a tour to the nursery school, where I read my book *More Spaghetti, I Say!* It's about a monkey who can't stop eating spaghetti. The pictures are silly. Ruth translates and the kids laugh. Then we're off to the milking barn. To the fields where the food is grown for kibbutz consumption. And to the factory where they are making machine parts. All part of the kibbutz enterprise.

When the tour is over, Ruth talks about when she first arrived from Austria in 1937. She was twenty-two years old. The kibbutz was a mosquito-infested swamp, and half of the early settlers, her friends and family, died of malaria. Now the kibbutz is a garden, lush with flowers and food and healthy people.

"My friend was right," she says to me after dinner in the communal dining room. "When I got your request, I was going to tell you I couldn't have any guests this week, but instead I took your letter to a friend who is a handwriting analyst. He said you were different and creative and I should meet you. I'm glad I did."

The next morning I go by bus from the kibbutz to Jerusalem, where I stay in a mother-in-law apartment next to the apartment home of a journalist who writes a column for the English-language *Jerusalem Post*. He brings me to the paper and introduces me to his colleagues. When my two days are up, he and his wife, who is a nurse, offer me the apartment for as long as I like.

But I've already made plans to celebrate Chanukah with a family that has recently immigrated from Argentina. I speak Spanish to the two young children. We light candles, sing songs, and eat potato pancakes, the traditional Chanukah meal. I give each kid one of my books as a Chanukah gift. When I leave, I decide to spend some time on my own. I've met some great people, but four families in nine days are too many.

I rent a room for two weeks in a private home where I write in the mornings and wander the city in the afternoons and evenings. One day I wander into the ultra-Orthodox walled community of Mea She'arim. I feel as though I have stepped into an eighteenth-century Polish ghetto, laced with courtyards, lined with paving blocks, and populated by pale-faced men and boys with side curls *(payot)*, long black coats, and broad-brimmed black hats. It is a culture within a culture.

I rush back to my room and look through my Servas book, but I can't identify any Mea She'arim hosts. I'm intrigued by this community of bearded scholars and women who wear wigs and cover their bodies so only their hands and faces are visible. Orthodox Jews are only 20 percent of the Israeli population, but they have considerable power; Orthodox votes frequently tip the balance in close elections.

It is a touchy issue among secular Jews that Orthodox young men do not have to serve in the Israeli army (exempt because they are supposedly studying the holy Torah). I have read also that ultra-Orthodox youths of Mea She'arim have been stoning cars in Jerusalem on Saturdays because they feel no one should be driving on the Sabbath. Mea She'arim is a world unto itself; I would like to visit it for a few days.

One day I take a walking tour of old Jerusalem. The guide is an American woman who now lives in Israel. As we are walking, I ask her if she knows anyone in Mea She'arim. Yes, the woman tells me, she knows an American woman named Zahava and her husband, Ephraim. The guide is sure they would be happy to have me for a few days.

When the tour is over, I buy a scarf for my head and a long skirt, which I slip over my khakis. I also put on a long-sleeved sweater. We walk together, from the elegant King David Hotel into Mea She'arim. It is

Thursday. Zahava, a tall, stocky woman in her late forties, invites me to come back the next morning and stay for the weekend. Good. I tell her that I am hoping to help her prepare for and welcome the Sabbath.

The next day, as we are peeling potatoes and carrots for the traditional Sabbath stew called *cholent,* Zahava tells me she has arranged for me to have Sabbath dinner that night with a big family who is celebrating the wedding of one of its seven children on Sunday.

"There will be guests from England and from other Orthodox communities in Israel," Zahava tells me, and she adds, almost shamefully, "My husband and I have no children. I want you to see the joy of a big family Sabbath."

The phone rings. Zahava picks it up. She speaks in English. "Oh, I'm sure she will be happy to help," I hear her say. "But she is going to the Steins for Shabbos dinner." A pause. "OK. We'll be over soon."

The call is from a friend, also an American in the community. Zahava explains that the man who called would like me to sleep at his house. His wife is not well and she is about to give birth. He needs someone to help take care of the other two children. And if the baby should come tonight or tomorrow, he will need someone to baby-sit in the house.

"He told me you were sent by God."

I'm not keen on the idea of baby-sitting, but it will certainly put me one step deeper into the culture.

Zahava delivers me. Two minutes later I am pushing a stroller on the stones in the courtyard, smiling at the other mothers, wheeling along a street filled with women buying meat and vegetables for the *cholent.*

When we get back to the house, my host, Steven, asks for help peeling the vegetables and making the stew. Turning on the stove on Sabbath is not permitted in Orthodox homes, so the stew must be put on early and kept on a low flame for twenty-four hours.

When the stew goes on the stove, Steven lights five Sabbath candles, one for each member of his family and one for me. Then he goes to the synagogue to pray. I feed the kids their dinner, bathe them, put on their pajamas, and get them into bed. All this time the mother is behind a closed door.

When Steven arrives home, the children are asleep for the night. If I were he, I too would think I'd been sent by God.

At the appropriate time, Steven walks me to my dinner. When I arrive, there are only women and children in the house. The men are off praying. Kids are running all over the place. Teenage girls are helping the women in the kitchen. The tables are set for thirty-two people. I help to fill water glasses and carry in platters.

Then the outside door opens and suddenly the room is filled with men in black with long sideburns and big furry circles of hats. The father of the home sits in a big chair, and one by one his children (seven of them) step before him to receive a Sabbath prayer. After the ceremony, the guests sit, women at one table, men at the other. By now I know several of the women by name; they all speak English. But among the men, I am introduced only to the father, who wishes me a good Sabbath but is not permitted to touch my hand nor look into my eyes.

I do not like feeling second class. In this super-Orthodox world, women are dangerous; their very presence can distract the men from their pursuit of knowledge. Women are not permitted in the places where men study Torah; and in the synagogue, they must sit upstairs, away from the more devout and distractible males. During the years I live in Hindu and Muslim communities in Indonesia, I will see similar practices. They all make me feel uncomfortable. But my journey is one of discovery and observation. Wherever I am, I try to participate in the culture, not judge it.

It is not difficult on this Sabbath night to participate in and share the joy of this family. It is all around me, in the laughter and in the pleasure they feel in being together for the celebration of Sabbath, and in the excited anticipation of the wedding two days from now. I cannot wait for the singing. I have read that when dinner is over, ultra-Orthodox families sing Hasidic songs.

I love the haunting melodies of Hasidic music; and I am excited that tonight, in one of the most religious communities in the world, I am going to join the family as they raise their voices in celebration of God. As a teenager, I was in the synagogue choir (*not* an Orthodox synagogue), where we occasionally sang Hasidic songs. They are filled with swaying and *Yaba-baba-bum, bum, bum, bum, Yaba-baba-bum.*

As much as I have always loved the singing, the camaraderie, the swaying, the richness of the harmony, I have never felt the presence of the God I was supposed to be singing to. Not in a synagogue, not in a gathering, not inside myself. Perhaps I will feel Him, the God of my ancestors, here in this most religious place.

But first the meal. The traditional meal. With gefilte fish, chicken soup with matzoh balls, brisket with prunes, broccoli, a sweet potato casserole, and four different desserts.

All of it familiar. All of it the food of my ancestors in eastern Europe. All of it binding me to the joy and warmth of this family.

And then, dinner is finished and one male voice begins. Soon, the others join him. And I feel the history of a people, the soul of a religion, the rapture of believers singing to their God. I slowly and softly begin to add my voice to their chorus.

The woman sitting next to me puts her hand on my arm.

"You cannot sing," she says.

"What?" I ask.

She repeats herself.

"But why?"

"The sound of a woman's voice is thought to be a temptation for the men. We can sing when we are by ourselves, but not when the men are present."

And suddenly, for me, the magic, the joy, the spirituality—and the bonding—is gone.

When I say goodnight and thank you to the family, they invite me to the wedding, which is in the Orthodox community of Bnei Brak, an hour away. Mrs. Stein tells me that she will ask her friend Shoshana (not her real name) to sit with me on the bus that will take us there. She will be my dinner partner at the reception (men and women sit separately).

Shoshana and I meet for the first time on the street corner where everyone is waiting for the bus. She is wearing a turquoise silk dress with a full-length matching jacket and a double strand of real pearls.

The other women are as exquisitely dressed. In gold and diamonds and pearls, strappy and stylish heels, and colorful silk dresses. In this community where a married woman may not show her hair, every woman is perfectly coifed, not a wig-hair out of place. Were a stranger to study the assembled women, it would be very clear who is the most devout person in the group. I am wearing what I have: a long black skirt over black tights, black ballet slippers, a white long-sleeved blouse, and a white lacy scarf on my head that I borrowed from Zahava.

Shoshana leads me to a double seat in the back of the bus. She is an immigrant from South Africa, she tells me, where her life was very different. She was born Jewish but not Orthodox. She and her friends in South Africa were modern and sophisticated. Twelve years ago she moved to Israel (she did not say why), became an Orthodox Jew, and moved into Mea She'arim. The community found her a husband.

As we talk, the loudspeaker is playing Hasidic music. I look around. The bus is filled with elegant women in wigs and men in big fur hats.

"See, there he is with our son." She points through the window to a thin, emaciated-looking man in long black Hasidic clothes and a black hat. He is holding the hand of a child.

Yaba-baba-bum. Yaba-baba-bum.

"We are divorced. He is taking care of our son for the day. Our marriage lasted five years."

I'm shocked. "Isn't divorce unusual in the Hasidic community?" I ask. "What happened?"

The music is still blaring religiously over the loudspeaker. The fur hats and wigs and elegant long-sleeved dresses surround us. Shoshana looks up with tears in her eyes and possibly, just possibly, a tiny smirk on her lips.

"Oh," she says. "The sex was terrible. He couldn't keep it up for more than a minute."

For the rest of the bus ride, the ceremony, the dinner, and the ride home, I listen to the story of her marriage, her sex life, and her divorce. This is a woman who is hungry for someone to talk to. I wonder if she too thinks I was sent by God.

The next day I have lunch with Zahava and her husband. It's the first time I've met him. He has brought two American tourists, teenage boys, home from the Wailing Wall, to join us. He is not permitted to shake my hand when we are introduced. During lunch, he does not talk to me nor look at me. And as I sit there listening to him proudly telling the guests that ten teens from Mea She'arim were out stoning cars on Saturday, I realize that the historical and religious bonds that he and I share are meaningless; we have little in common.

After four days in Mea She'arim, my anthropological perspective is askew. In this small community, I have encountered entitlement, arrogance, prejudice, and finally, violence. All in the name of religion. I cannot stop myself from judging. It is yet another instance of my inability to maintain the nonjudgmental role of participant-observer. Eight years later the issue will arise again in Bali, with much greater impact on my psyche and my life.

Before I leave Israel, I decide to visit a Druse village. The Druse are an Arabic-speaking people numbering approximately four hundred thousand, most of whom live in Syria and Lebanon. Their monotheistic religion, which dates from the eleventh century, combines Christianity and Islam, but the details are a well-kept secret. There are more than ninety thousand

Druse in seventeen villages in northern Israel. They usually marry within the community. Traditionally, a Druse man who marries a non-Druse woman is expelled from the community.

Most important for Israel is the fact that wherever Druse are in the world, they are loyal to the country they reside in. Druse are the only Arabic-speaking community in Israel in which the young people complete three years of military service in the Israeli army.

There are several Druse names in my Servas host book. The man who is expecting me is described in the book as the director of a children's home. I like visiting schools and orphanages where I can share my books with the children. And visiting a non-Jewish community will give me a chance to observe some of the diversity of Israel.

When I step off the bus, I am again in another world. The men are wearing long brown robes, white pillbox-style hats, and white shirts under their robes. The women are in long skirts or dresses, their arms covered. I ask a young man in the street if he can direct me to the children's home. He walks me to the door.

"Welcome," says my host, a robust man in his fifties with a warm smile. "I no speak English. You speak Arabic? Hebrew?"

Everyone I have met in Israel, until now, has spoken English. It is almost as though I am in an English-speaking country. But I did spend ten years of my childhood in Bridgeport, Connecticut, going to Hebrew school three times a week. I even had a scholarship one summer to a Hebrew-speaking camp. I know the alphabet and I can count, but I haven't spoken any Hebrew since I arrived two weeks ago. I silently review my conversational vocabulary, which has been dormant for thirty-five years.

From Hebrew school: Yes, no. Big girl, little boy. Mother is in the kitchen. Father is reading the book. Sit down. Close the door. Very good. I eat. He eats. Open your books.

And from camp: Bunk 18. Go to hell. I lost my yellow raincoat.

Nope. I don't speak Hebrew. Or Arabic.

I follow him to the room where I will be sleeping. I leave my bag and we go back outside.

"May I see the Home?" I ask. "The school? The children?" I manage to communicate in my word-Hebrew. There are four little girls following us around.

"*Shalom,*" I say to one of the girls. "What is your name?" I manage it in Hebrew. They only speak Arabic. I turn to my host and ask in awkward Hebrew.

"In Arabic? How say, What is your name?" He tells me. I say it five times. The children laugh and repeat it, making fun of my pronunciation. I laugh too and ask them the question one by one.

The girls are between eight and eleven. I can see from their eyes and mannerisms that they are mildly retarded. There are distortions in their faces and awkwardness in their movements. But they talk and laugh; and when I move on, they snuggle into the hugs I give them.

"May I visit the school?" I ask. I am thinking that I might read some books to the kids. I know the pictures will make them laugh. My host nods and smiles, and we walk toward a building that I think is a school. It is not.

We walk in and I am immediately accosted by the antiseptic hospital smell of clean . . . and the sound of distant groans and moans. This is not a school.

He takes me into the first room, where there are four beds with severely retarded children lying in strange positions and emitting noises that send chills through my body and tears to my eyes.

As we go from room to room, I realize that my language deficiency prevents me from asking the questions I would like to ask, like, Are these children all from Druse villages? From this village? If all these kids are from Druse families, is it inbreeding that has produced a disproportionate number of retarded children? I walk through room after room and look at the different afflictions. I am smiling at the children, saying hello, and wishing I were anywhere else.

Finally, after what seems like hours but is no more than fifteen minutes, we go outside. I breathe deeply. The girls I met earlier catch up with us. Their slight facial distortions seem so insignificant, their speech patterns so fine, their movements so miraculous. They are speaking and talking and walking. I remember their names but I pretend I have forgotten and I mix them all up. They laugh, their laughter loud and uninhibited. What a miracle to be able to laugh.

My host now takes me to meet Mohamed, my assigned day host, who speaks English. Mohamed and I walk along immaculately clean, unpaved streets, lined with white stucco houses. There is a dignity in the people as they walk gracefully in their long robes and dresses. Several of the men have full white beards and glasses, and many are carrying canes, though they walk erect. The women look strong and stout under their full, loose dresses.

Mohamed appears to be in his late seventies, a handsome man with a thin face, a white beard, and a friendly smile. In broken English he tells me he is responsible for Servas coming to his village.

"I first," he says. "All host sign because me. Now you meet all host." And I begin my two-day tour, going from one home to the next.

Druse literature says that they "are a friendly, reliable people, considered by many to be the most hospitable and courageous race in the world."

We knock on the door of the first host. I am greeted with a warm smile by a woman in a long maroon dress. There is a large tray on the coffee table in the simple living room, with three different kinds of nuts and assorted dried fruits and crunchy snacks.

Within two minutes of my arrival, people begin arriving from rooms in the back. The father, two teenage sons, a daughter about twenty, and several small children.

"Please," says the father, pointing to the tray. I eat some peanuts. And then some cashews. Everyone watches. I sip coffee and smile.

One of the teenage sons speaks some English. We discuss where I'm from, how old he is, how many brothers and sisters he has. One of his brothers, he tells me proudly, is in the Israeli army.

"Please," says the mother, gesturing toward the tray. I eat an apricot and a date.

As soon as I enter the second house, I hear things pouring into a tray from somewhere out of sight. And as I talk to the twelve-year-old daughter, who speaks a little English, the tray arrives, filled with nuts and fruits and more crunchy snacks.

As the day moves toward dusk, we visit more houses and the nuts continue to pour. And I continue to eat them and drink more coffee, but now there are also smells of dinners cooking. Onions frying. Meat stewing. Vegetables steaming. Blenders grinding.

"You will stay for dinner," say the hosts that we visit from five o'clock on.

"No, no," says Mohamed to all of them. "Thank you very much, but we have plans for dinner."

I just smile politely. I am in his hands.

When Mohamed decides my day is done, we walk to his home. I tell him I am so full of nuts and coffee that I can barely walk. We laugh. We have laughed much during the day. I make many mistakes trying to learn Arabic words and they come out funny. Then five minutes later I ask for the same word all over again . . . and make the same pronunciation errors. In the course of our day, Mohamed has told me that he has four children and that his wife is sick and staying with one of their daughters. She has been away for several months.

"We are here," he tells me and we climb a flight of stairs and enter a big room. It is everything in one: a kitchen, a sitting room, a bedroom. Mohamed tells me that he is going to prepare my dinner; he refuses my offer to help with the cooking.

Half an hour later Mohamed asks me to sit down at the table. There are humus and eggplant, string beans and pita and olives and tomatoes, and a very large fish. There is also only one setting of cutlery and one plate. He directs me to sit in front of it.

"Where is your plate?" I ask.

"I will eat later," he says and sits across from me to watch me eat.

When I am finished eating, he returns me to the Home.

When my two Servas days are up, Mohamed accompanies me to the bus stop. I thank him for the wonderful experience of getting to know him and the people of his village.

"Ah," he says. "Do not say thank you. I happy because you. Maybe wife die. We marry."

One week later, as I fly toward New York, I reflect on my Israeli experience. It was not what I expected. I enjoyed the Israelis; they were warm and hospitable and full of spirit. And they graciously welcomed me into their homes and their lives.

I was deeply moved by the stories of people who had lived through the Holocaust, the Israeli wars, and the founding of a country. But even though I kept seeing people on the street who looked like my uncles and cousins, in the end, they were not a religion or a nationality, but individuals, like people everywhere.

I am thankful for the fact that Israel exists, and I will fight and vote and contribute to keep it healthy. But my humanity is what ties me to others, and that goes much, much deeper than a shared history.

Galápagos
Islands

CHAPTER SEVEN

TRUE FREEDOM

It's been nearly three years since my first tentative steps into Mexico City, and people in the U.S. are asking me if I'm ready yet to end my wandering and resume my life. Some of them are sure that I'm still reacting to the divorce, running from reality, avoiding some abstract "real world."

"Perhaps," suggests one friend, "therapy would be better than getting on another plane."

They are all intelligent people who care about me, and I feel obligated to consider their comments. But no matter how often I ask myself if I'm running away from something, I always get the same answer. No, I'm not running away. On the contrary. I've discovered a new way to live.

My life is endlessly fascinating, filled with learning, adventure, interesting people, new and enlightening experiences. I laugh, sing, and dance more than I ever have. I am becoming the person inside me.

My life also offers opportunities to give as well. Wherever I am in the world, I read to children, visit classrooms, teach English, and bring food and laughter into homes.

And on top of all that, I'm existing on less than $10,000 a year, including airfares.

I'm embracing life, not running away from it. Why would I want to stop?

Jan is particularly happy to hear about my next destination. I have a contract to write a kids' book about the animals in the Galápagos Islands. I'll be writing it in the Charles Darwin Research Station Library on the island of Santa Cruz. Before I leave the States, Jan books her flight for a three-week visit.

I've come a long way since my first Galápagos trip eight years ago, the trip when I realized I wanted more than fine dinners and good theater in my life. I can't wait to revisit the islands, connect with the animals, swim in the warm, tropical waters.

While I am still in the U.S., I buy a portable computer, a tiny printer, and a ton of sunblock #15. Two weeks before I leave, I remember one of the subjects frequently discussed in the "backpacker network": the tyranny of customs people. They levy arbitrary taxes and fees at will, and they have been known to "hold" and "disappear" electronic gadgets.

My computer and printer are sure to be attractive to the guys behind the glass, so I decide to visit the press officer at the Ecuadorian Embassy in Washington, D.C. People like books about their countries. I'm hoping someone in the embassy will give me a letter that will move me through customs with no hassles.

The press officer at the embassy is intrigued that I'm writing a children's book about the Galápagos. I tell him my concern about bringing a computer into Ecuador, and he promises to have someone meet me at customs in Guayaquil. Then he offers me a free flight from Guayaquil to the Galápagos on a military plane. I accept.

He adds, as I walk out the door, "I will also make arrangements to have you met by one of our workers when you arrive in the Galápagos. He will take you to a government house where you can live as long as you like. I'm sorry but you will have to share the house with two government employees."

Wow! I never even asked.

I step off the plane in Guayaquil, my backpack a hump on my back, my gray computer-case and its eleven-pound contents weighing down my right shoulder, and my smaller printer case a lesser weight on my left shoulder. The first thing I see is someone in uniform waving my cardboard name. We speak a few words of introduction; he takes my computer and asks me to follow him. This guy is serious. No small talk here. I am high government business, even though I am wearing jeans.

We march past lines of people waiting to be interviewed by officials in glass booths. I feel the same smugness I felt many years ago when I first drove my new four-wheel-drive Jeep in a snowstorm, whizzing past all the cars that were stuck on the side of the road.

Even before the crew is off my plane, I am sitting in a room, holding a ticket for the free military flight, which, it turns out, goes to the military airport on the island of San Cristóbal. This is not the island where I thought I was going. On my other visit to the Galápagos, I flew into Baltra, which has an airstrip that the Americans built during World War II. In Baltra, there are boats and buses to take the passengers to the island of Santa Cruz. I just assumed that's where I'd be taken this time too. It's where tourists are delivered. It's where the Charles Darwin Research Station is. It's where I have to be. It never occurred to me to ask where the military plane landed.

As I sit there, I wonder if I should I say something. Nah. It'll be an adventure. The Ecuadorian government has come through brilliantly so far. When things are working, it's usually best not to break the rhythm with too many questions. It does occur to me, however, that I have no contact name, no address, and no paper proof that any arrangements have been made for me. All I have to go on is trust.

Interestingly, relying on trust and informality usually serves me better than when I ask for papers, stamps, and bureaucratic letters. I'm more comfortable operating on a personal level, asking about family, telling a little about my life, and often bringing one of my kids' books as a token gift. Moving things into a business mode changes everything. If I'd been formal with the press officer at the embassy, the offers of a plane trip and a house might never have happened. I like the handshake-and-smile school of doing business. I'm not going to say anything about flying to the wrong island. I'll just fly and see.

As usual, things work out. When the plane lands, there is another greeter with another Rita sign. Turns out that Felipe is one of the two men who lives in the house where I will be living. He's my height, swarthy, with a full mustache and smiling eyes. His voice is deep and sexy. He's probably close to forty. If I'd seen him on the street, I would have thought he was a farm worker. Actually, he's a scientist with a Ph.D. in biology.

He takes me to a little office just up from the dock, and we sip bottled water while we wait for the ferry. It's oppressively hot, with a little relief from the ceiling fan spinning over our heads. From time to time someone comes in and I am introduced. An hour after I arrive, Felipe and I climb onto the public ferry, a big motorboat, with about eight other people. When I nearly drop my computer into the water, there is a chorus of alarm.

"Déjeme ayudarle," Felipe says, smiling and reaching for the gray carrying case. Let me help you.

About half an hour later, we arrive in the town of Puerto Ayora on the island of Santa Cruz. Felipe carries my computer and printer and we walk through a plaza filled with souvenir shops, places to eat, small hotels, and boat repair and supply places. The plaza is busy with tourists shopping and eating and with locals hanging around. We pass through the plaza and walk up a dirt road past small houses, little stores, and lots of kids.

Our house is a white stucco cabin just off the main road about half a mile from the plaza. There's a kitchen, a bathroom, and three small bedrooms . . . all opening into a central room. There's also an enclosed porch in the front. The place smells of disinfectant and it's sparkling clean. There are sheets on my bed, dishes and pots in the cabinets, and plenty of ashtrays, but there's not a picture on a wall or a knick-knack on a table. There are no frills to these government accommodations.

The next day Felipe takes me to the beach along a path of sharp, black lava rocks. The Galápagos Islands are volcanic, having been spewed up from the ocean bottom. They became islands when the underwater mountains reached the air, millions of years ago, sputtering and hissing into being. Over millions of more years, dozens of craggy little islands and fourteen big ones established their presence in the vast ocean, six hundred miles away from the mainland and any form of terrestrial life. The birds arrived by air; the land animals on hunks of earth that broke off from the mainland and somehow bumped into the tiny masses in the vast Pacific.

As we walk along the path to the beach, Felipe gives me a lesson in how to negotiate lava. Every footstep has to be carefully placed; if you're moving, you have to look down all the time. From time to time he takes my hand and helps me over a rough spot.

We spend several hours on the beach. He asks as many questions as he answers, and we share our history, our interests, our families. Felipe refuses to speak English; he says he can't. But I know that someone with his education must have read books in English. Like many well-educated Hispanic men, he doesn't want to make mistakes, so he won't talk. We'll have to get along in my flawed Spanish. I have no problem mutilating his language.

That night we go out to dinner to a local hangout where I get a thick hamburger with avocado and sprouts.

The next day I begin researching. The Charles Darwin Research Station is about a mile or so from our house. Felipe carries my computer to the library before he goes off to work. And when I get home, he's cooked dinner and the table is set for two. Carlos, our housemate, is out.

I wonder, as I sit across from Felipe eating a wonderful stew made of *plátanos,* beef, and peanuts, if he is still on assignment: "Pick her up at the boat, take her to the house, and keep her happy." If so, he's doing a great job.

After I've been there for more than a week, all I can be certain of is that this ordinary-looking man, who reminds me of an Ecuadorian peasant, has sparked in me the pitter-patter sensations of a teenage crush. And then one night, when Felipe and I are sitting on the couch, my legs curled up under me, my knees slightly touching his legs, he asks, *"Puedo abrazarte?"* May I embrace you?

No one has ever asked before. Suddenly I feel shy and I don't know how to answer. Somehow, *"Sí"* feels uncomfortable and too short. *"Por favor,"* please, feels needy. *"Por supuesto,"* of course, sounds too eager. I am wordless.

Understandably, Felipe finds the silence awkward and he's too much of a gentleman to reach over without permission, which is of course what I want. He thinks I don't understand the Spanish, and he asks again.

Fortunately, it's one of those situations where language isn't necessary. Felipe turns out to be the best government gift of all, a thoughtful friend and an extraordinary lover.

My research is going well. The books in the library answer all my questions, and there are dozens of scientists (marine biologists, geologists, ecologists, zoologists, etc.) here from all over the world who are willing to sit with me and explain whatever I don't understand. I like being a part of this community of people who love what they're doing and where they're doing it.

Jan is on her way. Her timing is perfect. A day after she arrives, both Felipe and Carlos (my other housemate) are going on vacation. I do not have secrets from Jan; we are very close. Even before she arrives, I tell her about Felipe. But the fact that he will not be here will definitely make things more relaxed. When the guys return, Jan and I will be off on a two-week tour of the islands.

Touring the uninhabited (by people) islands is the essence of a Galápagos visit. The magic experience of these islands is observing the animals at close range: sitting on the ground just a couple of feet away from blue-footed boobies dancing their mating dance; swimming with sea lions when they brush you with their whiskers and swim around you as though you were a maypole; watching the big male marine iguanas jump into the water and swim for their algae food, looking like prehistoric aquatic dinosaurs; standing near the edge of a cliff while an albatross waits for the perfect wind to launch himself into the air.

The only way to see the animals in their environment is to visit them on *their* islands, islands where people are permitted only if they are touring on an Ecuadorian-registered boat with a government-certified guide. Islands where people are permitted only during the day. Islands that have paths where humans are permitted to walk. The Galápagos are well protected.

I make plans for Jan and me to take a two-week luxury tour, one that usually costs two hundred dollars per person per day. We are filling in the empty bunks and paying fifty dollars a day. I'm excited. I know Jan is going to love it.

Then, four days before she arrives, our luxury boat breaks down and the cruise is cancelled. So much for making reservations in advance.

It's time to test the pick-up-tour method. A pick-up tour is what the more adventurous and longer term travelers do. Instead of booking a boat in advance through a travel agent, they just book airfare to the islands. No one meets them. Instead, they settle into one of the mediocre hotels and wander the plaza looking for others like them who want to put together a group for a tour. I'm going to wait for Jan's arrival so we can find our pick-up group together.

I have to admit that being able to say to my kids "Come visit me in the Galápagos" makes me feel great (Mitch can't get away). I like being able to introduce Jan to new worlds while enriching our relationship.

The day after her arrival, Jan and I go off to the square. We talk to everyone we see. By afternoon, we've found our passengers: two women from Sweden, an Englishman, an Israeli couple, an American couple just finished with their Peace Corp duty in Peru, and the two of us. It's a good group. I'm the only one over thirty.

Together, the nine of us talk to various captains who are hanging around the dock. Finally, we book a seaworthy but slightly battered fishing boat that's been turned into a cruise boat. Then I talk to a friend who is an official guide and she agrees to come with us. We leave the next day. The cost per person is twenty-five dollars a day.

The first day out, Jan dives off the boat and loses both of her contact lenses. The whole point of being in the Galápagos, of course, is to observe the animals, and Jan can barely see. Her glasses are back in Santa Cruz.

It's been a long time since I've been called upon to sacrifice for my daughter; she's been independent since the age of eighteen, and stubborn about accepting help from adults since the age of fourteen. But this is serious. There's only one thing a mother can do.

It's not quite like giving her a kidney, but it's the best I can do in the circumstances. I have two lenses in my eyes and an extra one in my bag. I gallantly give her the extra lens . . . and the one in my right eye. *Voilà!* She can see again, albeit imperfectly since our prescriptions are not the same. I am only a little bit dizzy with one lens. And the blur disappears for both of us after two days. Somehow we are both able to adjust to our manufactured disabilities.

I have had two luxury trips before this one, both on the *Tigris,* a sleek sailing yacht. All the passengers on those trips were Americans who could afford $150 a day. And while the tours were great, on each tour there were at least two out of the six people who were unpleasant to be with. Some of my most vivid memories are of people not talking to people, others nonstop complaining, and one couple squabbling for two weeks.

This time we're on a beat-up converted fishing boat; there are no romantic sails fluttering in the wind, and no hints of luxury. The group is mostly European; all except me are young; and not one of them could have afforded $150 a day. But the dynamics are sensational. We sing songs in four different languages and play charades in sign language, desperately trying to come up with universal clichés and proverbs. No one complains about anything or criticizes a fellow passenger.

Our food is mostly fish caught by the crew while we are visiting the islands, and cooked to perfection, simple and moist. One day, the crew goes off and shoots a wild goat for our dinner. Twice, at night, they dive and catch lobsters. And we snack more than once on sea urchins, fresh from the bottom of the sea. Papaya, potatoes, *plátanos,* pasta, and other assorted non-*p* dishes are turned into great dinners.

Maybe it's being with Jan, maybe it's the contagious exuberance of the young passengers, but this trip is pure joy. There is a part of me that can't help but compare it to the hotel vs. backpacker syndrome. Do people who are spending more money have more brakes on their ability to have fun, are they more self-conscious, more demanding, more judgmental?

I'm the only one on the trip who is disappointed when the captain tells us that he is not planning to take us to Tower Island. I'm also the only one who knows what we're missing. Tower has all the birds of the other islands, plus. It's the plus that I fell in love with: hundreds of nesting frigatebirds.

A few hundred feet onto Tower Island from Darwin Bay is a flat area filled with trees and shrubs around four to eight feet high; and during the first six or so months of the year, there are spectacular great frigatebird colonies sitting on top of the vegetation. It's the males who are spectacular, resting their heads on what look like bright red basketball-size balloons (technically called gular sacs).

Normally these balloons are the size of a turkey's wattle, but when the male frigates want to attract a female, they blow up their balloons. When a female frigate flies overhead, the males turn their heads and wings upward, shake seductively, and cackle into the sky. The chorus of frigates sounds like a theme song from a witches' convention.

Hearing the call, the female flies around, surveying her suiters, flapping to the chorus of the cackles. If she's interested, she chooses one of the males and lands next to him. The rest of the birds stop cackling and go back to waiting. The "dating" pair do a short flirtation dance, waving their heads at each other, wiggling, the male shaking his balloon. Sometimes he puts his wing around her.

I have watched this ritual dozens of times on two visits to Tower, and I have never seen a female who liked what she saw. Once I watched for two hours as females flew over and males cackled and wiggled and wooed. Every time the female flew down, she flirted a bit, observed her suitor's technique, and then flew off in search of something better. As soon as she gave up, the cackle chorus began again.

It was obvious, however, that some females had stayed long enough to make the fluffy, puffy white babies that were perched in the trees waiting for their parents to arrive with food, but I never did see a female who stayed.

On both of my visits to the Galápagos, Tower was the highlight of my trip. If there were no iguanas, no sea lions, no boobies, no finches in the Galápagos, the extraordinary frigates of Tower would be worth the trip.

I think about those frigates often. In addition to their comedic courtship, they are also spectacular fliers. I have seen frigates poking and pulling on a booby in midair until it drops the fish in its beak; then the frigate with its ten-foot wingspan and forked tail swoops down, and catches the food in midair. I often fantasize about coming back in my next life as a frigate, riding the wind, pestering boobies, getting cackled at by whole colonies of males shaking their red balloons at me.

So, when our captain explains that Tower Island is too far and too flat (too easy to miss without radar), I am disappointed. He tells us that the last times he tried to get there, the island was fogged in and he missed it completely. The group lost two days of their tour and never made it to Tower. None of us is willing to risk losing two of our ten days.

Then, one evening, three days into our journey, the captain sends for me. "You have a call." A call? How exciting! This was before cell phones.

It's José. He was part of the crew on my second *Tigris* trip, and he's gone on to captain a very posh yacht. I happened to meet him in Santa Cruz a couple of days ago and I told him that my daughter and I would be touring on this boat. José tells me that he is moored just across the harbor from us. Would Jan and I like to come over for a drink? He'll send someone to pick us up.

I have no idea what his daily rate is, but the boat is gorgeous: the wood paneling in the parlor is polished to a mirror finish, the staterooms are spacious, and the equipment is state of the art. While the passengers watch a movie on the VCR, the three of us talk and drink. José and I reminisce about his dalliance with one of the passengers on our last trip. When we leave, I ask José where he's headed next. "We're leaving for Tower in a couple of hours."

His luxury craft is navigating by radar, he says, and he'd be happy to have us follow him.

I wake up our captain when I get back to our boat. He's not too happy, but he gets on the line to José, and in a couple of hours, we're off to Tower, following José. Most boats do the long distances at night while the passengers sleep. The islands are far apart and we'd miss too much if the traveling were done during the day. You get used to sleeping to the rumble of the motor, and when you wake up, you're moored off another island.

Our pick-up trip is wonderful for everyone. The amazing experiences with the animals, the camaraderie, the sea. The singing and games and snorkeling. The fresh fish every day for dinner. When the trip is over, Jan and I are closer than we've ever been. Sharing friends and experiences, watching and enjoying each other in a new and intriguing setting, has brought our relationship to another level. We've become good friends.

When her three weeks are over, I return to the library for another week of research; and then, there's one last experience I need in order to finish the book.

I want to write about the lives of the animals . . . around the clock. I've observed them during the daylight hours, but I've never been on an island at night. It isn't allowed . . . except for scientists. My only chance is to get permission from the National Park Service. I go see them.

"No way," they say, closing the subject before it is even opened.

There's got to be a way, I think, and I go talk to some of the scientists. Turns out there's a group of four Germans—three men and a woman—who are about to go off to one of the islands for several weeks to study marine iguana hatchlings that will emerge soon from white leathery eggs that were buried three months ago. I ask if I can join them for a week. It's no problem for them.

I'm called in to talk to the head of the National Park Service. Under the sponsorship of the German iguana team, I'm given permission to go with them to the island and to stay for a week, not a minute longer. I promise—on my life—to be off the island after seven days. I don't know at the time, but it's a promise that will be almost impossible to fulfill.

Felipe makes arrangements for the interisland boat to pick me up after a week. He gives me a number to call via the scientists' shortwave radio so I can confirm the day before. My return trip is set before I leave—day, time, and place.

The bay where we debark is on the side of the island where tourists never come. The team has been here before, when the iguanas were laying the eggs. One of the scientists gives me a little tour. He shows me a deep crevasse in the rocky cliff, about fifty yards away from where we set up camp. "Here's where we shit," I'm told. I peer down the crack, which is an opening in the rocks about three feet long, eight inches wide, and probably thirty feet deep. The roar of the ocean echoes from the depths.

The group sets up tents, including one for me, and they take out a grill and a tank of gas. We have meat that first night and rice and salad. I wander around looking for animals to observe. I want to know what the boobies do at night, what time they wake up, what noises they make. It's a long walk to the booby colony. Maybe it'll be enough to write about their early morning rituals, stretching and combing their feathers, and doing whatever else they do.

Close by camp, about a hundred yards away, is a sea lion colony. I'll definitely spend a night watching and listening and sleeping with them.

One of the scientists and I talk until we go to sleep. He's a hang glider back home, and he offers, if I come to Germany, to take me hang gliding. I like the idea.

It's peaceful snuggled in my sleeping bag, listening to the waves crash into the rocks and to the bull sea lion honking every five minutes to let the world know that his harem is well protected. There's an owl nearby and her hoot pierces the waves. I sleep soundly.

By the time I get out of my tent in the morning, there is a yeast bread cooking on the fire. Breakfast is bread, melted butter, and sliced, raw garlic. I try, but raw garlic in the morning makes me vomit. That's something I never knew until now.

The next night I take my sleeping bag and spread it on the rocks next to the sea lions. The sky is flooded with stars; the moon is dark. I have my flashlight with me. There is a mother and her baby less than three feet away from me. They don't seem to care at all that I am sleeping with them. They don't even mind that every fifteen minutes I scan the area with my flashlight. The bull's honking goes on all night long. Every now and then I hear a splash as one of the females dives into the water. A few minutes later, she waddles back up.

Another day, with the sun's earliest rays, I wander over to watch the blue-footed boobies waking up. Seabirds, the boobies dive for their food, so they have to spend a lot of time waterproofing their feathers. At all times, in all booby colonies, birds are oiling their beaks by rubbing a gland just under their tailfeathers and spreading the oil onto their body feathers. In the early morning, every bird in the colony is oiling and combing. Frigates are seabirds too, but they don't dive. They catch flying fish in the air, surface-swimming fish with their long beaks, and from time to time they do their pirate trick of stealing from the divers; but they don't dive because their feathers are not sufficiently oily.

The week goes quickly. Then, the day before I'm supposed to leave, I get a call on the radio. The boat that is supposed to pick me up has broken down. It can't pick me up for at least five days. I tell the person at the other end that I promised the National Park Service I'd be off this island tomorrow. He apologizes, but there's nothing he can do.

I confer with the scientists and they tell me that tour boats stop in the bay on the other side of the island. They decide that we should all walk across in the morning. Hopefully I'll be able to hitch a ride.

Everyone comes for the walk. I'm flattered because it's a long, hot walk in the early morning sun, and we have to climb two big, rocky hills. After a two-hour trek, we get there, but there's no one in sight. We wait in the hot sun.

Then, an hour after we arrive, a boat comes into the bay and the passengers are brought to shore.

The guide, the passengers, and Enrico, the crew member who is ferrying everybody, are surprised to see people on the island without a boat. I explain my predicament and ask if I can hitch a ride back to Santa Cruz.

"We have another three days," says the guide, "before we go to Santa Cruz. We do have an empty bunk, but you'll have to ask the captain."

Enrico ferries me to the boat. The captain is OK with my joining the tour, but he is worried that the passengers might object. He tells me that they are a group from Canada. I promise the captain, if I get their OK, that I will entertain them with stories of my adventures in Mexico and Guatemala and Nicaragua.

"If they agree, it's OK with you?" I ask.

"Por supuesto. Cómo no?" Sure, why not?

So I am ferried back to the island to pitch my proposal to the passengers. And that's how I end up a hitchhiker on a twenty-person luxury cruise ship.

When I get back to Santa Cruz, I feel explosively free. I have slept with sea lions, sailed with strangers, cooked bread on a fire in the middle of nowhere. I feel as though the ties that have forever bound me to a place, a culture, a way of life, have finally been cut, and I am free to be me in the world.

I love this place and the way it makes me feel. When the book is completed, I get a brilliant idea: I'll become a Galápagos guide and live here.

Every boat that takes tourists around the island has to have a registered guide. I'll take the course, which is given here on Santa Cruz. Guides have to be bilingual; I'm almost there. I like the sound of the academic part . . . studying the geology of the islands, animal behavior, weather, marine biology. All subjects I love, a lot of which I already know from my research. I'm a very good swimmer and a former lifeguard, which would be useful skills on a boat. I also like the laid-back life of the guides, hanging out with the locals, going out on yachts, lecturing to groups of tourists. I could get used to that.

I have to admit that part of the appeal of becoming a guide is thinking about telling people in the States that I'm a guide in the Galápagos Islands. I love the idea. It would be fun, safe, and healthy. *Cómo no?*

I actually fill out the application and talk to some guides and the National Park Service, but in the end, I decide to wait and think about it. I never officially apply. Waiting and thinking is not a good strategy for making decisions; all sorts of practical matters get added into the process. Spontaneity is better. For me. But, hey, just the thought that I was considering becoming a guide in the Galápagos is exhilarating.

Indonesia

Chapter Eight

The Forests of Borneo

By the time I leave the Galápagos Islands, I feel ready to conquer the world. But I don't know where to go. The answer comes to me at my college reunion in Waltham, Massachusetts.

It's been thirty years since I've seen my Brandeis classmates, and my eyes keep flipping from the familiar names on the tags everyone is wearing to the less familiar faces. We were a small, coed class of around 217 and the ambiance at the Friday night cocktail hour is friendly and easy. Yet, it is here in this warm and accepting setting, while I am sipping my red wine and smiling a lot, that I realize for the first time that I am a threat to tenuous marriages.

David L. was a friend when we were both students. I remember vividly the many lazy afternoons when we'd sat in our jeans and turtleneck shirts under a tree on the hill overlooking the library, talking about things like the existential meaning of life, and arguing about which was the best pizza at Saldi's. Now, thirty years later, we both sneak a look at the other's name tag before we commit to a hug.

Today, David is a successful, distinguished, graying lawyer, sharply dressed in creased khaki pants, a navy blazer, a silk tie, and a crisp white shirt that has flown in a suitcase from the West Coast without getting a wrinkle. He introduces me to his wife, who, like most spouses at reunions, is standing a half step behind her mate. As I talk about my three years in Central America, and my idyllic stay in the Galápagos, I notice a tightening around David's mouth and a simultaneous widening of his wife's eyes.

"You're doing this alone?" she asks.

Their physical positions have altered. She is leaning toward me, animatedly asking questions, and he is a half step back. It happens three more times that night and many times over the next years. Usually it's the women who identify with me and ask the questions. It isn't the details of my travels that intrigue them; it's the fact that I am living a rich, fulfilling life. And I'm doing it without a man. For many women, my story awakens buried dreams or stimulates new ones. I can tell by reading eyes and body language when I've touched a sensitive nerve.

The second day of the reunion there's an informal session where we are asked to talk about our lives, our thoughts, whatever. So I tell my story. I conclude by saying that I don't know where I'll be going next.

"If anyone has any ideas, I'd love to talk."

Only one former classmate has a suggestion about where I might go.

"I've heard Indonesia is fascinating," she says.

As soon as she mentions Indonesia, I remember a conversation I had with a Norwegian man from UNICEF when I was in Guatemala.

"Indonesian is an easy language to learn," he told me more than a year ago. He suggested I start out in Yogyakarta, where there are more than fifty schools of higher learning and plenty of classes to choose from.

That's it! I make up my mind before I ever leave the campus. I'm going to Indonesia. The minute I get back to my mother's house, where I've been staying, I locate Indonesia in her atlas. It's a country of islands, including most of Borneo, half of New Guinea, and all of Bali. I know nothing about its politics, its history, or its culture. I can't wait to learn.

Two days later I walk into the Indonesian Consulate in New York and I'm directed to the office of Soehardjono, the man in charge of the press.

Soehardjono, Jono for short, is in his late twenties. A small, sturdy man with a warm crooked smile. I have brought him one of my books as proof that I'm a legitimate writer. He tells me that his wife collects children's books.

Jono and I talk about our families, our background, and the difficulty of being a foreigner in the United States. He and his wife have been in New York for nearly a year and they've never been invited to an American home.

I tell him that I will be house-sitting in a beautiful area of Pennsylvania when I return from Indonesia in four months. I invite him and his wife to visit me for a weekend. (They do come and we have a great time, barbecuing, talking, and tubing down a river.)

Finally, we get to business. I tell him that I would like to know his country and that I am planning to begin by studying the Indonesian language in Yogyakarta.

Jono looks pleased. "I am from Yogya. How can I help you?"

There are two things I'm hoping he will help me with. I'd like him to talk to me about appropriate and inappropriate behavior. The customs are very different and I don't want to insult anyone by mistake. And second, I'm hoping he can give me some hints about how I can arrange to live with a family.

He tells me to come back in a week.

The following week, Jono greets me like an old friend. Then he gets down to business.

"The first thing that you must never forget is you cannot give or receive with your left hand. It is considered rude and dirty.

"Another important thing to remember is that ours is a culture that has a great deal of respect for older people. If you are walking by an elderly person, you should lower your head and shoulder as you pass."

Jono gets up from behind his desk and walks by me, bending his knees, and lowering the shoulder that is closest to me. His head too is lowered.

"Years ago, servants would crawl on the floor so that their heads would be lower than the person they were respecting. Today it is more symbolic, but still expected."

"And you don't think it would look as if I am mocking the custom if I do it?"

"Don't crawl on the floor. But lowering your head and shoulder would be seen as a sign of respect. You don't have to exaggerate; just show your respect. Also, never point your feet at anyone or rub a child's head. Feet are dirty and the head is sacred."

This is going to be interesting. I cannot imagine myself lowering my body before anyone. Will I do it or will I use the exemption that is given to foreigners?

"And now about a place to stay in Yogya. I have sent a letter in our diplomatic pouch to an old friend of mine from school. He owns a travel agency. I have asked him to find two families who might be interested in having you as a guest in their homes. Here is his name and the address of his agency. He will be expecting you. Good luck."

Jono's friend has done his homework. His agency is off the lobby of a starred hotel and he greets me warmly.

"As Jono suggested," he tells me, "I have found two families who would like very much to have you. One is a retired couple who live in the center of Yogya, near everything. One of them speaks a little bit of English. The other family is a young couple, English teachers, who live in a suburb about fifteen minutes away from town. They work every day and have a baby who is cared for by a maid, so you would not be alone. You may stay with whichever family you want. The choice is up to you."

I choose the English teachers. My first priority is learning Indonesian, and it seems to me that learning a language from scratch might be easier if I could ask questions and get answers from English speakers.

Jono's friend drives me to the house, which is compact and immaculate. All the rooms are through doors off the living room: three small bedrooms and a kitchen. The couple is formal, in their early thirties, and a bit stiff compared to the effusiveness of the Hispanic families I have been living with. There is no question that I have entered another culture. I tell them that I am hoping to study Indonesian while I am with them.

"Bambang and I leave for work at eight each day," says Diana. "We return at four. Didi is the maid. She will be happy to help you. Our baby is one and a half years old. He is also learning Indonesian. Didi will be a teacher to both of you."

My room is small, clean, and spare, and there is even a light on a table next to the bed. This is obviously a well-ordered home with a routine. There will not be much adventure here, but that can come after I have learned to speak the language. We negotiate a price of eight U.S. dollars per night, including food. I move in that afternoon.

Within minutes of my arrival, Inid, Diana's sixteen-year-old sister, bursts through the door holding a tiny white *Shih Tzu*. Tall, slim, and model-beautiful with shoulder-length black hair, Inid rushes over to me, hand out for a shake.

"Hi, my name is Inid. This is Fifi. Come. I will take you for a ride."

Inid is stealing me. I'm not sure her sister and brother-in-law are happy about it, but when I look to them for permission, they gesture that I should go.

Inid and I walk up the street to the house where she lives with her mother. She brings me in for a quick introduction and a dog drop-off. Then she hands me a helmet. Yay! It's not going to be all that stuffy after all.

We shoot through the quiet tree-lined streets on her motorcycle, me holding onto Inid's waist, and Inid pointing and calling out the Indonesian names of things like *dokar* (horse and carriage), *ojek* (motorcycle taxi), *masjid* (mosque), *gereja* (church). I repeat the words into the wind and promptly forget them. This is not going to be an easy language to learn.

"House my friend," says Inid as she stops in front of a typical suburban home. I hop off the back and follow her inside. She introduces me to a beautiful girl with shoulder-length, shiny black hair that smells sweet from the perfume of a recent shampoo. We sit in the living room for five minutes as the girls giggle and chatter in Javanese, the language of Java; nearly everyone in Indonesia speaks two languages, the language of their island and the language of the country. Minutes after we arrive, Inid jumps up and takes my hand. "Come."

We ride around several more streets and stop again. "House my friend," says Inid, and we repeat the routine. Finally, after I have been shown off to her three best friends, we pull into the parking lot of a big Catholic church. I am surprised to find out that Inid and her family are Catholics in a Muslim country.

"Come."

My little dictator-guide takes my hand and we go into a huge hall for a choir rehearsal. Inid is in the choir. The choir director tells me in English that the group is going to be touring Europe in a few months and she invites me to sit and listen. They sing "Ave Maria" and "Greensleeves," and some wonderful tribal songs with drums and exotic instruments.

When the rehearsal is over, we whiz home, pick up Fifi, the dog, at Inid's, and report on our afternoon to Bambang and Diana. I have learned how to say good afternoon, thank you, traffic light, motorcycle taxi, and horse-drawn carriage.

The next morning I hear Bambang and Diana drive off in their car as I am lying in bed doing leg lifts, holding *Indonesian Made Easy* in my hands. I count to five over and over again, staring at the book and counting my legs lifts. Five times five on each side and then five more sets of five on each leg while lying on my back. *Satu, dua, tiga, empat, lima. Satu, dua, tiga, empat, lima. Satu, dua, tiga, empat, lima.* By the time I've finished my leg lifts, I can count to five. I dress and go out the door.

Didi is in the living room sweeping the floor. She greets me with a big smile and says, *"Saya menyapu."* Then she points to herself and says, *"Saya."* She begins to sweep and says, *"Me . . . nya . . . pu. Saya menyapu."* Again she points to herself, *"Saya."* To the broom, *"Sapu. Saya menyapu."*

I take the broom and do exactly what she did, saying the words she has taught me. She smiles, proud to be such a good teacher. We both laugh. I decide on the spot that I will not go to a school. I will learn from Didi and Inid, and, I discover later, the neighborhood children.

During the week I do errands and walk and wander with Didi and the baby. As we walk, she points and names, alerting both me and the baby that we are about to learn a new word. I learn goat and swing and kite and nose and mouth and eyes. We have a little trouble when she says something conversational, something that she can't point to. *"Saya capet"* (pronounced "chapet"), she says one day during our afternoon walk. I know it's descriptive of herself—*saya* means *I*. The *am* is understood; there is no verb *to be*. But since there is nothing she can point to, I have to guess at the meaning of *capet*. *"Saya capet,"* she says again, this time bending her knees and sort of rolling her eyes. I still don't get it.

Capet, I discover later when I look it up in the dictionary that is too heavy to take on our walks, means tired.

I usually spend an hour or two in my room with *Indonesian Made Easy,* repeating phrases and words out loud, wondering if Didi thinks I'm a little crazy or if she understands that saying things out loud is the only way to learn a language. And I keep strengthening both my thighs and my numbers every morning as I continue counting leg lifts.

One morning I take a motorcycle taxi into town and rent a bike for two weeks. Then I pedal for about half an hour to Gadjah Mada University. I have always loved the feeling of a university campus. I wander among the big buildings, among the students rushing to their next classes. I sit on a stone bench, breathing in the excitement of learning, and I decide that I'm going to study my Indonesian in the campus library.

But first I have to find the library. I look up the word and groan. Library is *perbustakaan.* Where is the library? *Di mana perbustakaan?* I walk around for half an hour, saying it over and over again. Finally, when I am saying it easily, I ask a young woman who is passing by. I nod at her answer, but I don't understand a word she says. I ask three more people until finally someone answers me in English.

"I will take you there," says Hamid, and we talk as we walk. He is about twenty, a third-year student in the English faculty, and thrilled that he has found me. He has been dreaming of meeting a native speaker, and suddenly I appear. Hamid takes me to one of the inner reading rooms.

"If you study here, I will come to visit you every day. Perhaps I can help you with your Indonesian. And I hope we can have conversations in English. Good luck."

The next morning as we eat our breakfast of rice and *tempeh* (fermented soybean), I ask Diana and Bambang to help me write some sentences about myself that I can use in conversation: I am a writer from America (no one knows the United States). I write children's books. I am living in Yogya with a family. I am in Indonesia to learn the language and get to know the people.

In the afternoon I bike to Gadja Mada and sit in my reading room. I write and whisper the sentences, each one hundreds of times. Hamid picks me up at four and I recite my words. Then we talk in English. Hamid is applying for a student exchange program in Canada. We work on his application.

Each day I bike to the university and sit in the same place. Some of the regulars in the room talk to me after a while, and Hamid always comes to see me in the late afternoon when I am ready to quit. We have coffee and I adjust his too perfect English by adding idioms and teaching him how to slur his words together so he doesn't sound stilted. He also listens to my lesson of the day.

The second weekend that I am in the house, Diana tells me that she is going to take me to meet the head of the neighborhood organization. He is an architect and he has four children. I smile and nod and indicate that I would like that.

Ten minutes later she tells me again, adding that he lives in a particular house down the street.

"He is an important leader in the community," she tells me. I smile and nod.

Ten minutes later, she points to two little girls who are playing in front of our house. They are dressed in crisply ironed, flowery cotton dresses, and their hair is freshly washed and combed.

"These are the architect's children. They are freshly bathed for your visit."

"When will we be going?" I ask, aware that there is some unspoken message that I'm not getting.

"As soon as you bathe."

Bathing is not an optional thing in Indonesia. People bathe in the morning, in the afternoon, and before ceremonies and visits and special activities. Every bathroom has a built-in cement "tub" about three feet high and two to three feet square. It is usually filled with clean cold water that you scoop out with a plastic container and throw over your body before you soap up. All bathroom floors have drains. Those first few scoops are always a shock and you often hear exclamations of "Aaah!" and "Ooooo!" accompanying the splashes.

When I am bathed and dressed in clean clothes, we are ready to go.

The architect tells me that he very much wants his children to learn English and I offer to teach them. He nods with pleasure, and we make a plan for an English class two afternoons a week. The other thing that comes out of our visit is that the architect tells his daughters, and they tell all the neighborhood children, that they have to help me with my Indonesian.

From that day on, whenever I walk out the door, I step into the neighborhood classroom. Children come running up to me, pointing. "*Rumah*," they say slowly, separating the syllables and pointing to a house, as though I were their baby brother or sister. "*Pohon*," they say, pointing to a tree.

One afternoon I return from the library and Inid is sitting alone in the living room. She greets me, but her bouncy effusiveness is missing. So is her dog.

"Fifi was killed by a car this morning," she tells me, and like all Indonesians, she delivers her bad news with a smile.

I use my exemption. As a foreigner, I do not have to smile. Instead, I hold her and she allows herself to cry.

After I have been in Yogya for nearly a month, I begin to get itchy. I'm ready for an adventure. I ask Bambang and Diana if they have any ideas. Two days later, they sit me down and translate an article from the newspaper. In one week, the vice-governor of the province of Kalimantan (the Indonesian part of the island of Borneo) is having a ceremony for his long-dead grandmother, who was never properly sent off to the next world. The traditional ceremony is to take place deep in the rain forest in the village where his tribal ancestors lived, many miles by boat into the interior.

Perfect. I will go to the ceremony. And when the festivities are over, I shall ask permission to stay for a month . . . in the interior of Borneo.

The next day I bike to Gadjah Mada and study in the library, looking up every few minutes, waiting, watching for Hamid. Finally, late in the afternoon, he arrives.

"Hamid, I am going to Kalimantan in a week and I would like to hire you as my tutor. I have to learn some sentences that I will need as I travel. If you have the time, perhaps we could have a formal class for two hours each afternoon until I leave."

Like every other student I've known, Hamid is happy to have a way of earning money. We begin that day.

I have read in the guidebooks that when you travel in Indonesia, you have to register with the police or headman of each village you visit. I need the polite words and mannerisms to introduce myself to a headman. And

I need to learn how to ask permission to stay and whether there is a family in the village that would put me up overnight. I have no idea what kind of travel will be involved or how I will get around. I do know that the rivers of Borneo are the routes from one place to another. I will have to inquire about boat transportation.

Hamid teaches and drills me on things like "It is an honor to meet you," accompanied by putting my hands together and lowering my head. "Your country is very beautiful." "It is a privilege for me to be here." "Do you know of a place where I can sleep tonight?"

I learn how to ask about children and school and work. And I practice saying that I am from America, that I write books for children, and that I have children of my own. Several people have suggested that I tell people I am married and that my husband could not come with me. The lie is not for safety, but rather to avoid pity. With Hamid's help, I create a husband who is a teacher.

By the time I step onto the plane for Pangkalan Bun, my head is swirling with words and sentences that I'm sure I'll forget at the crucial moment.

In Pangkalan Bun, I check into a cheap hotel and register with the police. They tell me that I will need permission from the mayor to go into the interior.

The mayor's private office is a big room, perhaps fifteen feet square. Facing the entrance door is a huge desk, ten feet long and very wide. Staring down at me from the wall behind the desk are two enormous framed photographs, one of President Suharto and the other of his vice-president. And under the portraits, barely visible behind the giant desk, is a small man who looks as though he is playing in his father's office. He is smiling broadly.

I begin my well-practiced monologue. First I lift my hands and lower my head and tell him, with a smile, what an honor it is to be in his presence. Then I move into the fact that I am a writer from America and that I find his country very beautiful. I continue to smile.

"I was living in Yogyakarta," I continue, "when I read in the newspaper about the ceremony for the vice-governor's grandmother. I would consider it an honor and a privilege if you would give me permission to go to the ceremony and then remain in the interior for a month."

He smiles back at me and says with a nod, "*Tidak.*" No.

I am certain he did not understand me; maybe the words were wrong, maybe the accent was too strong or my speech too quick, so I begin again, pronouncing the words carefully, smiling broadly. Once again I recite my memorized introduction, my practiced compliments, and my request.

He smiles again and says, *"Tidak."*

I ask why. He answers in Indonesian, some of which I understand.

"It is dangerous," he tells me, "for a woman to be alone in that part of Kalimantan . . . I am responsible for you. I invite you to join the government party that is going to the ceremony. You may travel on the boats with them at government expense and you may eat with them and sleep where they sleep. You will be our guest. But when the ceremony is over, you must return with them. You may not stay."

I smile and thank him, hands in front of my lowered face as I back out the door. "Thank you. Thank you very much. It will be an honor to travel with the government party."

His assistant gives me information on where the group will assemble. They are leaving tomorrow morning. The good news is that my trip is set; I was wondering how I was going to do it on my own. The bad news is that I was hoping to settle into the village and stay for a while. Now I don't know what I'll do for the rest of the month.

Damn. I don't like being told what I can do and where I can go. It dredges up the adolescent rebel in me. As I walk back to my hotel, I have to remind myself that I am in Indonesia, where my every move has to be recorded and approved by the police. If I'm going to survive here, I have to learn to live with rules.

The next morning I arrive early. Already the lobby of the hotel meeting place is packed. I introduce myself to the coordinator of the trip, who is expecting me; then I step back and observe the group . . . all Indonesian men. They are chattering noisily. The speech is too fast and the people too many; I don't understand a word. Then my ear picks up English and women's voices.

Behind a noisy clump of men, surrounded by five young Indonesian men, are two white women, one fairly heavy and tall with long gray hair pulled back, and the other, a slim woman with reddish hair. I stare at them long enough to know they have seen me, but they make no effort to return my smile.

After about fifteen minutes, the smaller woman walks over to me and asks who I am and what I am doing there. I answer and ask the same questions. When she finishes answering, she walks away and I watch her pass the information on to the other woman. Neither of them initiates another conversation for the remainder of the trip.

The bigger woman is Biruté Galdikas. I know her name from the physical anthropology classes I took at UCLA. Galdikas is one of Louis Leakey's primate women: there are Dian Fossey and her gorillas, Jane Goodall and her chimpanzees, both of them household words; and Biruté Galdikas and her orangutans, whom few have heard of. A few years ago the three of them went on a speaking tour as "The Trimates."

When I hear her name, I remember that Dr. Galdikas has been studying the lives of orangutans here in the rain forest of Kalimantan since 1971. She is highly respected in academic circles and I would very much like to walk over and introduce myself, but every time I am able to catch her eye and smile, she turns away.

The other woman is from the zoo in San Francisco, and she never again looks my way. She is in Borneo to assist Dr. Galdikas. The young men around them are students and Dayak tribesmen. Dr. Galdikas towers over her all-male entourage like a great white queen. She is engrossed in the group and it is obvious that she is not planning to acknowledge my presence.

The smaller woman, I find out later, approached me at the request of Dr. Galdikas. Once Dr. Galdikas knows that I have no official status, I am never approached again. The message I get is clear: I have invaded her world and I am not welcome.

There are six boats lined up at the dock, and about twenty-five people. The coordinator of the trip directs me to a small powerboat that seats eight. Our boat is the third in the caravan; Dr. Galdikas and her entourage are three boats behind us.

I am feeling uncomfortable, rejected, and very alone. I watch others climb into my boat and sit down, but the seat next to me remains empty. Like that first night in Mexico three years ago when I couldn't go out to dinner alone, it isn't being alone that's the problem. It's watching everyone else's reaction to my being alone. I sit, trying to smile but wanting to cry. I can see the unasked question that is in everyone's eyes: Why have you been isolated by those women?

Finally, a young, handsome Indonesian man sits next to me. He is taller by a head than the local Dayak men; he has a small, neat mustache, well-trimmed hair, and he's wearing jeans and a white T-shirt. He is carrying three cameras around his neck and two black leather bags over his shoulder.

"Hi. I am Abdul. Where are you from?"

Oh, my God! He's speaking English.

"Hello. I'm Rita. I'm a writer from America, but I've just come in from Yogya. Are you part of the government group?"

"No. I'm a photographer for *Tempo* (Indonesia's *Time* magazine)." A journalist. I can feel the tears welling up in my eyes; I have been saved.

"You don't know how happy I am to see you."

Abdul and I are nearly inseparable for the next four days.

We have been moving inland and upriver for two days. This morning, after a torrential rainstorm overnight, the river is brown and swirling and more powerful than our motor. We move to the edge and pull the boat against the current, gripping the vines and branches, moving ourselves upstream, stopping occasionally to rest by holding onto a branch until we catch our breath. A trip that should have taken half a day takes twice as long; and then, long after dark, we are told to get out. Miraculously, deep in the rain forest, in a place that is accessible only by river, a truck is waiting for us.

We drive for what seems like hours in bright moonlight on a road built by a Korean logging company, a dusty, smooth road that winds its way through fields of stumps as far as the eye can see. I have no idea where we are, but I know I am witnessing the destruction of the rain forest. We ride on and on until finally, in the middle of the night, we arrive in a village that is sound asleep. But not for long. We are important guests that must be honored.

While the chickens are being killed for our midnight meal, chairs are brought in and placed along the walls of a big room. We are welcomed with speeches, entertained with music, songs, and dancing, and the local brew. The night before, we slept in another village and we were purified and welcomed individually by the touch of a tiny chicken on key places of our bodies, and prayers, and a sip of a brandylike liquor. Then we were invited to dance. This night we are welcomed with speeches; and when the speeches are finished, we are again invited to dance. Finally we are left to sit in chairs lined up against the walls while we wait for our dinner.

I am overwhelmed, hungry, tired . . . and feeling extraordinarily privileged to be here. I look around the room at the guests; all but three of us are Indonesian citizens; many are native tribespeople of Kalimantan. I have talked to most of them, thanks to Abdul, my journalist-photographer friend and translator. The only people in the room I have not spoken to are Biruté Galdikas and her entourage. I glance over to where she is sitting.

There is an empty chair next to her. Abdul notices the empty chair at the same time as I do.

"Go ahead," he says. "What can she do to you?"

He and I and probably many others in the room have been talking about how odd it is that she and I have not exchanged even one word. Indonesians do not understand overt rudeness; whatever the circumstances, the impression of civility must always be maintained.

I walk over and sit down.

"Dr. Galdikas," I say. "I admire your work very much. What you are doing is very important to the worlds of primatology and anthropology. Have you ever considered writing a book for children explaining what you do? It is, after all, the children who will carry on your work some day."

"Why are you asking me that?"

"I have written many books for children, both fiction and nonfiction. And I have a master's degree in anthropology. If you are interested, I would like very much to talk to you about working together on a book. I would do the writing, but I would write in your voice, in the first person, and the author would be you. I can stay here in Kalimantan for as long as it takes us to finish it."

She does not smile; nor does she ask me my name . . . or anything else.

"I will discuss it with you after this trip is over. When you get back to Pangkalan Bun, stay in the Blue Kecubung Hotel. I will send for you when I am ready to talk."

And I am dismissed.

The village where the ceremony is to take place is still getting ready when we arrive, but the air is bursting with celebration. It is clear that preparations for this event have been in process for months. Small wooden houses have been whitewashed. A new footpath has been constructed through the center and out toward the cemetery. And throughout the area of the ceremony, there are small, decorative constructions of fringed bamboo poles wearing hats, flags made of batik fabrics, tall teepeelike structures, and old weathered wood sculptures of taller-than-life humans from another era. There are traditional houses on stilts, tables with fringed skirts filled with cups and glasses and baskets, and mats and gong instruments waiting for players.

The local people are dressed in jeans and T-shirts with collars, dark pants, skirts, blouses, dresses. The children are dressed in school uniforms, maroon shorts and crisply ironed white shirts. The attire is not what I had expected in the middle of the Borneo jungle. There are no grass skirts or nose bones. These people could have been my neighbors in Yogya.

"It is time to go and get the bones," says the teacher who has attached himself to me. He's a charming man in his forties who sees to it that I am fed and educated.

We walk along a newly made footpath that stands about two inches taller than the rest of the road. The new path is edged in timber and filled in with light-colored sandy soil. Just a few hundred yards away from the village center is the cemetery. There is a small roof over a deep hole that has recently been dug. Grandma's remains are about to be exhumed. I stand near the edge of the pit, thinking I am going to see a wooden coffin. Instead, two men climb into the pit and one emerges carrying a small green Naugahyde suitcase about two feet square. Grandma's bones are inside.

The suitcase is much too small to have held a full-grown woman, and too clean to have been buried for thirty years, so I assume that the bones were removed from whatever receptacle originally held them.

There is a procession to the main area of the village, led by a man carrying the little green suitcase. The place where the ceremony is to take place is elaborately decorated with bamboo poles, spears, colorful flags and fringes. For a while, the main activity is drinking from hollow bamboo cups, glasses, regular cups. Everyone drinks, including the guests, from cups that are passed around with growing enthusiasm. I sip the *tuak,* the liquor made from palm trees, and pass it on to the person next to me.

Abdul tells me that we are awaiting the arrival by canoe of a neighboring tribe. Long ago, no one can or will be specific about when, a man from this neighboring tribe was killed whenever this ceremony was performed. Today, the arrival of the canoes symbolizes a new era. Instead of sacrificing a person, the tribe has been invited to join in the festivities, and the victim is a cow.

Well decorated for the occasion with paper fringes on his legs and tail and ears, the cow waits in the center of a small ring. Soon after the guests arrive, the stabbing begins. One after another, men from the village take their turns stabbing the cow with spears. The animal squeals and shrieks and squirts blood. The killing process takes more than half an hour, the longer the bloodier, until the cow finally falls to the ground, at first twitching and finally dead.

I stand in the crowd, breathing heavily, trying not to watch, but compelled to look. The violence of the act is repulsive to me. I look around and see that there are others, mostly women, who are grimacing and turning away. Even walking away. And still other women who are gathered at a distance totally avoiding the event. It is yet another instance of the universal bonds that tie women together. We give birth, we nurture, we love. We are creators and not destroyers. These women in the forest of Borneo and I are one.

There is a feast following the stabbing, with dishes of noodles, rice, *sate,* and an assortment of chopped vegetables, meats, poultry, fish flavored with soy sauce and garlic and chili peppers. I am guided through the meal by the teacher who has adopted me. When the meal is over, he takes me through the school and talks about his world.

"Why don't you stay when the others leave?" he asks. "You can live with my family and I will see that you are well taken care of."

I tell him that the mayor has ordered me to return with the government group. The teacher tells the representative of the mayor that he will be responsible for my safety; but it is too late. The mayor's delegates have orders to bring me back.

The drinking never stops. *Tuak* is drunk from glasses, from cups, from bamboo, from animal horns, small and large. And finally, in the middle of the night, when everyone is dancing and laughing and passing a bull's horn, the chief of the village brings out the skull of the last human to have been sacrificed for this ceremony. It was a long time ago, they say, but no one gets specific about when. The skull, looking exactly like what it is, will bring power and spirituality to each of us. It is filled with *tuak* and passed around the dance floor.

All day I have been sipping *tuak* from communal cups, sharing saliva and tipsy smiles and moving my body to the beat of the drums. But now, as I take the skull in my two hands, I am shaking. It is as though I am drinking the brains of a human being, sipping his spirit, gaining his power. I am nearly in a trance, moving, sipping, feeling my lips on the smooth bone, dipping my tongue into this other person's fluids, absorbing his soul.

I am trembling with the taste of cannibalism.

THE ORANGUTAN CAMP

I have been a prisoner at the Blue Kecubung Hotel for three days. I cannot afford the rates (it costs nearly three times as much a night as the dumpier hotel a few blocks away), but I don't dare defy my orders: "Stay in the Blue Kecubung Hotel. I will send for you when I am ready to talk."

The more I think about it, the more excited I become about the chance to stay in the orangutan camp for a couple of months. I've always loved studying primates (I've written five books starring monkeys and apes, two of them nonfiction). Their habitat, the rain forests of the world, is rapidly disappearing. Maybe a children's book will help to create a more responsible world population. In any event, it's my only ticket into Camp Leakey. And I know from my Nicaragua and Galápagos books that both the emotional and intellectual experience of a place greatly intensifies when I am writing about it.

It is clear that Dr. Galdikas will not be easy to work with. The fact that we just spent five days together in the interior of Borneo and she never once initiated a conversation indicates that she does not want me in her life as a friend. But if I am there to write her book, it's a different relationship. I'm more than willing to honor her in whatever way she wants. I am not bothered by the fact that Dr. Galdikas seems to be the great white goddess here and I, like everyone else, must pay appropriate obeisance. She's earned it.

So I sit in the Blue Kecubung, in my room, in the lobby, or in the restaurant . . . all day and all night, waiting.

After three days I wonder if Dr. Galdikas has forgotten me. The hotel manager, who is a friend at this point, tells me that Ibu (mother, in Indonesian) Professor Galdikas is still at her home in Pasir Panjang, the village of her Dayak husband's family, a fifteen-minute ride from the hotel. She has not yet gone back to Camp Leakey, which is a day's trip up the Sekonyer River. It's time, I decide, before my money runs out, for me to contact her.

The taxi driver that the hotel recommends knows who she is and where she lives. This large western woman married to a small Dayak man is very much a local celebrity, my driver tells me as we drive; everyone knows her. Finally we pull up in front of a big wooden house. I ask the driver to wait and I ring the doorbell.

Galdikas's graduate student answers the bell. I recognize him from last week's journey, but we've never talked.

"Is Professor Dr. Galdikas in?" I ask.

"Just a minute," he says. "I'll see."

A few minutes later he returns. "She's busy right now. She will call you when she is ready." I smile and say thank you, and the door closes. I have been dismissed again.

I get back in the cab, quietly fuming, but smiling all the while. I am determined to make this happen. The next morning I get a message. Dr. Galdikas will be sending a car for me at eleven.

The graduate student ushers me into her presence. I smile and nod and say something about what an honor it is to meet her again.

"How do I know that you really are a writer?" she asks.

I show her three of my books that I have brought with me to prove the point.

"But I still don't know that you are this person, Rita Golden Gelman." She reads my name from the cover of one of the books.

I show her my passport.

"You say you studied anthropology?"

"With some of the same people that you studied with. My master's degree is from UCLA. My area was psychological anthropology, but along the way I took two classes in physical anthropology where we studied primates and early humans."

I tell her the names of my committee members and we talk about the physical anthropology faculty members. I have studied with people she knows well.

"Something interesting just happened," she says. "In today's mail I received a letter from a publisher in Canada asking me if I would write a children's book for them. I think the fact that you are here at this moment is a sign that I should do a book."

I tell her that I will write the book in her voice, take an "edited by" credit, and that we would split the money, fifty-fifty. She's fine with that. Then she tells me that I cannot stay in the camp, that I will have to write the book while staying in Pangkalan Bun.

What? For starters, I'd suggested the book so I could stay in the camp; that is the whole point . . . for me. But even more absurd is the idea that somehow I could write about something I've never seen or experienced. I have to live her life in order to write about it. In the end, she agrees to let me stay in the camp, but asks that I pay for room and board. Not quite what I had in mind, but we settle on something I can afford.

We leave the next day.

The Sekonyer River is a black mirror that reflects a world of such extraordinary beauty that it is almost a cliché. Directly in the water ahead are white clouds, a sky as blue as the one above, a hot orange sun, and giant tropical trees and twisted vines that have parted the forest to let the river through. I am so overwhelmed by the perfection of this environment that I can barely talk.

The river narrows and widens; sometimes it is filled with grasses; other times it is as clear as polished glass. About four hours into our trip, I am sitting in the sun in the front of the boat, staring straight ahead, when I see a wall of gray, several hundred yards away. It's a rainstorm that looks as though it has been created for a movie. Literally a gray wall that stretches across the set from one side to the other. We move toward each other, the boat and the storm, two distinct entities. Then almost ghostlike but a good deal wetter, we pass through each other, intersect briefly, and move on. And our boat is in the sun once again.

Twice during the final two hours of our trip, we see crocodiles sunning themselves on the riverbank. Looking like ancient amphibians soaking up the sun, they are at least six feet long with gray bumpy skin and an ominous presence. They become even more ominous when one of the young Dayaks on our boat tells me that this is the river I am going to bathe in during my stay at Camp Leakey. Then, not confident of my Indonesian, he shows me in vivid charades, how crocodiles attack and eat little monkeys. And he laughs.

Late in the afternoon the same young man points to some trees. Sitting on the leafy branches, fifty feet up, is a troop of proboscis monkeys, with their long pendulous noses, peering down at us. They are the noses of comical Halloween masks, banana-shaped blobs hanging down in the middle of monkey faces. The brown, white, and gray monkeys, about two feet tall, with long white tails, nestle into their sleep trees along the river at dusk every night.

I am overwhelmed by the river trip. I feel as though I am motoring through the pages of a *National Geographic* magazine. It is another piece of a dream come true.

We arrive at the camp and tie up next to a two-hundred-foot wooden walkway in time for the orangutans' dinner. Pak Achyar, a Dayak man, is standing on the walkway next to mounds of rice and bananas and sugar cane stalks, calling the orangutans by name, calling into distant trees.

"Siswoyo, Mellie, Pola, Tutut, Hani, Kusai." The sound of their names alerts the orangutans that dinner is ready. More than ten orangutans are in sight, large and small, some already squatting next to the rice, feeding themselves and their babies, some ambling down the boardwalk. Others are swinging out of nearby trees, responding to Pak Achyar's call.

A few young orangutans greet our boat, climbing all over Dr. Galdikas and the supplies. She greets them by name, sweetly, lovingly; they are her babies. I swing myself up onto the dock and slip my arms into the straps of my backpack. I am wearing an Indonesian army hat and sunglasses, and my hands are swinging loosely at my sides . . . until a furry orange youth takes my left hand and another hops on my shoulders, takes off my hat and glasses, and puts them both on his head.

These orangutans, the ones that are responding to Pak Achyar's call, and the ones that are climbing on me, are not wild. They are ex-captives that have been confiscated and brought to Dr. Galdikas. In Indonesia it is illegal to keep an orangutan as a pet, but until Dr. Galdikas set up camp, there was nowhere to bring a confiscated pet; they can't just be released into the forest. Many of the pets were babies still clinging when poachers shot their mothers. Others lost their canopy home when loggers cut down the trees. Most of the orangutans who were taken into homes as babies have never been with other orangutans. They have grown up in human homes and learned human ways. They have no idea what orangutans do.

Orangutans are great mimics. Some of the ex-captives can smoke. One can wash clothes. But they don't know how to climb trees, pick fruit, or interact with others of their species. So now, in Camp Leakey, they are learning.

In the beginning, the ex-captives learned from Dr. Galdikas, who first arrived in 1971. She climbed trees and picked fruit to show them how it was done. Today, many of the babies learn from the older ex-captives who adopt them.

There is one baby in the nursery who has had to be adopted by one of the Dayak workers. There was no female ex-captive to adopt and nurse her, so Dr. Galdikas assigned a human man with a bottle to be the mother. Day and night, while the human "mother" eats, sleeps, reads, bathes in the river, and walks in the forest, the baby clings to his clothes, and defecates and urinates on him. In the wild, orangutan babies do not leave their mothers for two years.

It is five-thirty in the morning, two days after we arrive. I am settled into a dormitory that is one of several buildings in the clearing known as Camp Leakey. I am about to accompany two Dayak men into the forest. As instructed, I am dressed in a long-sleeved shirt over a turtleneck, long pants, two pairs of socks, the outside pair pulled up over the pants, and gloves. We have sprayed Deet insect repellant on our clothes wherever they overlap: where the gloves meet the sleeves, where the socks meet the pants, and where the socks disappear into the sneakers. It's leech protection. (I am also taking one doxycycline a day for malaria prevention. After my Mexican skin-peeling experience, I won't go near anything with quinine in it, not even tonic, as in "gin and.")

For the last two days our guides have been following an orangutan mother and her baby, noting everything they do, every tree they feed in, and every fruit and leaf they eat. There are several teams of Dayaks who are helping Dr. Galdikas record the details of the orangutans' lives in the wild. Last night, at six-thirty, the pair of orangutans went to sleep and the young men returned to camp in the dark. Today, we are going to follow again and take notes. We have to be at their tree, which is one hour away, when they wake up.

It is still dark when we walk the few hundred feet across the clearing and enter the forest. We are stepping carefully, lighting our way with flashlights. Already, even before dawn, there is a noisy cacophony of songs coming from the forest. From our right, there is a cackling staccato voice.

"*Monyet,*" monkey, whispers one of our guides.

Gibbons, those long-armed aerial gymnasts, also sing their musical greetings to the world, unforgettable songs that get louder and louder until the gibbons are singing to miles of forest creatures that they are there and a new day has begun.

While I concentrate on where my next step will be placed, the ubiquitous cicadas, sounding like dozens of chainsaws chopping down the forest, whine and tick and whirr and buzz. Day and night, sometimes so loudly that you want to hold your ears, other times no louder than a hum, millions of male cicadas vibrate a membrane at the base of their abdomens and score the background music of the tropical forest. Every minute of every day the cicadas play their endless concert.

As dawn appears tentatively and sparsely through the overlapping leaves a hundred feet above our heads, we step carefully on slippery logs and planks and twisted roots that mark the path. In the depths of the forest, the air, heavy and damp, smells like mildew and signals that we have passed into another world, where our human senses will be challenged by a new way of experiencing the environment.

Dr. Galdikas has a rule: no talking in the forest. Our silence magnifies the voices of the forest creatures and focuses our attention on the magical world we have passed into. A world of exquisite spiderwebs woven in the sparse underbrush, still wet with diamond drops of dew. Moss. Leaves. Branches. Monstrous roots. Massive trees. And the chorus of gibbons and monkeys and cicadas and birds. From time to time we stop and stand motionless, listening, looking, observing. From the songs and the sounds, I know I am surrounded by animals, but I see none.

Finally the guides stop and indicate that we have arrived at the tree where the orangutans are sleeping, a mother and her baby. When we arrive, there is no orangutan in sight. And then, about fifteen minutes later, leaves rustle and one of the guides points. I see nothing, but I am looking for a big red orangutan, three feet tall, carrying a baby. It's the wrong "search image."

What I should be looking for is a black spot in the leafy canopy, a big clump where no light is coming through. That means a body is blocking the spaces between the leaves. Since the body is not lit from below, there is no reflected light, and the big red orangutan is a big black shadow. If we were searching for an orangutan to follow (as opposed to one whose location we already know), we would also be listening for rustling leaves, cracking and falling branches, and fruit pits and inedible bits of bark dropping to the ground.

One of the young men hands me the binoculars. I know exactly where this orangutan is and I know what to look for, and still it takes me five minutes to find her. But I do. She is there with her baby, more than one hundred feet up, holding onto a branch over her head with one hand and gripping two other branches with her feet. The baby is nursing.

My heart is pounding. No matter how bright the day, the tropical rain forest is a shadowy, eerie, magical world. A world where the sun is reduced to streaks of light that filter through masses of leaves. I am overwhelmed by a sense of awe. Suddenly I understand Dr. Galdikas's obsession. There are tears streaming down my cheeks.

All day we follow Georgina (for purposes of her study, Dr. Galdikas has given names to the different orangutans whose lives she is tracking) as she moves from tree to tree looking for fruit or leaves or bark to eat. When she finds a cache she likes, we tie up our hammocks and watch from below. We are not permitted to sit on logs or lean on trees. The dangers range from acids that can burn through your clothes to poisonous snakes and fire ants. The tropical rain forest is not a friendly place, but it is mesmerizing in its otherworldliness.

A few days later I go out with another Dayak team. This time we are searching for an orangutan that hasn't been followed lately. All of the orangutans in Dr. Galdikas's study live most of the time in the area around Camp Leakey. Her work, with the help of her staff and volunteers, is to track their lives. What do they eat? How do they mate? How many children does an orangutan have in the course of her lifetime and how long do babies stay with their mothers? The questions are endless, and until Dr. Galdikas devoted her life to these studies, very little was known about orangutans in the wild.

Year after year, since 1971, volumes of observations have been recorded. Our mission today is to find an orangutan and follow it. We leave in the light, since our only hope of finding one is to hear it moving around or eating in the course of the day. All day we listen in silence for leaves rustling, branches falling, things dropping to the ground. We are constantly looking up into the canopy for that black spot or those moving leaves. But when the day comes to an end, we have not found an orangutan.

When I get back to the camp, I change clothes and discover a big fat leech sucking away at my ankle.

I pull it off and watch the watery blood pour out of my wound. Leeches have three jaws, and each jaw has ninety teeth that saw open the skin so the leech can secrete an anticoagulant that helps him/her (they are hermaphrodites) suck blood. I have no idea how the little guy/girl got through the pants that were tucked into two pair of overlapping socks and heavily sprayed with Deet. Although, he/she was a lot smaller when he/she started out.

After I have been in the camp for two weeks, I am ready to begin writing. I have a good sense of what it is like to live and work at Camp Leakey, and from the articles and papers Dr. Galdikas has given me, I understand the purpose and process and passion of her work. I've been into the forest three times (we did find an orangutan the third time out), and I've spent hours in the nursery where the newly confiscated pets undergo their education.

I have also been eating in the dining hall where ex-captives climb the chain-link fencing that cages us in. Like people at a zoo, the orangutans watch us eat. If they are given a plate, they hang on, often upside down, and eat at the same time, knowing instinctively how to hold the plate so the food doesn't slide off. (It is extremely convenient to have four hands.)

I have a lot of material to work with, and I can begin writing; but I am missing the voice, the passion, the intensity of Dr. Galdikas. I have not met with her yet.

There is a small cabin about a hundred yards away from the dining hall. I am set up with a desk, a chair, an old manual typewriter, and a stack of paper. Each day now, after breakfast, while the gibbons are still calling and the cicada chorus fills the air, I go to my office and write. I no longer go into the forest or even to the nursery where baby orangutans are clinging to people as though they were their real mothers. I do occasionally stop by the bridge for the morning and afternoon feedings, but mostly I stick to a rigid writing schedule. I don't even go back to the dormitory to go to the bathroom. When the urge comes, I hide behind a bush. One day I discover that my "offering" of the day before has completely disappeared. The next day I watch as dung beetles consume every crumb, just minutes after I deposit it.

The writing moves well, but since I am writing as Dr. Galdikas in the first person, I reach a point where she and I must talk. We have barely had a conversation since I arrived. I am willing to meet anytime, morning, noon, or night, but she is always too busy. There are the graduate students, the local staff, the cataloguing of the "follow" information, the tending to a sick ex-captive, the education of the twenty or so volunteers from Earthwatch (there were three of these volunteer groups during my tenure in the camp), and the occasional trip to Pasir Panjang to see her children and her husband, and on and on and on. All legitimate, all important, and all keeping the book on hold.

I am about halfway through the book when my two-month visa expires. Indonesia gives an automatic two-month visa when you enter, and you have to leave the country and reenter in order to renew it. Singapore is close by. I'm there for two days.

When I return, I discover that in my absence, a tree near my office has burst into white bloom. Like a magnet, the blossoms are attracting thousands of white butterflies. The butterflies are swarming around the tree the way bees swarm around a hive. I have time to sit and stare because I can go no further with the book until I meet with Dr. Galdikas; and she continues to be inaccessible.

One of the highlights of my visit is a boat ride and a walk with Pak Bohap, Dr. Galdikas's husband, a native of the area. We are walking silently across an open field when there is a sound from the tall grasses nearby, a sort of *blurp*. He smiles.

"That was a snake eating a frog," he says.

Pak Bohap can read the world he grew up in like a mechanic can read the sounds of a motor. Pak Bohap's hearing is fine-tuned to the natural world. Every movement creates a noise and every noise records an action. Pak Bohap is fluent in "forest."

After attempting for more than three weeks to get an hour or two with Dr. Galdikas, I finally write her a note:

> Dear Dr. Galdikas,
>
> My weeks here in Camp Leakey have been an extraordinary experience. I will never forget them. I consider it an honor and a privilege to have had the opportunity to visit the forest, to live with the orangutans, and to read about and watch your work.
>
> But in order to write a book under your byline, I need your words, your observations, your comments, your emotions. I will need at least four hours of your time during my final two weeks here.
>
> I will understand if you cannot find the time to meet with me; the beauty of the experience will more than compensate me for my time. But I do want you to know that unless we meet, there will not be a book.
>
> Thank you for opening my eyes to a new world.

We finally meet. Late at night. After all her other obligations are asleep. By the time I leave, there is a draft of the book. Six months later, we have a sale, to Little Brown, the publisher that has contracted with Dr. Galdikas for her autobiography.

But there are strings. Our book will not be published until a year after her autobiography is out. And we agree that we will not write anything else about the orangutan camp for children.

But the autobiography is not finished for several years. During those years, another book for children about Dr. Galdikas and Camp Leakey is published, by a different publisher, with an afterword by Dr. Galdikas. The book is similar to the one we have written, and because of the material by Dr. Galdikas, Little Brown feels justified in canceling our contract. The book is never published.

I am disappointed. I wanted to introduce children to orangutans in the wild, to the passion of Dr. Galdikas, to the intensity and fulfillment that comes with committing one's life to a cause, and to the extraordinary tropical rain forest.

My experience of the tropical rain forest was like stepping into another dimension of life on earth. The muted color of the light, filtered by a canopy of leaves; the heaviness of the air hovering over the swampland; the sounds of insects and primates and birds filling the forest with their music; and the overwhelming knowledge that all around me were hidden eyes peering down or across or up at me. The only world I will ever enter that is as extraordinary as the tropical rain forest is the world on the bottom of the ocean. And it will be eight years before I will dive with a tank on my back into that watery paradise.

CHAPTER TEN

ARRIVING IN BALI

I have always loved New York and its creative, pulsing energy; but going from the forest in Borneo to the streets of New York is not a good plan. Every civilized sound is offensive. Garbage trucks grinding their refuse replace gibbons calling out their morning songs. Horns honk where only hours ago cicadas were buzzing. And people screaming at each other have replaced the gentle sound of the soft-spoken Indonesians. A part of me wonders if my explorations on one end of the spectrum will ultimately reduce my ability to enjoy the pleasures at the other end.

I race through my visits with family, friends, and editors, just a little off-balance and impatient to be somewhere else. I suspect that with a little more time, I would slip back into the delights of the city, but I don't wait around to find out. I stay for two weeks and get on another plane for Indonesia.

This time, I'm going to Bali. Noted for its art, music, and dance, Bali is an island the size of Connecticut with a population of about 3 million, 95 percent of them Hindu. Main industry: tourism. Main attraction for me: the Balinese people, who are known for their spirituality, something that has always eluded me.

As a kid I sought spirituality in the synagogue, but I found words, music, social events, and fundraising. The rituals, the social stuff, and the camaraderie were great, but I never felt spiritual.

I have also looked in Protestant, Catholic, Unitarian, and Quaker churches. I looked in Nicaragua at the First Communion of Marco's daughter. The setting was right: the chapel was dimly lit, the voice of the priest was soothing, and the sun-illuminated stained-glass windows told me that this was a holy place. But I didn't feel anything spiritual. Not inside or outside. And my Israeli experience wasn't even close.

In Palenque, considered by many to be a particularly spiritual place, I felt the presence of the ancient Mayans, but it was the dramatic history of the people that set off my imagination, and not really anything spiritual.

Little do I know, as my plane flies over the Pacific Ocean, how deep and intensely spiritual my Bali experience is going to be. There's not even a hint that Bali is about to become my home for eight years and that its spirit will change forever how I look at the world.

The plane lands for a forty-five-minute stop on the island of Biak in Irian Jaya, the easternmost province of Indonesia and the western half of the island of New Guinea. As I step onto the metal stairway that has been wheeled up to the exit door, I am greeted by the earthy smell of forest and the intense heat and humidity of this equatorial island.

The flight attendant standing on the tarmac at the bottom of the steps hands me a plastic transit card that I stick into the black nylon passport case that I always wear around my neck when I'm on the road. Walking next to me is a couple, American missionaries, who tell me they are planning to live and proselytize (my word, not theirs) here in the highlands for two years. As we chat, I make a mental note to visit the tribal people who live in those mountains before they have totally abandoned their native religions and customs.

Inside the terminal, a group of grass-skirted women and guitar-and-drum-playing men are singing and dancing for the transit passengers. I watch for a while and then walk to the back of the room, where I join a dignified-looking Indonesian man who is studying a topographical map of Indonesia. Dr. Djelantik is a Balinese doctor returning home after doing malaria research in Irian Jaya. His English is nearly perfect.

I ask him about his research. He asks about my destination. For forty-five minutes we talk about Bali and its uniqueness as a Hindu province in a Muslim (88 percent) country. We talk about the music and art and history and religion of Bali. And we discuss customs and ceremonies and life in general. We continue our conversation on the plane.

When we land in Bali, Dr. Djelantik asks me where I am planning to stay. I tell him that I am going to Ubud, that the guidebooks say Ubud is the center of music and dance and culture on the island.

"Oh no," he tells me. "Don't go there. You are interested in anthropology, culture, religion. Ubud is too touristy for you."

Then he writes on a small piece of paper: *I Gusti Ngurah Ketut Sangka, Puri Gede, Kerambitan, Tabanan.* I have no idea what it means.

"Go to this man. He is a scholar and as close to an anthropologist as you will find in Bali. He is a friend of mine. Enjoy your visit."

I collect my bags, climb into a cab, and hand the paper to the driver. Without a word, he takes off. Soon we join hundreds of motorcycles and bicycles and honking horns as he drives through the tourist town of Kuta, which is filled with shops, tourists in shorts, and rock music blaring from loudspeakers.

But as we move north along the western part of the island, we begin to pass through towns where there are no tourists, just Balinese people and shops selling altars for family temples, pots for the kitchens, and pottery and stone carvings for gardens. We have moved into a part of the island that still belongs to the Balinese.

An hour after we leave the airport, we turn off the main road and wind for another fifteen minutes between terraced rice fields that stretch as far as I can see in every direction. Then, finally, we enter a village.

The driver pulls up to a group of men who are clustered in front of an open pavilion. He reads from the paper I gave him, listens to directions, then backs up and drives about a hundred yards down a side road and stops. We have arrived.

I have no idea where we are or who it is that I'm about to meet. I leave my bags in the car and hold off paying for the cab. At least I'll have transportation out if I need it.

I walk through an arched gate into a grassy garden and am welcomed by the sweet perfume of a gardenia bush that is nearly as tall as I and filled with fragrant white flowers. A tiny old woman, topless, her waist-length gray hair hanging down her back, is stooped over, sweeping leaves and flowers off the grass with a three-foot-long broom. The noisy swish of the bristles, made of palm-leaf veins tied together, allows me to watch unnoticed for a few minutes. Her waiflike body is wrapped from the waist down in a faded brown-and-tan sarong. As she sweeps, she hunches over, holding her left hand behind her back. With her right hand she brushes pink petals and brown leaves into little piles.

I step onto the stone path in front of her. She looks up, smiles toothlessly, and, feeling modest in front of a western stranger, puts her hand across her naked chest. I smile back and read the paper to her: *I Gusti Ngurah Ketut Sangka, Puri Gede, Kerambitan, Tabanan.*

She nods, smiles, and rushes off. Soon, two younger women, one in her thirties, the other in her forties, approach, smiling. (There is a lot of smiling in Bali.) They are dressed in western skirts, flip-flop rubber sandals, and T-shirts. The older and heavier of the two is wearing a T-shirt that says "We are the world."

I show them the paper. They nod. The older one, Dayu Biang, walks me to a nearby patio, sits me down on a bamboo chair, and asks me if I want *kopi.* I nod, smiling. The other goes off, deeper into the compound.

A few minutes later, two cups of coffee appear, one for me and the other for a tiny beautiful woman who looks about forty years old (I later learn that she is nearly fifty-seven). She sits in a chair across from me, dressed in an earth-colored batik sarong that is wrapped around her small body like a stocking. A yellow-and-purple flowered top sets off her shiny black hair and her wrinkle-free bronze skin. She sits straight, smiles at me, and I show her the paper. She nods. Then she places her hand on her chest.

"Tu Biang," she says slowly, enunciating clearly. Her name means, literally, a princess who has children.

"Rita," I say. "America."

She looks toward the old woman who is sweeping nearby.

"Ibu saya," she says. My mother.

"Ibu Tu Biang," I repeat. Tu Biang's mother.

"Ya, ya," she says, laughing, with an endearing, inclusive glee. *"Ibu saya."* My mother. "Tu Nini." A princess who is a grandmother.

When I show her the paper, she smiles. *"Suami saya."* My husband. She reads his name, which is I Gusti Ngurah Ketut Sangka.

As we sit and sip, we do not speak much, but we smile a lot. Then, after about ten minutes, a tall and distinguished-looking man approaches. He is wearing a patterned scarf tied artistically around his head in traditional Balinese fashion. His sarong is the same earth colors as his wife's sarong, but unlike her skin-tight wrap, his is loose and tied with a roll of fabric at the waist, and a soft flow of folds in the front. He is also wearing a long-sleeved white shirt. He is in his late sixties.

"May I help you?" he asks in English, smiling.

"My name is Rita," I say through my smile, my prayer hands, and my nodding head. "I have just arrived from America. I met Dr. Djelantik on the airplane and he suggested I come here."

The man's smile gets even bigger and spreads to his eyes. "Welcome," he says. "Let me show you your room."

I live there for four years.

I Gusti Ngurah Ketut Sangka, Puri Gede, Kerambitan, Tabanan are the words Dr. Djelantik wrote on my paper.

I Gusti Ngurah Ketut Sangka is the name of the man I have just met, the doctor's friend.

I indicates a male.

Gusti indicates high caste.

Ngurah means he was born in a palace.

Ketut says he is the fourth born.

Sangka, his personal name, means "big shell."

Puri Gede means "great palace."

Kerambitan is the village.

And *Tabanan* is both a city and a country.

The man who has invited me to stay, addressed as Tu Aji, a prince who has children, is the unofficial scholar of the Kerambitan dynasty, the son and brother of a king. Everyone in this royal family is called *Tu* something, usually translated as "prince" or "princess." It's an indicator that says this person is from a high caste.

Dr. Djelantik, who, Tu Aji tells me, is a prince of a different dynasty, directed me to a royal palace, though this section of the palace does not look very royal. There are three traditional buildings: a pavilion—the Balinese call it a *bale,* with two open sides and nine columns holding up a tiled roof (the *bale,* which measures about ten by eighteen feet, is frequently used for ceremonies)—and two other buildings about the same size, one-room closed structures, each with a porch and columns. The other three buildings are simple one-story white stucco houses that contain bedrooms.

There are no gilded statues royally proclaiming wealth, nor elaborate friezes broadcasting grandeur. Instead, in this part of the palace, there is a feeling of serenity conveyed by grassy stretches with flowering trees and bushes, and stone pathways that are lined with flowers of every possible color. The gentleness of this family compound is a reflection of the people who live here.

My room is in a small house consisting of two rooms, with an open, covered patio between them that faces the garden. Behind the rooms, accessible from the patio, are a toilet and bathroom. I will be paying the family eight dollars a day for the room and three meals.

I step into the bathroom with my towel. There is a big tiled tub nearly four feet high and two and a half feet square in the corner, filled with clean water. On the rim of the tub there's a red plastic scoop with a handle for scooping out the water (you never climb in).

The water is cold compared to the air, and I squeal with the first few scoops. But, like jumping into a lake, after a few minutes of splashing, the water feels refreshing.

"*Sudah segar ya?*" Are you refreshed? asks Tu Nini, who is still sweeping when I come out in clean clothes and sit on the patio. "*Sudah minum?*" she asks. Have you had something to drink?

"*Ya, terima kasih,*" I answer. Yes, thank you.

These are the first of thousands of similar questions Tu Nini asks me over the months I am there, all of them concerned with my comfort as a guest. *Sudah makan?* Have you eaten? *Sudah mandi?* Have you bathed? This last is a common question around five o'clock in the afternoon. Everyone bathes for the second time before dinner. "Have you bathed?" is a late afternoon greeting.

There is another open patio with a dining table and chairs about thirty feet from my room. At quarter to seven in the evening, just as it is getting dark, Dayu Biang (Dayu means she is a *brahmana,* from the highest, priestly caste; Biang means she has children) passes by my patio en route to the table, with a big bowl of rice. A servant in the palace and one of the women who greeted me earlier, she is a large woman, taller and rounder than the others. And more relaxed and open. Though she has said very little, I sense immediately that she and I will be friends.

A minute later, the other woman who met me when I first arrived, Jero Made (Jero means she is of low caste married to someone "higher" than she—the title *Jero* raises her status; Made means she is the second born) passes my patio carrying a tray with bowls full of accompaniments to the rice: eggplant, shredded chicken with garlic, pork *sate,* a dark green dish of something that looks like spinach, a plate of sliced cucumbers, and a bowl of roasted peanuts.

When the food and dishes are set up, Tu Aji appears and leads me to the table. There are only two places set. He sits across from me. Dinner tonight, and most nights, is just the two of us. Neither of Tu Aji's wives ever eats with us.

I begin our conversation by asking Tu Aji if he and Tu Biang have any children.

"I have seven sons with Tu Biang and two sons with my other wife. Nine sons." He laughs a round deep laugh. "When I married, I prayed that

I would not have any girls. I thought that girls brought too many problems. And now I am sorry because my prayer has come true and I will never know what it is like to have a daughter." He laughs again. "*Ya*, better laughing than crying."

Among Tu Aji's sons are two mechanical engineers, two agronomists, one economist, one doctor, one architect, and two still in high school planning to become economists like their older brother. Only three of them are still in Kerambitan.

"Of course, I would like them all to be nearby," he tells me, like every other parent in the world, "but that is not to be. I have five grandchildren who live in Jakarta. They do not even speak Balinese. But," he lifts his hands in the air, "the river must flow. You cannot stop it. My children are part of the modern world."

There is a quiet wisdom about this man. We talk that first night for more than three hours. He is eager to share his life stories with me.

"You are more direct than the other westerners I have known. And not so stiff. Also," he laughs, "you ask me many more personal questions. The others are only interested in academic things."

It is clear that he is not offended by this. He is pleased.

As he tells me about his family, I feel an excitement surging through me. This is a prince, a real prince! The scholar brother of the king of the Kerambitan dynasty. And a self-proclaimed educator. What an honor.

I ask him what it means to be a king in twentieth-century Bali.

Today, he explains, kings do not have any political power. But the dynasties still function. Tu Aji's brother, who has twenty-nine children, lives in another section of this six-acre compound with his five wives. As king, he is the head of 157 families in Kerambitan; and the families must do as he orders. The rest of the people in the village, the ones of lower caste, pay him homage.

"My brother has a special spiritual power," says Tu Aji. "We call that power, *sakti*. You would probably call it magic. He can use it for good and for bad. People who do not give him what he wants will suffer. Everyone in the village knows that he has this power. They are afraid of him."

He goes on.

"My father was the king in the last generation. He was a very wise man, a literary man, strict but kind. As king, he honored his obligation to the people of the village and to the people who served the *puri* (the compound of a royal family is called a *puri*, which is translated as "palace"). But my brother is not the same as our father. He is demanding and vindictive. He only cares what others can do for him. He cares nothing for our family and the people of our village."

As Tu Aji speaks, I am smiling appropriately on the outside. But inside, I am leaping with joy. He is the teacher I have been seeking, the wise man I had hoped to find. After only a few moments, I know he will lead me to knowledge, to depths I have never known, to spirituality. Thank you, Dr. Djelantik.

"How is it that you speak English so well?"

"I studied. At first, with a teacher; later by myself. For many years I have been working with European and Australian scholars, helping them to know Bali; so I have had much practice. But I will speak to you in Indonesian; you must learn."

Tu Aji also speaks fluent Dutch and some German as well as Balinese and Indonesian. And he has a reading and praying knowledge of ancient Kawi, akin to Sanskrit.

"Have you been to Europe?" I ask.

He laughs. "I have been invited many times. 'Come to Holland. I will pay.' But, I always say no. I will not go. I am a frog in a coconut shell and I must stay in my small world, even if it is sometimes not so comfortable. A person will be bewildered if he goes in another's road. Rich or poor, you must seek happiness in your own world. We can all reach the same happiness, but you must go in your world and I must go in mine. That is life. Three times three is not always nine. Sometimes it is four."

I think about my life as a nomad, always living in other worlds.

"Tu Aji, don't you think we can learn from visiting other worlds, from sharing experiences, from living in other places?"

"The answer to your question is, Of course. But I am lucky. Other worlds come to me. I have to accept that my sons will leave Kerambitan. That is logic. For me, I cannot. I have *adat* (tradition). I will live as my family has always lived. And I will die in Kerambitan. I must. Maybe my generation is the last to have this feeling."

Then he laughs again. "*Adoo.* Rita, I am old. According to the Hindu religion, I have completed my duties and my life is finished. *Ya.* I have studied and learned and married. I have had children and worked to see that they are all educated. Now I am ready to die and I am not afraid. You know that we Balinese live in two worlds, the *sekala,* the one we can see, and the *niskala,* the one we cannot see. My spirit is ready to move on to the next world, the *niskala.*"

I am uncomfortable with his statement. "But, Tu Aji, isn't it possible that now that your tasks are completed, there are other duties that you can do?"

He laughs again. It is a laughter that I can see in his eyes. It says life will continue, the world will change, and we must be open to whatever passes before us, because, well, what other choice do we have? It is a laughter of acceptance.

I have just met this man, but I feel as though I have known him forever. His gentle manner, his innate wisdom, his soft but penetrating eyes have touched something inside of me that I cannot define. Is it possible that already, on my first day in Bali, I have tapped into my spirit?

By ten o'clock, we are both exhausted, from talking and listening so intensely.

"Rita," he says, rolling the *r* and extending the *a,* "you have much to learn about Bali and our beliefs and traditions. I will be your teacher. I will show you Bali from the inside."

With those words my education becomes Tu Aji's final duty in life.

The next morning Tu Aji comes to my patio.

"You are in good luck," he says. "In three days there will be a cremation, and tomorrow they are washing the body. You must buy traditional clothes. Dayu Biang will help you."

A few minutes later, Dayu Biang and I are walking toward the market about a hundred yards away, past two barking dogs and many small white stucco houses with flowering white frangipani trees in their front yards. On the left is a wall that seals off a part of the *puri* that I have not seen yet.

There is a sweet smell in the air and a curiosity in the people when they see me. I smile and nod to everyone we pass. They smile back and talk to Dayu Biang. I know they are asking about me because I hear the word *Amerika* in Dayu Biang's answer. And *kebaya,* which is the traditional blouse we are going to have made for me. But they are talking in Balinese, which I do not understand.

Balinese and Indonesian are not the same. I have been studying Indonesian; it is the language I began when I was in Yogya and continued in Kalimantan. It is the official language of the country, of the government, of schools, of banks, of television. It is spoken on all of the Indonesian islands. But each island also has at least one island-language, the language spoken in the homes, on the streets, at informal gatherings. Nearly every

Balinese person speaks two languages. Indonesian, which is similar to the Malaysian language, was adopted in 1928.

I have decided not to study Balinese, the language mothers use with their children, and men and women use when they meet on the street. It is a language that reinforces the caste system that has characterized Balinese society since the arrival of the India-influenced Majapahit empire from the neighboring island of Java in 1343. This Hindu empire brought with it music and dance, art and religion. And a caste system based on blood.

Brahmana are the priestly caste.

Kesatria are the royals.

Wesia are descended from warriors.

Sudra are everyone else.

Whatever a *sudra* may achieve in life, he or she will always be a *sudra*. The barriers between the castes can never be crossed. And when that *sudra* speaks to a *brahmana* (or a *kesatria* or a *wesia*) he or she must speak in high Balinese. And when my *kesatria* friends of the *puri* speak to the *sudra* of the village, they speak a low language.

Often there is no similarity between the words in high and low Balinese: *toyoh* is the word for water if you are talking to someone of high caste. *Yeh* is the word if you are speaking to someone lower than you. If you use a "low" word to a high person, you can get into trouble.

I have always been uncomfortable slotting people into hierarchies, whatever the qualifications for inclusion . . . or exclusion; so, during the years I live in Bali, I do not learn the island's language. Instead, I continue learning Indonesian, which means I cannot talk to preschool children and elderly people who have not learned the country language. But it also means that I am not walking around insulting people. I do learn a few high phrases, like, "May I have some coffee," "Excuse me," and "Good-bye" (actually, "May I have permission to leave?") that I use around the *puri* and at royal events.

During my first years on the island, I am able to accept, from an anthropological, nonjudgmental perspective, the hierarchical ways of the culture. Later, years later, the caste system, the impermeable walls between the classes, and the feudalistic relationship that the wealthy have with the poor, are the reasons I leave the island. But for now, and for many years, my love affair with Bali is intense and passionate.

Dayu Biang begins my shopping trip for traditional clothes at the seamstress's shop where I look at *kebaya* fabric. A *kebaya* has long sleeves, a square neckline, and buttons down the front. Dayu Biang jokes that I will need a whole roll of fabric to cover my ample body and that maybe I should make a sexy strapless top instead of a *kebaya*. She's funny; I like her a lot.

I choose a solid blue nylon fabric that is certain to be hot. The seamstress takes my measurements and promises to deliver my *kebaya* tomorrow morning.

Then Dayu Biang and I walk into the main part of the market. It is crowded with women buying and selling fruits, vegetables, meats, dried fish, colorful cakes, cooked-rice breakfasts wrapped in a banana leaf, and flower petals for offerings. There are also stalls selling pots, fabrics, sarongs, hats, and ready-made clothes.

The ground is sloshy from last night's rain and we are walking in mud. Every person in the market is wearing flip-flops; I am wearing sneakers that are getting muddier by the minute. My first purchase is a pair of blue flip-flops, which I put on immediately and let the warm, wet, muddy water slosh through my toes. My other purchases are a *sarong* and a sash, both necessary parts of a traditional outfit.

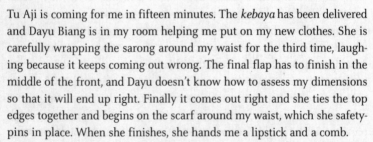

Tu Aji is coming for me in fifteen minutes. The *kebaya* has been delivered and Dayu Biang is in my room helping me put on my new clothes. She is carefully wrapping the sarong around my waist for the third time, laughing because it keeps coming out wrong. The final flap has to finish in the middle of the front, and Dayu doesn't know how to assess my dimensions so that it will end up right. Finally it comes out right and she ties the top edges together and begins on the scarf around my waist, which she safety-pins in place. When she finishes, she hands me a lipstick and a comb.

"You cannot go if you look like a chicken," she comments, pointing to my hastily combed hair. We both laugh.

Tu Aji and Tu Biang exclaim their approval when they see me. Then, accompanied by Dayu Biang, who is carrying a basket on her head with rice and sugar and a folded-up long white cloth, a traditional gift for the family of a dead person, we walk around the corner and enter a courtyard where there is a big crowd. Tu Aji walks through the crowd, telling me to follow. As soon as the crowd sees Tu Aji, everyone moves to let us through; and soon, he and I are standing in the front row looking down at the naked body of a withered old woman stretched out on a bamboo table.

"The people close to her must wash and purify the body before they wrap it up," Tu Aji explains.

A brother and a sister, four children, and two teenage grandsons all step up to pour holy water over the corpse. The huge crowd represents the *banjar,* the neighborhood organization that provides community support on such occasions. Everyone is on tiptoes, children on shoulders, straining to see the body being washed.

Before they wrap the body in white cloth, they wash it with soapy root and place flowers, coins, mirrors, spices, and leaves on and in designated parts of the body. Many months later, when Tu Aji tells me that if I should die in Bali, he would arrange for my cremation, I picture the craning necks of the villagers straining to see my withered corpse as it is washed in holy water, and I have to admit that in spite of the modesty that I conquered in Mexico, I cringe. It is easier for me to imagine the flames of cremation consuming my body than the village peering at my naked corpse.

The cremation is two days later. Accompanied by a syncopated brass percussion band, we walk through the streets alongside a procession of people holding onto a long white cloth, perhaps two hundred feet long (which explains why we brought cloth to the family). One end of the cloth is attached to the body, which is being carried in a decorated tower by dozens of young men from the *banjar.* The long cloth allows everyone to be connected to the deceased.

As in most ceremonies, everyone in the *banjar* participates ... in the preparation, in the procession, and in the celebration at home after the cremation. The *banjar* is a bond that ties the community together from birth to death. People who leave the *banjar* to work or live somewhere else usually make monthly contributions in lieu of their participation, so that the *banjar* will be there for them during rites of passage. Our *banjar* has 250 families, two orchestras, a women's group, and many small committees for every possible community need.

"Come," says Tu Aji when we get to the cemetery, which is less than a mile from where we started. Once again he takes me through a crowd. This time we climb up a little mound to the center of the activity. The body has been placed in the bottom half of a papier-mâché bull that was part of the procession; the top half of the bull has been cut away, opening up a cavity for the body. There is a gas tank nearby, and three men are fiddling with the connections that will lead the gas through a hose to a place where it will ignite the wood and fuel the fire that will burn the body.

Women are pouring holy water and sprinkling flower petals on the body and placing sarongs and personal belongings next to the corpse. The dead woman and her possessions will burn together.

After the body ceremonies are done, we all step down, and the gas burners begin to hiss and shoot fire under the body. I cannot take my eyes away from the fire or my thoughts away from the fact that I am watching a human body engulfed in flames. In the West, cremations are done behind the scenes and the family is presented with the ashes; here, we watch as the body turns into ashes. It is so matter-of-fact.

When Tu Aji says that we are watching a practical way to get rid of the shell that has housed her spirit, it feels right. The spirit has moved on. I need time to live with the idea; but it seems so natural when he says it.

Within half an hour, the crowd is gone. A few hours later, so is the body.

A couple of days later, Tu Aji comes by my patio, where I am reading.

"It is time for you to have a tour of the *puri*," he says. "And while we walk, I will tell you about my family."

I am wearing a sarong and a short-sleeved T-shirt with a picture of a blue-footed booby on the front.

"Do I need to dress in traditional clothes?" I ask.

"You are fine," he tells me. "Just tie a scarf around your waist."

As we walk through an archway into another section of the compound, Tu Aji explains that his father, the previous king, had two wives. One of the wives was low caste; Tu Aji and his older brother (who is dead) were children of that wife. The only child of the high-caste wife, Tu Aji's younger brother is the one who became the next and current king.

We enter the king's section of the palace; it is ornate and gilded, the way a palace should be. There are fountains and carvings and paintings and statues. As we pass by his royal-looking home, the king steps off his porch and walks toward us, leaning on a cane and limping. Tu Aji whispers that the king suffers from arthritis.

The king is a big man around and short; he has a heavy scar that slashes across one side of his face. Tu Aji introduces us. I lift my hands and lower my head in greeting. He tells me that he doesn't speak English, and we converse briefly in Indonesian.

"Perhaps," he says to me, "you can give me and my wives English lessons." I nod and smile.

When we shake hands in parting, I discover he is missing two fingers on his right hand. A few years ago, Tu Aji explains as we walk, a crazy man slashed the king's face and cut off his fingers. The man had been coming onto the palace grounds through a back entrance to consult the king's Wife Number Two, who, secretly and against the king's orders, had set up a business as a trance medium. One day the king saw the man and ordered him off of the palace property. The man returned the next night with a knife and slashed the king . . . and Wife Number Two as well. (After the incident, the man was put into an asylum.)

Now we are in the holy part of the compound, the part that contains the temple of the dynasty. Tu Aji points to a small white building with no windows, about twelve feet square. It is here that the family heirlooms are stored, gold and silver bowls, precious krisses (knives) that have been in the family for generations, jewels, and other royal treasures. Tu Aji tells me that he is worried the king may have sold some of the family inheritance, things that belong to everyone, things that he is obligated to pass on to future generations.

Tu Aji also advises me that if I teach English to the king and his wives, I should do it in our section of the compound.

"The king is used to getting whatever he wants," says Tu Aji. "And that includes women." And then he adds, using an expression I will hear from him many times over the next years, "A king must what he will."

Apparently, ever since they were children, Tu Aji was told that his royal little brother, king-to-be, could have anything he wanted. "Including my food, my bike, my friends, and my wife."

My friend is matter-of-fact when he talks about his younger brother's behavior. Tu Aji is smarter, gentler, and far more compassionate than the king; but while he often questions his brother's behavior, he is firmly rooted in the royal culture, and he always observes its traditions.

After I have been in the *puri* for about a month, I develop a routine. Before breakfast, I bike to the beach, which is six kilometers away. I leave at six, as soon as it is light enough to ride. As I pedal between miles of rice fields, there is a steady stream of women with baskets on their heads walking toward the market to sell and buy.

And there are men along the road, staring into the street in meditative tranquility, feet flat on the ground, thighs resting on calves, backs more or less straight. I have often tried to crouch that way. The minute I flatten my heels onto the ground, I fall over backward.

There are also fathers and grandfathers on the side of the road holding babies, some in silence, some in a one-way conversation with the babies. When I pass by, many of the younger men tell the tots to wave to the tourist. I smile and wave back.

When I get to the beach, I leave my bike on the road and walk onto the black sand. If the tide is out, there are long stretches of wet sand with thousands of tiny sand pictures made by miniature crabs. They are exquisite little pictures, symmetrical and balanced; some are circular, others are angular. Always, when I first arrive, there is no sign of the artists. They have felt my movement and run for cover. If I stand motionless for a few minutes, hundreds of them reappear and continue processing the algae and spitting out the sand in the little balls that create the pictures.

Every morning I sit cross-legged on a clump of grass, facing the sea, alone and at peace. I close my eyes and meditate. When I finish, I feel one with the world. I have always loved the sensation of meditation and the peaceful feeling it brings. For years I promised myself I would meditate daily, but I never did. Here in Bali, I'm doing it.

On the way back to the *puri,* I bike past preschool children beginning to assemble for their morning playgroup. *"Elo, turis!"* they call. *"Elo!"* I answer back.

There are other kids, older, hair wet from the morning washing, dressed in well-ironed uniforms, navy shorts on the bottom, white shirts on the top, on their way to school; some are walking, some biking. Often someone calls out, "Hello, Mister, I love you." His pals giggle.

By the time I get back to the *puri,* breakfast is waiting for me: sliced papaya (the most orange and best I have ever eaten, picked from a tree near my room), a newspaper-and-banana-leaf-wrapped rice package with bits of vegetables, half a hard-boiled egg, and a sprinkle of crisply fried shallots. And coffee.

The rice breakfast is what the family eats each morning, minus the fruit. I am the only one who eats fruit. The Balinese assert that fruit in the morning is bad for the stomach; but they accept that my western stomach is different.

After breakfast, unless there is a ceremony or a procession in the village, I plug in my computer and work. Tu Aji usually joins me for lunch and continues my education. One day I give Tu Aji a photograph with my left hand.

"Rita, you must never give or take anything with your left hand."

"Oops. Sorry, I forgot. You know that we do not have this prohibition in America. There is not a distinction between a dirty hand and a clean hand."

In all of Indonesia the left hand is used to wipe one's bottom, and the right hand is used for interaction. The training begins at birth. An infant who reaches out with the wrong hand is corrected by the parent.

"No, no," says the parent, moving the left hand back and putting the right hand forward. "Use your sweet hand."

Tu Aji has apparently never been told that westerners have no hand etiquette.

"What if you are giving something to the president?" he asks, reaching for the most formal situation he can think of.

"It would not matter," I say. "In fact, at graduation ceremonies, it is traditional for the president of the university to hand the student the diploma with the left hand and shake congratulations with the right hand."

Tu Aji is shocked.

One day when we are talking about marriage in Bali, Tu Aji tells me that Balinese men often have women other than their wives. (Although Tu Aji has two wives and his brother has five, it is no longer legal for a man to marry more than one woman, unless the first wife gives permission, or if she cannot have children. The courts decide.)

I ask Tu Aji if the wives know about the other women.

"The wives know and don't know," he says. "They see but they don't see." He holds his hand, the fingers wide open, in front of his eyes.

One of the reasons Balinese wives choose not to see is that there is little they can do about it. Women are second-class citizens. They do not inherit; instead, when a woman marries, she must move from her father's home to the home of her husband's family, where she is totally dependent on them. There is a tearful ceremony at which the bride, flanked by her parents, says good-bye to her ancestors, to whom she has always prayed. From that point on, she will pray and give offerings to her husband's ancestors, and serve her mother-in-law as well.

The place of women is obvious at celebrations, on the street, in the homes. On ceremonial occasions, they sit lower (pavilions have different heights) and are served their meals after the men. And I have also heard stories about wife beatings. Yet, divorce in Bali is only about 2 percent, probably because if the woman leaves the marriage, the children are legally the property of the husband's family.

It is difficult for me to accept this inequality, but I do not permit myself to dwell on it. I too must learn how to see and not see. As a guest in this culture, my role is to observe, not to judge.

One day, when our conversation centers on women, Tu Aji tells me that, like all women in Bali, Tu Biang has a much closer relationship with the gods and the ancestors than he does. She communicates with them daily.

Every morning Tu Biang pours coffee, sweetened with sugar, into twenty-five tiny orange cups that are arranged on a tray. Then she puts the coffee and sticks of incense into the altars, most of which are in the family temple. (Every home in Bali has a family temple with altars to the gods and the ancestors.) The smell of the incense alerts the spirits that coffee has been served. Being spirits, they only take the essence of the coffee, and later of the rice, which explains why there is still coffee in the cups and rice in the containers at the end of the day.

In addition to their special relationship with the ancestors, women also have close connections to what is going on in this world. Each morning before eight, vendors arrive in the *puri* with their wares on their heads and the village secrets on their tongues. Women selling vegetables, fruit, and squirming eels snatched from the rice paddies also carry with them the news and gossip of the night before. Who climbed through whose bedroom window, who was beaten by her husband, who was drunk, and who got into a fight.

Often, later in the day, the women sit together making offerings, sharing their secrets, and passing on the gossip. In spite of their second-class citizenship, women get strength and sisterhood from the bonding that takes place daily as they sit together weaving palm leaves and assembling offerings.

One morning, after I have been in the *puri* for nearly two months, Jero Made is making the eggplant dish we often have as part of dinner. I tell her I want to learn how to cook it. She has already added chopped garlic, onion, and chili pepper to hot coconut oil. "You cook this until it releases a good smell," she tells me. "Then you add a little shrimp paste mixed with water and wait again until it releases another good smell."

Noting my reaction to the unpleasant smell of the shrimp paste, she adds with a smile, "According to a Balinese nose."

As she moves things around in the wok, she says, "You will probably sneeze from this aroma."

Then she adds the eggplant and salt.

Like all Balinese food, the eggplant is cut into small pieces and eaten over rice with the fingers or with a spoon in the right hand and a fork in the left. In a Balinese home, the eater never needs a knife.

I take a little taste. It's great. Jero Made watches my face, hears my sigh, and smiles with pride. As I am tasting, a servant from the king's compound arrives with a message for me. The wives would very much like to have English lessons, and they would be happy to come here.

We begin lessons that night. The king's five wives arrive at five o'clock, and they are joined by Tu Aji's two wives. Just before they get here, Dayu Biang puts eight jasmine blossoms in the middle of the big dining table, "for a sweet lesson."

The wives are very different from one another. Wife Number Two and Wife Number Five are big women. Wife Number One is lean. Wife Number Four wears glasses. Wife Number Three, delicate and tiny, is the only one who has studied English before.

I pass out a sheet on which I have printed a short conversation, and I read it. Then we read together. Then I read it again and call upon them to repeat the words.

They are lovely students, some much quicker than others. My biggest problem is calling on them to answer a question. All seven wives are called Tu Biang, a princess who has children. It is not polite for me to call them anything else. I ask if I can call them Wife Number One, Wife Number Two, etc., but they definitely don't want that. I suspect they like the idea that they can avoid being called upon by lowering their eyes. Pointing is impolite.

After the first week, they acknowledge my frustration and give me their individual names: Tu Biang Sandat, Tu Biang Adi, etc. Our lessons continue. I feel like Anna in Siam.

After I have been in the *puri* for several months, Tu Biang and Tu Aji arrive at my patio one morning in formal dress.

"If you will excuse us," says Tu Aji, "we would like to talk to you about something."

Tu Biang, whose trademark is laughter, is not even smiling. This is serious.

"Please," I say, lowering my head and putting my hands together.

"Rita, you have been here for more than three months," says Tu Aji. "Every day we talk and share our lives. You have brought your joy into our *puri*, and you have helped us in many ways. We are here to tell you that you have become family. We can no longer take money from you."

I cannot stop the tears or the swelling of pride I feel inside. I have come to Bali to seek spirituality and to learn about the Balinese world; but most important, wherever I am, I want to feel a part of the culture, to be accepted on the inside.

Now as a family member, I want even more to know about the *puri* family. Tu Aji frequently talks about his father, who, when he became blind several years before he died, was writing a family history. He continued to dictate the history to Tu Aji until it was completed. One day I ask Tu Aji if he plans to write the family history of his generation. He apologizes, to me and to his father. He has not written anything. We both know that if Tu Aji does not write it, no one will. The written story of the dynasty will end, which would be sad, because Tu Aji is a wonderful storyteller.

During our frequent conversations, Tu Aji tells me stories that make me feel as though I am living in a fairy tale.

He tells me how he happened to marry Tu Biang. His father, the king, and her father were brothers, the only male siblings of their generation. The family wealth was split, half and half, between the two brothers.

Tu Aji's father had three sons. His brother had only one child, Tu Biang. Since wealth is passed on to sons, not to daughters, Tu Biang could not inherit her father's half of the *puri*. Like all women, she had to "marry out" and live with her husband's family.

But the Balinese are very practical. And when a royal family is in such a situation, the woman (a teenage Tu Biang, in this case) officially becomes a man and takes on the duties and responsibilities of a man. She inherits and chooses a "wife," who moves into her *puri*. She also assumes economic responsibility for the family and the education of the children. There was a tricky clause that was thrown into the deal: she had to marry one of her three first cousins.

The teenage Tu Biang chose Tu Aji, who already had a wife and child, which of course angered Tu Aji's younger brother, the king. He wanted her and her half of the wealth.

Together Tu Aji's first family moved into Tu Biang's part of the *puri*.

The two wives never got along. Today they barely talk, though they live within fifty yards of each other.

Many years after they were married, Tu Biang was swindled out of all her money. She went crazy. For several years the beautiful princess from the *puri* ran insanely on the streets at night trying to win her money back by gambling.

Tu Aji could not help. As a "wife," he had no money. But the king did, and he promised to assist . . . if Tu Biang would sleep with him.

Tu Biang and her mother, Tu Nini, chose instead to beg for rice from house to house, rather than give her cousin, the king, what he wanted. (Eventually, foreign guests in the *puri* helped her get back her life, some money, and her dignity.)

Tu Aji tells me that because of Tu Biang's "fall," one of his sons had a nervous breakdown and was hospitalized. (He's fine now.)

Tu Aji also tells me an intriguing story about the king's Wife Number Two. She went into a trance one day and received orders from the king's dead father that the mother, who was still living, should adopt her, thus placing Wife Number Two into the highest caste.

Tu Aji told his brother that it would be a crazy thing to do; there was no precedent. Surely it was a scheme of Wife Number Two and not a message from their father.

The king, in that great royal tradition of punishing the messenger, cut off all relations with Tu Aji and his family for several years, sending out orders to all the extended 157 families in Kerambitan that they were to have nothing to do with Tu Aji, his wives, or his sons.

Against Tu Aji's advice, Wife Number Two was adopted by the king's mother, who began coughing during the ceremony, spit blood soon after, and died the next week. (The adoption didn't work either. Bad things started to happen to the family, and a few years later it was undone.)

I am swept into Tu Aji's stories like a child in a fairy tale. It is an enchanted world, and sinister. When Tu Aji talks about the special powers that his brother, the king, possesses, there is something ominous in the air. I have to keep reminding myself that these tales are not fiction or folklore. They are true stories about Tu Aji's family, about people I know. People I talk to every day.

The tales are so addictive that I cannot wait to get up every morning. Something extraordinary is always lurking just minutes away in Tu Aji's stories. Finally, I cannot stand it any more.

"Tu Aji," I say. "Your stories are wonderful and I agree with your father:

they should be recorded. Would you like to write a book with me? It will be a lot of work, many months, maybe years. Would you like to try?"

"I have been thinking about the same thing," he says. "I would like that very much."

And we plunge in with a fury. Every day we meet for hours. Now I am taking notes and asking questions, filling in gaps, and expanding on details. There are days when Tu Aji says, "I am tired today." And we do not work. Often on those days he asks me questions, as interested in my stories as I am in his. I love it when his enthusiasm bursts into my dramatic pauses with "And then? And then?"

But mostly Tu Aji talks. I never get tired of listening. I cannot get enough.

Then one day I realize that there has never been anything like the book we are constructing . . . a true story of life in a real kingdom that reads like a fairy tale. I am suddenly frightened.

"Tu Aji, I do not want you to work today. I would like you to think about something instead. I have just realized that our book has the potential of becoming a bestseller. That means it will be read all over the world . . . and it will certainly find its way back to Bali. The story of your family will be read by millions of people. They will read about your children, your brother, your wives. The good, the bad, and the embarrassing will be there in print for everyone to know. Please think carefully about the consequences. If you decide that you do not want to do it, I will understand."

The next morning Tu Aji joins me on my patio. "I have made a decision," he says. "I am not worried about the stories we tell about my sons. They have all passed through their difficulties. Besides, I am their father and I can tell their stories. My wives' stories too, I can tell. Those stories are my stories as well. But I have decided that the stories about my brother cannot be told while we are both alive. The book cannot be published until one of us is dead."

"No problem," I say, hoping that his brother will be the first to go. "We can do all the work; we can even look for a publisher. We will just stipulate that the publication will have to wait until you or your brother dies."

"Good, then," he says. "Let's continue."

Four days later I walk out of my room at six in the morning. Tu Aji is sitting on my patio.

"Why are you here so early?" I ask.

"I had a heart attack in the middle of the night. I am waiting for a car to take me to the hospital."

His face is pale and his eyes are dull. He has already told me that he had a heart attack several years before I met him.

"How do you know it was a heart attack?" I ask. "What were your symptoms?"

"They were the same as the last time. A terrible pressure, like squeezing, in the middle of my chest. Then it spread into my shoulder and my neck and my arm and I started to sweat. Adoo. Rita, I have told you many times that I am not afraid to die; but last night, when I thought I was dying, I did not want to go. I am not ready."

"And I am not ready either for you to leave."

We are sitting across from each other. I am not sure what his heart is doing at this moment, but my head is close to exploding. How is it possible that we are discussing a heart attack he is having as we speak, so calmly, without emotion. It is the Balinese way: as a subject gets more intense, more charged, the voices always get softer.

I continue in the tone he has set, though it feels strange to be sitting there asking questions when inside I want to be screaming for the car and driver. Where are they? Somebody, please, get this man to a hospital.

"Tu Aji, did you have other thoughts? Was anything else going through your head?"

"Yes. I have told you my brother has special powers. When I thought I was dying, I thought, 'My brother is doing this to me because I am telling too many family secrets.'"

My eyes fill with tears and my body begins to shake. I realize for the first time that I love this man. It is a deep spiritual love, something I have never felt before. He cannot die; he is needed still, by his wives, his children, his family, his village . . . and me. If our book is really the target of his brother's powers, then I am responsible for Tu Aji's heart attack.

"Tu Aji, you must go to the hospital and get well and never think about the book again. I promise you we will never write it." He does and we don't.

CHAPTER ELEVEN

THE TRANCE

It's been several months since Tu Aji's heart attack. Things are back to normal. He and I are still very close; we talk all the time. But I no longer ask for intimate details about his family, and he no longer volunteers them.

One morning, as Tu Aji and I are sitting on my patio, the mailman, who only comes when there is a letter (no junk mail here), arrives with news from Jan. She's on her way to Bali. I'm the second stop (after Hong Kong) on her one-year round-the-world trip. Perhaps there *is* a travel gene. I can't wait for her to get here.

Tu Aji is as excited as I am about her four-month visit. There is something about meeting family that intensifies a friendship.

Jan arrives a few weeks after the turkeys. Tu Aji likes having animals around. Our menagerie consists of two dogs, four nursing puppies, an ordinary hen with six chickens, two black-and-white guinea hens, five birds in cages, a very green parrot on a chain, two pigs in pens, and the two recently arrived turkeys.

Everyone agrees that one of the turkeys is *galak,* fierce; and he doesn't like Jan. Whenever she steps off the patio, he spreads his feathers out like a peacock, cackles like a demented rooster, and runs straight at her. Jan, an animal lover, shouts and swings her leg as though she is going to kick the big ugly bird with his off-color wattle and his shabby array of feathers, but he is not fooled. Instead, when he is close enough, he leaps off the ground and crashes into her. The scene is straight out of a slapstick comedy, and Tu Biang, Dayu Biang, and I cannot help laughing. Jan is not amused.

Neither is eighty-pound Tu Nini, Tu Biang's mother, who has added to her sweeping chores the job of protecting Jan from the turkey. Whenever the sound of turkey cackle announces an imminent attack, Tu Nini comes running and screaming and swinging her broom. And if that doesn't send him off into the bushes, she's not afraid to give him a good whack . . . and a kick as well.

One day, as Jan and I are safely sitting on the patio (the turkey doesn't leave the dirt), Tu Aji tells us that on Sunday we will be going to Bulung Daya.

"You are very lucky to be here at this time," he tells us. "Many years ago my ancestors built a temple next to the beach there, to thank the gods for the treasure they found in the cave."

"Treasure?" Jan asks, thinking gold and jewels.

"At Bulung Daya there is a huge cave. My ancestors discovered that the cave was home to thousands of little birds, swiftlets, who built the kinds of nests that are considered a delicacy by the Chinese. My family became wealthy selling the nests to Chinese traders, so we built a temple at the site to thank the gods for our good fortune. Today, the birds are gone, but the cave is still there; to us, it represents wealth and good fortune. So once every 210 days (a Balinese calendar year), we go to the temple to thank the spirits of the cave for their gifts, and we ask for continued success. And," he pauses to laugh the deep rich laughter I have grown to love, "we have a picnic and the children play in the sand and the water. It is always a wonderful day."

Though he has never seen them, Tu Aji tells us that the nests look like shiny shredded coconut. They are made of seaweed and held together by thick bird saliva. In China, they are thought to strengthen a man's sexual drive and cure many different kinds of illnesses. There are still many caves in Indonesia where these birds exist. It is said that fifty pounds of nests sell today for fifty thousand U.S. dollars. Unfortunately, the birds abandoned the *puri*'s cave several generations ago.

When Jan and I awake at dawn on Sunday, Tu Biang is assembling casserole-size containers, which will be filled with the various dishes of our picnic lunch and then locked together in metal carrying frames, three containers to a frame.

Dayu Biang is reviewing the hundreds of palm-leaf woven baskets filled with offerings. Besides being a servant in the *puri,* Dayu Biang, a *brahmana,* is an "offering expert." She is called upon by many different families in our neighborhood to advise the women about what offerings they need for their ceremonies, how many, how big, and how to present them.

There is nothing haphazard about offerings. Each kind of weaving has a name; each type of flower or leaf combination is specific. Some offerings require a slice of banana or sugarcane; others require four different colors of flowers; still others need eggs or rocks or tiny modeled Buddhas.

I once joined some women who were shaping colored rice dough (very much like play dough) into figures and symbols for a wedding offering. When I showed my carefully sculpted, two-inch-high Buddha to Dayu Biang, she held it out, turned it around, and, noticing that the head was a bit askew and the mouth slightly twisted, announced to me and ten other women, "Your Buddha has a toothache!" As with the *tortillas* in Mexico, my contributions in Bali bring laughter to my hosts.

When the offerings and the food and the people are loaded into the van, we take off toward the north. An hour later, our drive comes to an end in a grove of coconut trees that overlooks the sea.

We walk, single file, down a muddy hill toward a sandy beach, all of us carrying as much as we can: food, offerings, clothes, paraphernalia for the ceremony. I am carrying a giant birthday-type cake about the size of a large pizza, only taller. It is my western contribution to the picnic, purchased after long and serious consultation with Tu Biang. My flip-flops are slithering in the downhill mud and I am desperately praying that I and my cake don't fall. After about ten minutes on the muddy hill, we step onto the sand.

It's a few hundred yards in the hot sun to the temple, a distance that could be dangerous for a cake with a gooey frosting. I stop, take out a sarong from my book bag, and put it, folded, on top of the cake box. About five minutes later, I see that Tu Biang is waiting for me. When I catch up, she looks with horror at my improvised insulation. Quickly looking around to be sure no one else has noticed, she takes the sarong off of the cake box.

"It is clean," I tell her.

"You cannot put it near food," she tells me. "It has been worn around the bottom half of your body."

I turn around to see if anyone is looking. I can imagine word going out that no one should eat my polluted contribution to the afternoon. Tu Biang looks too and then she signals that no one has seen and I must not tell anyone this has happened. It's our secret.

The beach ends when the sand meets a huge cliff that reaches out into the water. Waves are pounding into the cliff and covering the rocky path that leads to the end of the promontory where the cave is located. Tu Aji explains to Jan and me that the first part of the ceremony will be held out on the rocks and that we cannot begin until the tide goes out. First, we will have lunch.

By the time the ceremony begins, the king's family has arrived. Eight of his children, their spouses, and their children are here. And all of the five wives. The *banjar* (neighborhood organization) gamelan orchestra has also arrived. Twenty men carry the heavy brass instruments across the sand. Bulung Daya represents wealth and success. Even the *banjar* is hoping the family, and the village, will thrive in the coming year.

During lunch, the gamelan plays. The kids run in the waves. The adults talk. We all eat. Then, finally, someone signals that the tide has gone out far enough. It is time to begin.

We walk in a long procession on the rocky path that abuts the cliff. There are men and boys carrying colorful flags on bamboo poles and others rhythmically clapping their cymbal-like instruments, surrounding us with a syncopated brass-percussive beat. There is a lay priest in white sitting at the end of the path, surrounded by offerings and waves crashing into the cave about twenty feet to his left.

It is not an easy walk from the beach to the cave entrance. Some of the younger men help the women over places where the rocks are rough and the step up or down is steep. The women's sarongs are wrapped so tightly around our legs that our stride is barely six inches.

We all sit on the rocky ground facing the cave, the men cross-legged, the women with their legs to the side. The chanting begins and the sweet ringing of the priest's bell. We hold a stick of incense between our fingers as the priest chants. And then we hold flower petals. We are praying to the spirits of the cave. The waves are roaring in the background, splashing us all, but lightly.

When the praying is over, and we have paid our respects to the benevolent spirits, it is time to acknowledge and placate the evil spirits.

Three men, one son from each of the three brothers, walk to the edge of the cliff and face the cave. The first, son of the king's Wife Number Three, an officer of one of the major banks in Denpasar, is holding a live duck. The second, a lawyer and a judge, son of the oldest, deceased brother, is holding a chicken. The third, Tu Aji's son, a doctor, is carrying a squawking chicken. One by one they throw their animal sacrifices into the waves, sending them to their death as the waves crash into the rocky promontory.

And the evil spirits, who like fresh blood, are pacified. Hopefully all has gone well, and the spirits, both good and bad, are happy.

"Now we will go into the temple to pray," says Tu Aji to Jan and me, rushing us along the rocky, wet path. "Oh, you are so lucky to be able to see this. Hurry. The women are going to dance now, from the beach to the temple entrance."

How proud he is of his ceremonies; how much he loves his culture. His enthusiasm is contagious.

As the five wives of the king, several of his daughters and daughters-in-law, a few teenage grandchildren, the wives of the lawyer, the doctor, the banker, and Tu Biang step from the rocky path onto the sand, they turn to face the water and begin to dance backward, inviting, enticing the spirits of the cave to come to the temple and receive our prayers.

Tu Aji stands between me and Jan near the entrance to the temple, which is about forty feet from the water. The dancing women approach, their fluid movements flowing through their bodies from their fingertips through their hands and arms and hips as though they were all of one boneless, rubbery piece.

As they come closer, Tu Aji exclaims, "Oh, no. It's happening again."

He is looking at Tu Biang and calling for two of his sons to help their mother. Her dancing is no longer smooth and flowing, it is jerky and angular. Her feet are stabbing the sand, her arms are cutting through the air. The muscles in her neck are tight and visible. Tu Biang has gone into trance.

Tu Aji is upset. He does not want her in this state. Two of her sons are supporting Tu Biang, one on each side, as she trance-dances toward the temple. The king's Wife Number Two is also in trance. The two women dance next to each other into the temple and sit down together on a mat.

Soon we are all sitting on mats, silently facing the many altars that are filled with offerings and decorated with black-and-white checkered cloths. There is an energy in the air, a tension among the players.

Then a scream pierces the moment. Tu Biang and her sister-in-law jump up and begin to call out in eerie voices, shrill and demanding.

"What are they saying?" I ask Tu Aji.

"They are calling for the king to come before them."

Jan and I sit there, frightened and fascinated. No one "calls for the king"; it isn't done. It's the king who "calls for" things and people and services. But the king is walking, with his severely arthritic body, leaning on a cane, moving from his comfortable, shaded seat on the other side of the altars toward the two women. And soon he is standing before Tu Biang and Wife Number Two.

The sounds coming out of their mouths are not at all like their everyday voices. Tu Aji translates from the Balinese. They are telling this vindictive, powerful man that he is not fulfilling his responsibilities to the family. They are saying that he is destroying the dynasty, ruining the family name by not being honest. He must attend more family functions, they tell him, and treat the people in the village with more kindness.

"You have to be true, not false in your heart, to bind the family together," are the words coming out of Tu Biang's mouth, but she does not sound like Tu Biang. The king is standing in front of her, nodding his head. He does not look like a king.

When the two women are finished, they sit down, the king returns to his seat, and the prayer ceremony takes place.

As we walk back to the van an hour later, I ask Tu Aji, "What will happen to Tu Biang tomorrow? Will he punish her?"

Tu Aji looks at me as if I have not learned anything in all these months. "No, he will not punish her. That was not Tu Biang, it was the spirit of our father speaking through her. Nothing will happen to Tu Biang. She was not responsible for what she said. She was the empty vessel that was used by my father's spirit."

On the ride back to the *puri,* Tu Biang, apparently exhausted, sleeps in the front. Jan and I sit in the back, stunned and silent. As soon as we are home, we huddle in Jan's room. Neither of us knows what to think. Have we seen and heard a voice from another world or are these women faking? There's no question that the Balinese around us, including Tu Aji and the king, believed they were hearing from the spirit world.

Tu Biang was definitely in trance, but it could have been self-hypnosis, which I have seen many times in dance performances here. Perhaps Tu Biang is using trance as an escape valve, to release emotions she is not permitted to have. She has many good reasons to dislike her cousin the king.

Or perhaps we have heard the voice of an unseen world, the world inhabited by spirits?

In recent weeks, I have often found myself thinking about "spirits." It's unavoidable. All those offerings and altars and prayers. All that talk about different worlds.

There's no doubt that my spiritual development is still rather primitive; but since my arrival in Bali more than nine months ago, I've come to believe that there is such a thing as a spirit. That we are not just flesh and bones and blood.

Once I have accepted the existence of a spirit, anything is possible. If the spirit leaves the body when we die, why wouldn't it want to visit now and then to see what's happening? And why not step in from time to time with advice?

If I were Tu Aji's kind and benevolent father watching his son the king damage the name of the dynasty, the ceremony at Bulung Daya would be the perfect place to send a message.

Jan and I talk into the morning. Neither one of us knows what to think, but there's no doubt that we're both in a place, spiritually, that we've never been before. At this point, we are both convinced that there is such a thing as a spirit. It's a slippery concept and we are not altogether comfortable with the implications, but we work on it together for most of the night. I'm so glad she's here. Today would have been difficult to handle alone. I'm going to miss her. She leaves next week.

While Jan is moving west around the world, Mitch is honored by his peers in the New York Press Club as Nellie Bly Cub Reporter of the Year for stories he wrote in 1989. He is presented with a plaque at a banquet at the posh Water Club restaurant in Manhattan. My ex is there to support and cheer him. So are my parents. I am not. When I find out about the honor several months later, I feel both proud and sad. I would have liked to have shared that moment with my son, and I know I was missed.

Years later, when Jan, Mitch, and I talk about the fact that I was a very peripheral part of their lives for many years, I hear for the first time how much they missed a traditional mom. They were twenty-two and twenty-three when I began my travels. My mothering years were over. My kids were adults and they didn't need me any more, I thought. They saw it differently. They missed not being able to talk to me and share what was going on in their lives.

In the early years of my travels, I wrote letters frequently, and I spent as least two weeks every year with each of them. But I wasn't a part of their daily lives, and I wasn't at the other end of a phone for those supportive conversations that kids (even adult kids) need from time to time.

I thought at the time they were pleased not to have a hovering mother nearby. I was flattered, surprised, and pained to learn that they both wished I'd been closer.

The last few years have been easier. I've had both a phone and e-mail.

After Jan leaves, friends of friends arrive from the U.S. and I spend a month introducing them to Bali. A few months after that, I join Jan in

Thailand and we tour the country together. When I return to Bali, I spend some time at an ashram on the eastern coast of the island.

When I finally come back to the *puri,* I discover that Tu Biang's mother, the tiny Tu Nini, is dying.

Her room is filled with the earthy smell of incense, rising from an offering that has just been placed on the floor at the foot of her bed. In the palm-leaf container are rice and meat and vegetables and sweets, the ingredients for a betel-nut chew, a glass of liquor, and a cigarette, bribes for the evil spirits who are killing her; perhaps they will reverse their curse. Evil spirits get their offerings on the ground. Ancestors and gods get theirs on raised altars.

The room is hot, and heavy with humidity; the fan in the corner is still. Tu Nini, dressed in her *kebaya* and sarong, is in bed, her head and chest propped up on pillows. She is surrounded by four women, each one massaging a limb. I relieve Tu Biang and take the tiny right arm in my hand, gently moving my fingers across skin and bone. There is no flesh.

The IV, assembled by her grandson, Dr. Rai, is standing on the floor, its plastic tube ending in a needle in Tu Nini's arm. From time to time, a family member studies the drip and decides she's not getting enough to eat. During the half hour I sit there, two people, separately, adjust the clip. The IV is not a sacred medical tool; it's food. Why not give her a little more?

Tu Nini cannot move her arms or lift her head, but in spite of the cancer that is swelling in her stomach like an eight-month-old fetus, she can see and speak.

"Did you bring me a *manggis?*" she asks when she sees me.

She and I share a passion for the purple-skinned fruit (mangosteen in English). It is the juiciest, sweetest, whitest, most wonderful fruit in the world, and she remembers that I have just returned from the eastern part of the island where *manggis* grow.

I am devastated at having to say no to a dying woman. There is a custom in Bali that when you go away, you return with *oleh oleh,* often some food that is specific to the part of the island where you've just been. *Manggis* are not in season. Instead I have brought cookies and crunchy soybean snacks. If I were dying, however, I would want *manggis* too.

When I am replaced at her side, I run to the small outdoor market in Kerambitan. No *manggis.* I hire a car to drive me to the town twenty minutes away, where there is a huge market. I check dozens of fruit sellers. No *manggis.* I return to the *puri* empty-handed.

Tu Biang laughs her infectious giggle as she tells everyone that I have been running around trying to find a *manggis,* which Tu Nini cannot even eat. There are probably some imports in the big supermarkets in Denpasar, more than an hour from here, but I cannot go. There is not enough time. In a few hours we are going to a trance medium, a special one who can undo curses.

Tu Biang has visited trance mediums twice in the last two weeks. She is certain that the cancer growing in her mother was planted by a particular woman who, it is said, does black magic. The woman, whom I know well, *is* different. She rarely sits with the other women when they weave their offerings and gossip, hour after hour. And I have often seen her sitting on her porch, reading a book, something one rarely sees Balinese, female or male, doing. And she always wants to talk with me about world problems and history and philosophy and religion. I like her. Whenever I go to see her, Tu Biang warns me that I shouldn't.

I once asked this woman's husband if he thinks his wife performs black magic.

"I have seen her sleeping upside down in her bed, her head to the ocean and her feet to the holy mountain of the gods. They say that is something a *leyak* would do. But how can I know? I can't."

Leyak, it is thought, are the human collaborators of evil spirits. By day they look like everyone else, but at night they become cats or monkeys or even bright lights. Most of their evil is done after dark, when they cause hideous things to happen . . . illness, death, pain. Nearly everyone I know in Bali claims to have "seen" a *leyak.* They hang out at night in cemeteries, at crossroads, near banyan or fruit trees, and in places where two rivers meet.

One night a few weeks ago I asked Tu Aji if he thought black magic was real.

"Let me tell you a story," he said. "Once, many years ago, when Tu Nini was a young mother, her marriage was in trouble. She went to a special priest who, like other *brahmana* priests, had access to the palm-leaf books that hold the secrets of both white and black magic. She asked him to make her attractive to her husband. The priest chanted and lit incense; he used herbs and leaves and flowers and fire as he sang. Then he wrote Sanskrit letters and drew a picture on a small white cloth. 'Tie this next to your body, under your sarong,' he told her. 'It will make your husband love you.'

"Soon after she put on the cloth," Tu Aji continued, "she started waking up in the mornings with knowledge of things she should not have known, like who had become sick during the night, and who had died. She knew who had had secret liaisons the night before and with whom, but she had no idea how she came by the knowledge. Then one night Tu Nini turned into a cat. She ran through the village on tops of walls, peered into family compounds, entered bedrooms. All night she observed events that only a cat could see."

The next morning, terrified by the memory of the experience, the young Tu Nini returned the magic cloth to the priest.

I do not know what I think about all this. Does accepting a world of spirits mean that I have to accept a world where black magic exists? I'm not ready for that. But I imagine that mischievous spirits can cause mischief, and evil spirits can cause more serious trouble. Spirits probably don't change their individual personalities. That's why the Balinese entertain them with music and dance, feed them rice, and create beautiful art objects for their aesthetic enjoyment. It's important that the spirits stay happy.

I'm still skeptical about the cats and bright lights and curses of the *leyak.*

Tonight, Tu Biang, Dayu Biang, and I are bringing the dying Tu Nini to a *balian taksu* to ask for help. A *balian taksu* is a healer who is able to go into a trance by emptying his body of his own soul and filling the space with the soul of a spirit from the other world. Most *balian taksu* work with one particular spirit who guides them through the invisible world. Through that spirit, the *balian* can talk to all the dead spirits, the good and the bad.

Last week a different *balian* said there were *leyak* hanging around the *puri,* and that they were attracted by certain fruit trees that were planted in the wrong places. Tu Biang came back to the *puri* and ordered the trees to be cut down, including the papaya tree near my room. Tu Biang is hoping tonight's *balian* will be able to undo the curse that is causing Tu Nini's illness. For the first time, she is bringing Tu Nini.

The healer is a small man in his fifties with curly black hair and a jovial face, creased with laugh lines. He greets us warmly and loudly, like an old, somewhat coarse, friend. Tu Nini is carried in and placed on her mattress on one side of the healer. Tu Biang is on a mat near her mother's head. Dayu Biang and I are sitting on a mat across from them.

The smell of incense mixes with the sweet perfume of jasmine flowers and the rich smokiness of sandalwood burning. After his effusive greeting, the *balian* sits quietly with his eyes closed. Then he begins to twitch, his face, his shoulders, his whole body. Then he grunts. And mutters. And jerks some more. And then he is still and silent. Minutes pass.

Suddenly, the silence is slashed by a howling animal noise. The healer leaps up and runs back and forth in front of us. He cackles and howls and jumps as though he is pouncing on prey.

Don't laugh, I tell myself as he begins to snort and squeal like a pig. Then he begins uttering nonsense words. I fight the urge to giggle, feeling guilty and traitorous until I look at Dayu Biang. She too is struggling to keep from laughing. I relax.

The noises, the words, the pouncing, the sitting continue for ten minutes. Tu Nini is silent and motionless, her eyes closed. Then the healer sits. He lifts a knife and passes it over the smoke of the burning sandalwood. He takes a stack of incense and waves it over the knife and then over a bowl of holy water. Then he talks to Tu Biang, giving her the consecrated incense. She nods as he speaks. Then he closes his eyes, twitches some more, and then is calm, back in the room with us, chatting as though nothing has happened, though he appears tired. We return to the *puri*.

The next morning I wake up at seven and walk to Tu Nini's room. Tu Biang is standing outside the door, crying. A relative from across the street is standing with her, also crying. I am not sure if I am supposed to see their tears, so I don't. Instead I go inside.

There are two women massaging Tu Nini. Her breathing is a choking, guttural sound. I know, though I have never heard it before, that this must be what they call a death rattle. I quickly leave and sit outside my room with a cup of coffee. My heart is the only thing I can hear until Tu Biang arrives ten minutes later and stands before me.

There is a fixed smile on her face through which she says, "My mother has just died."

I do not know how to receive the news. I nod and smile back. Tears are filling my eyes.

"When I went in to her," says this small, beautiful woman still smiling through her pain, "Tu Nini asked me for permission to leave. I told her, 'The western doctors have told me there is nothing they can do. Last night the *balian* said it was in the hands of the gods.' I told her, 'If you are ready to go, Mother, I give you permission.' Then she lifted both arms into prayer position above her chest, and she died."

As I am hugging Tu Biang, not a Balinese gesture but one they have become used to from me, I hear the metal *kulkul* clanging the news of Tu Nini's death from the center of the village. The sound is an eerie contrast to the hollowed trunk that serves as the wooden *kulkul* that calls people to meetings and rehearsals.

Minutes later our compound is filled with people from the *banjar*. Women gather and begin making offerings. Men climb ladders to decorate the *bale* where Tu Nini will lie in state: they are draping white cloth over the ceiling, wrapping gold-painted strips of red cloth around the columns, placing mats and carpeting on the floor.

While they are working, Tu Nini's body is laid out, naked, on the wooden platform, and a young cousin and neighbor, with a container of formalin and a hypodermic needle, injects the preserving agent into her still warm body, piercing the skin over and over again until suddenly he calls out in pain. Somehow he has squirted formalin into his own face and he is blinded (temporarily). Two men, their arms supporting him, lead him down the street to the doctor.

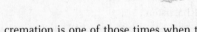

A cremation is one of those times when the *banjar* takes over. If you are Balinese, you spend your life helping your neighbors as a member of the *banjar,* so that the *banjar* will be there for you when you need it. You cannot die in Bali without a *banjar*. *Banjar* men build the tower in which the body is transported to the cemetery, they decorate the family compound, deliver chairs for the guests to sit on, whittle the *sate* sticks, break open the coconuts, build the structures that are necessary for a proper cremation. And it is the men of the *banjar* who make the meat dishes that are served during the festivities.

Banjar women make the offerings and cook the meals that all the workers will eat. Each of the approximately 250 families in our *banjar* will contribute three working days to the event. There are work charts, schedules, assignments, and meetings. The *banjar* is like a big public caterer. How many pots, how many chairs, how many gas burners will be needed to cook the food? How many pigs have to be killed? How many *sate* sticks have to be whittled?

One night a procession of men marches into the *puri,* each man carrying two woven palm-leaf "shade tiles" that will be used to construct a roof. Under the roof, the men, chopping and cooking all day long, will be protected from the hot sun. Some of the "tiles" will be used to make a second shaded area so the guests who come to the cremation can eat their meals in the shade.

All day for three days, there are women sitting in groups, weaving the offerings, peeling shallots and garlics, making coconut milk by grating hundreds of coconuts and soaking the bits in water and finally squeezing the "milk" out of the shredded "meat."

I peel shallots with the shallot peelers and stay far away from the women grating coconuts; every time I try to grate coconuts, I grate my fingers. The women around me peeling shallots are pleased that I am helping. They do not believe me when I tell them I have always done my own cooking. They assume that anyone with enough money to come to Bali must have a staff of servants back home.

Each woman who spends the day helping is given rice and food to take home to her family. More than one hundred people are fed during each of the three preparation days, and more than five hundred, including guests, on the day of the cremation.

On the second night I take my turn keeping Tu Nini's body company; it can never be left alone. I am sitting there when Tu Man, Tu Aji's architect son, comes over and says, "Rita, listen."

A dog is howling like a wolf. *Aaaaaooooo. Aaaaaooooo.*

"When dogs howl like that, *leyak* are about. They are attracted by the blood of the newly dead."

A few minutes later, Tu Aji tells me that a special ceremony is about to begin. Each member of the immediate family will take a turn cutting a string that symbolically holds Tu Nini's spirit to the earth. It is one way the family says to the spirit that they are ready to let her go. Tu Aji, Tu Biang, and their sons are all called to cut off a piece of the string (divided into six-inch segments by tied-on coins) and throw the snipped segment over their shoulders. I am observing from a distance, moved by the beauty of the ceremony, when I hear my name, and join the immediate family in releasing Tu Nini's spirit.

By the third night, my eyes can barely stay open. All night long there are neighborhood men sitting all over the compound, including outside my room, playing cards, eating the crackers and snacks, smoking the cigarettes, drinking the coffee and tea that the *puri* supplies, and talking loudly. Evil spirits would not dare to come to a place where there is so much activity.

Exhausted by the sleepless nights, I head for my room, about a hundred feet from Tu Nini. No amount of noise will keep me up tonight.

Tu Aji follows me to my patio. "Rita, there is a *kekawin* tonight at three in the morning. I would like you to come."

A *kekawin* is a wondrous thing. Four people sit on mats around a table, each with an open book containing the text of the *Mahabharata,* a sacred Hindu epic poem. They choose a portion of the text and one by one they chant in ancient Sanskrit. The first person sings a few lines in Sanskrit. Then he or she stops and someone sitting off to one side of the table chants the same passage in Balinese, so those who are gathered around will understand it. Occasionally, one of the listeners or singers will halt the process and discuss the meaning of the passage or the nuance of a particular word.

A *kekawin* is a beautiful ceremony, but for me, it is tedious because I don't understand Sanskrit or Balinese, and it can go on and on and on.

I have never said no to Tu Aji. Out of respect, out of curiosity, and because he has a keen sense of what will intrigue and interest me. But I have seen a *kekawin* before; tonight, all I want to do is sleep.

"Tu Aji, I am so tired. I don't know if I can stay awake."

"Don't stay awake," he says. "I will call you when we are ready to begin."

In the middle of the night one of the servants wakes me up. At the *bale,* Tu Aji motions for me to sit next to him on the mat. We are surrounded by protective spears that surround the *bale* and keep the evil spirits away from Tu Nini. The draped white cloth covering the ceiling adds a touch of purity to a solemn event. From where I am sitting I can see the mat-wrapped bundle that is Tu Nini. Tomorrow she will be cremated. Tonight she will be entertained.

The people who will be chanting are seated on mats around a low wooden table. They have finished their coffee and the books are opened. The chanting begins. It sounds like the chant of Torah scholars. Or the call to prayer from the top of a Muslim mosque. Or a Catholic priest intoning Latin to his congregation. The sound is otherwordly and deeply spiritual.

Then the first singer stops and the same passage is sung in Balinese by a man sitting on the other side of Tu Aji. And then the people at the table turn to Tu Aji. There is a pause as Tu Aji turns to me with a smile . . . and chants in English.

Several months after Tu Nini's death, I am making offerings with Dayu Biang, trying to figure out which bit of leaf to weave in next, when my friend Ida Bagus walks in the gate. He and his family live more than an hour away. As soon as I see his face, I know something is wrong.

There are no phones in Kerambitan. My family in the States has instructions to call Ida Bagus or his wife if there is ever a family emergency. They have a phone in their house. They speak English. And they have a car.

The phone call came in the middle of the night. First thing in the morning Ida Bagus has driven over with the news that my father has had a heart attack.

My hands are shaking as I toss some underwear and a change of clothes in a bag. Three hours later I am on a plane. And twenty-eight hours after that I am standing over my father in the hospital. He is pasty white and weak, but he smiles when he sees me.

"Where'd you come from?" he asks.

"Around the corner," I say. "I heard you were sick."

Later that day he slips into a coma, and a few days after that, it is clear that he is not going to make it through the night.

"Dad," I tell him aloud, holding his hand. "You've been a wonderful father and you've lived a good and caring life. If you are ready to leave us, I give you permission. I am certain that your spirit will live on and someday we will meet again. Go in peace. I love you."

I hear myself speaking the words and I realize that I believe them. Tu Aji, Tu Biang, and Tu Nini have helped me accept my father's leaving. I hope my words will help him through his transition.

That night, he dies. When the call comes from the hospital, I find myself wishing there were concrete rituals to help me say good-bye to his spirit and wish it well on its journey, the way there are in Bali. But here there is no body washing, no cutting the spirit loose by symbolically snipping a string. After comforting my mother and calling my brother, I sit up in bed and meditate, creating my own private ritual.

The funeral home is overflowing into the parking lot; there are hundreds of people. My father was a pharmacist on the same corner on the east side of Bridgeport, Connecticut, for fifty-two years. He was "Doc" to all the people whose splinters he removed and the thousands of customers who came in for medical advice. He and my mother were born and lived in one city all of their lives. They are both known and loved for their years of civic leadership.

My mother takes comfort in the outpouring of sympathy, and so do the rest of us. It is a celebration of a life well lived, a person well loved. After the funeral, for a full week, hundreds of people come to the house to comfort my family. There is no neighborhood organization like the Balinese *banjar,* but there is food and the supportive company of friends, family, and community.

As I sit in my mother's living room, surrounded by friends and relatives, I think about the fact that I have chosen to live my life without a community. I will not have hundreds of people at my funeral like my father and Tu Nini. I am overwhelmed by a rush of loneliness. I fear that I have given up something significant.

But as I think about it, I realize that I do have communities; I create them wherever I live. They are not communities of people with whom I have shared experiences over time; but rather, they are communities where I have made new and intense connections. Community is important to me; and my kind of travel does not preclude being a part of a group. In Mexico, it was the backpacker community; in Nicaragua, it was Marco and Doña Juana and their family; in Israel, it was Servas. And in Bali, my community is the *puri.* There is more than one kind of community.

I remain in the U.S. for several months. My mother has Parkinson's; and though she is fully functioning, she cannot live alone. I put a two-by-two-inch ad in three suburban papers, and I post notices in local churches:

> *I am looking for a gentle, intelligent woman to live in and be a companion to my mother, someone who will share her interests in art, classical music, current affairs, and good conversation. Mother is suffering from Parkinson's and cannot drive or cook or take care of her house, but she is still interested in the world, in the community, and in people. If you are interested in meeting and being a friend to someone very special, please call me.*

There are lots of calls and interviews; most of the applicants are all wrong. Then Amparo walks in. She is from Colombia and has five sons and four grandchildren in the area. She is articulate, literary, cultured, and she and my mother click immediately. I stay around for a while, giving support to Amparo and working with my brother, Dick, on taxes, on the house, and on all the bureaucratic paperwork that death carries with it. When I leave, I tell Amparo to keep the place lively. Her children and grandchildren and friends are welcome. Houses need children and healthy people.

I go back to Bali knowing that my brother and his family will be there if there are problems, either major or minor. With Dick, his wife Margaret, and their daughters, Michelle and Danielle, just a few towns over, I feel secure in leaving. And I also have a feeling that my mother is in for new, happy adventures with Amparo.

~~~~

I have been away for three months. During my absence, Tu Aji has bought a refrigerator. The women who cook have no interest in ruining perfectly good food by putting it in a refrigerator. They continue to shop for fresh ingredients just before they cook. And if there is leftover food, they continue to give it away or feed it to the dog. Everyone tells me that food doesn't taste good if it is kept in a refrigerator overnight. I am the only one in the *puri* willing to eat last night's dinner the next day. They are amused at my lack of taste.

Tu Aji has not bought the refrigerator to preserve food. The refrigerator is for making ice. He has been seduced by the iced juices in the tourist restaurants around the island: fresh fruits, like pineapple, banana, and papaya, swirled in a blender with water, sugar, and ice. They are thick and fruity and healthy, and *"enak sekali"* (delicious).

Tu Aji has also bought a blender. And he has instructed his architect-son, Tu Man, to learn how to make juices. An architect, Tu Aji tells me, unlike the women in the kitchen, has mechanical skills.

"Would you like a juice?" he asks me while we are sitting and talking on my patio late one afternoon. And when I say yes, he calls across the courtyard, "Tu Man? Man? Tu Man?"

And from wherever he was, Tu Man arrives and takes his father's order. Then he disappears into the kitchen, where he plugs in the blender. The sound of a machine in the kitchen is new and strange. In this kitchen there have never been machines . . . no blender or processer, no coffee grinder, no toaster. Even rice makers are years away for this family.

When the whirling stops, Tu Man delivers a tall, fruity, icy glass of papaya-banana juice; and then he goes back to the other side of the garden, where he was trimming hedges (with hand-clippers).

Every day Tu Aji has a glass of juice, and each time, he calls for his son, loudly across the courtyard. "Tu Man? Man? Tu Man?" And Tu Man, who is over thirty, arrives to serve his father.

I have been back for two weeks when one evening, Tu Aji, Tu Biang, and I are talking and Tu Aji's craving hits. He wants a juice.

"Ah," he says, "but I remember now that Tu Man is not here. I cannot have it."

I smile, happy for the chance to serve him. "I will make your juice," I offer.

"Do you really know how?" he asks.

"Of course," I say. Then I turn to Tu Biang. "And I will be happy to show you how to do it."

I go to the kitchen and plug in the blender. I look around for Tu Biang but she has gone to her room. I peel and cut some papaya and banana and put it in the container. Then I add water and sugar and ice. Tu Aji is waiting at the table when I bring him his juice.

Later that night Tu Biang joins me on the patio outside my room. "What happened to you?" I say. "I was going to show you how to make juice in the blender."

She giggles. "Rita, you don't understand. If I learn how to make the juice, Tu Aji will stop calling, 'Tu Man? Tu Man?' And he will begin calling, 'Tu Biang? Tu Biang?' Thank you very much, but I don't want to learn."

After a few weeks, I settle into my old routine. I bike to the beach and meditate early each day. I write every morning. And I study Indonesian and read in the afternoons. I usually have lunch and dinner with Tu Aji.

Late one morning, as I am sitting in front of my computer, Dayu Biang hands me a banana-leaf package. There's a sparkle in her eyes as she tells me she has brought me a present.

Yesterday, when I asked her about the kids and the old people I had seen in the rice fields who were "fishing" for dragonflies, she told me how she wishes she were young enough, or old enough, to catch dragonflies again. Then she stopped her chores and we went "fishing" in the yard. Our pole was the spine of a palm leaf, tapered to toothpick-size at one end. The hook was the tarlike sap that came out when she scraped a frangipani tree trunk.

We smeared the thin tip of the spine with the sap and went after dragonflies, who are apparently attracted to it. And when they didn't come to us, we tapped them as they rested on a wire, and they stuck. Dayu removed the wings and skewered the bodies, piling up seven tiny dragonflies on a stick. Fortunately there weren't enough for a meal.

But today, Dayu Biang's nephew spent the morning on assignment in the rice fields; he came home with fifty dragonflies. And while I was writing, Dayu Biang sautéed them in coconut oil with onion, shallots, garlic, hot pepper, and salt. Now she can't wait to watch me eat them.

My friend Dayu Biang, who wouldn't even take a bite of the French toast I made the other day, and who told me a few weeks ago that she wasn't brave enough ("*tidak berani*") to get into my hammock, is awaiting my first crunch of dragonflies with a smirk on her face.

Once, long ago, I ate chocolate-covered ants, but they didn't look any different from chocolate-covered peanuts. The dragonflies in my package look exactly like what they are: wingless dragonflies. I pop one into my mouth and bite into it. It tastes like a crispy vegetable sautéed in garlic and shallots and hot pepper. There's nothing wrong with the taste. It's the tiny legs tickling my tongue that I'm not too fond of. Dayu stands there while I eat the dragonflies like potato chips. I do get her to eat a few.

After I have been back in Bali for four months, I decide to go to the U.S. My brother reports that Mom is doing fine, but I want to see for myself.

United States

CHAPTER TWELVE

BACK IN
THE UNITED STATES

Mom has a new haircut, her nails are painted, and she looks well. She never did discuss feelings with me, nor has she, like most of her generation, shared her pain. This time is no different. She doesn't say anything about how she is adjusting to being without my father, but both she and Amparo tell me about the meetings and lectures and concerts they've attended, the dinner parties they've given, the friends they've shared. Amparo is taping my mother's stories about her life and family, and with my mother's help, she is putting together an album of pictures, with captions.

I don't know if I am projecting or if there really is an excitement in my mother's tone that suggests she is reveling in the companionship of someone, unlike my father, that she does not have to drag to concerts and lectures, sometimes kicking and screaming. She and Amparo are enjoying their time together. At seventy-seven, Mom is experiencing her own version of liberation.

Amparo has hired Gera, an Italian woman from Argentina, to come every Wednesday to do my mother's hair and nails. Sometimes Gera brings her six-year-old daughter, Romina; and while Amparo enjoys a few hours away from the house, Gera and my mom and Romina bake cakes and quiches and make pasta from scratch.

Amparo's children and grandchildren come frequently as well. My mother's house, which had gotten old and stodgy in recent years, is a pulsing, multigenerational community.

I stay in the States for several months, taking care of business, both mine and my mother's, getting health checkups, meeting with my agent and my publishers . . . and most important, catching up with Mitch and Jan. They are both successful journalists in New York. I love seeing them in their adult worlds, wrapped in glamorous, high-profile lives.

Mitch has just reported the inside story of how a drunk motorman caused a subway crash in New York City. (That reporting would help his paper win a Pulitzer Prize.)

Jan is working on the popular gossip column in *New York* magazine called "Intelligencer." She talks to celebrities every day and is building an impressive list of "informants." Jan and Mitch are both interesting and talented people. I enjoy being with them. They have active and full lives; I'm glad I do too. I'm going back to Bali.

Garuda, the Indonesian airline, flies out of Los Angeles to Bali. I decide to stop and visit a friend in L.A. for a week before I return to Bali. On the last day, as I am getting ready to leave for the airport, my mail package from Connecticut arrives at my friend's house. My brother waited until the last minute to send it so that I'd be up-to-date. One of the envelopes contains a telegram from a woman friend in the Netherlands whom I met at the *puri*. It was delivered to my mother's house four days ago. No one noticed it was a telegram, so it was tossed into the Rita pile, to be FedEx'd with everything else.

A second telegram was sent to Jan's address, this one from Tu Biang and her sons. It is in one of those red striped envelopes that says, "Open immediately. Urgent information inside." Or something like that. It was delivered to Jan with the regular mail four days ago, and Jan figured it was a solicitation letter for starving children in Ethiopia or pandas in China, something that could wait a day or two. Her mail package arrived in the same FedEx delivery.

I open both telegrams on the day I am returning to Bali . . . the day of Tu Aji's cremation.

I remember nothing about the twenty-two-hour journey from L.A. to Bali except watery eyes and the recurring thought that something very deep and important has been taken from me. In the taxi riding to Kerambitan, I am disoriented. Everything looks strange; it is as though I have never been here before.

I have no idea what I will find in the *puri*. Tu Aji *is* the *puri*. Tu Aji is Bali. And now, suddenly, he isn't. I am hurt. He knew I was coming back today. Why didn't he wait so I could have said good-bye? Perhaps he knew that I could not have given him permission to leave.

I am dreading my reentry. I won't even have the comfort of the rituals.

They are over. So are the processions. All those things that make death easier. The family has spent the last five days releasing his spirit from this world and wishing him well in the next one. I don't even believe he is dead.

I arrive in Kerambitan from the airport at eleven o'clock at night. The *puri* is full of people. Tu Biang, the nine sons, and all their wives and children are there. And friends and family and two women from the Netherlands who studied with him, one of whom had sent me the telegram I received too late. We all hug and cry. I sleep that night on a mattress on the floor next to Tu Biang and four of her grandchildren.

Three months later I am still in Kerambitan. It is not the same. Without Tu Aji, the essence of the *puri* is gone. But I cannot abandon his family. Tu Biang has said that she feels stronger because I am there; she is frightened that all the westerners who have always come to study with Tu Aji will stop coming. She is right to worry. The intellectual elegance that he brought to the *puri* is gone. I feel his loss intensely. From time to time I am overwhelmed with sadness.

There is a small altar in Tu Aji's library where I can stand among his books and papers, light a stick of incense, and have a conversation. I bring him the chocolate he was not supposed to eat while he was alive. I tell him about ideas I have for books. One day I spend half an hour communicating with Tu Aji, and then I walk out of the library and begin writing. I can't stop. It is as though I am possessed. I'm writing an allegory about animals who live in a banyan tree in Bali. Tu Aji is in it. So am I. We are a mouse and a bird, from opposite ends of the world, who become the best of friends. The words are pouring out of me. I can barely do anything else.

For three weeks I write fiendishly. Then, in the middle of my inspired writing, I get word by mail that I have sold a book to an American publisher. A few hours later, a young man from the village arrives at my patio with two tourists from Germany.

Bali is loaded with tourists, but very few of them ever find their way to Kerambitan, which is nothing more than a comma in the guidebooks. The ones who do have chosen to detour from the recommended itineraries. They're rarely American, usually interesting, and always a touch adventurous. And since I am the only westerner in residence, when tourists appear in the village, they are brought to me. I think of it as holding court in my little part of the palace.

Michael, the German tourist (who is with his mother), has just come from leading a tour on the southern rivers of Irian Jaya, the easternmost province in Indonesia. For a long time I have been wanting to tour Irian

Jaya, the western half of the island of New Guinea. Only two things were lacking: a guide and the money. That day they walked in together. After a dinner of nonstop questions from me, I tell Michael to sign me up for his next trip, which is several months from now.

When he leaves, I try to settle into a routine, but it is difficult; my head is still racing and often disoriented. Sometimes I fill my days with writing. Other times I sit with the women and make offerings. In the early mornings I bike to the beach and walk alone on the black sand, watching the waves and staring out into the vast sea.

In the evenings I often have a young visitor. Wayan is one of the few Kerambitan youths who is brave enough to visit me in the *puri*. At first he comes to practice English, and we talk after dinner for an hour or two a few times a week. Wayan has worked hard on his English, memorizing lyrics, accompanying himself on a guitar as he sings pop American songs. His vocabulary includes the graphic and colorful language of heavy metal and the beautiful romantic words of love songs.

Gradually our friendship deepens and I often ask him for favors, to take me on his motorcycle to the Telecom center at odd hours, or to deliver me to a tourist part of the island where I can watch CNN or eat a Thai dinner. Over the next years, Wayan is one of the most stable parts of my life. Along the way he graduates from a school of tourism and becomes a certified guide. I introduce him to visiting friends, both old and new, and he guides them around the island. He also helps me do the research for a children's book about how rice grows in Bali, whizzing me from one rice field to another on the back of his motorcycle, looking for stages of plant development.

Wayan and I laugh a lot. It is important for me to have a friend outside of the *puri*. There is little laughter these days within. Among the people in Tu Aji's family, I talk most often to Tu Man. He is trying to find out who he is without his father. Most Balinese men his age (thirty-four) are married, but I have never seen Tu Man with a woman. I have never even seen him look at a woman. From time to time he and I go off on his motorcycle to do errands: we buy birds in the bird market in Denpasar (two parakeets die in their paper bags before we get them home); we buy a table for the garden; we buy tiles for the bathroom. We often pass beautiful women, but Tu Man never looks.

Tu Man moves slowly and talks slowly. He spends hours clipping hedges, planting cuttings, thinning flowers. Often in the early morning I see him standing in the garden staring at his plants for long periods of time in a sort of meditation. He is an architect by training, but his love is taking care of the garden and the birds. Unlike his father, whose laughter frequently filled the *puri* with his love of life and his enthusiasm for discovery, Tu Man has a weighty demeanor.

One of the only times I have ever seen Tu Man laughing was when Jan was here. She and I involved him in a cross-cultural comparison of animal noises. Tu Aji was still alive, but he was out for the evening. Tu Man does not speak English, and he has never been interested in learning. So, during the four months Jan was in Bali, they never talked. But one night, Jan and I were sitting at the table after dinner and Tu Man joined us. The night air was filled with the mating calls of frogs. I imitated them with the American version of a frog call.

"What does a Balinese frog say?" I asked Tu Man.

He made a frog sound. "*Dokodokodok.*"

"And a goat?" I said, making an American goat noise. He did a goat in Balinese, "*Mbeek, mbeek.*"

Cats in Bali say, "*Meong, meong.*" Dogs say, "*Ngongkong, ngongkong.*" Pigs, "*eeleng.*" Horses, "*Hiiiiik, hiiiiik.*" Ducks, "*Kwek, kwek, kwek.*"

The three of us laughed and oinked and meowed and meonged and kweked.

In those days, Tu Man didn't mix much with guests. People came to see Tu Aji, and Tu Man was far in the background. That night of animal noises was the only time he ever interacted with Jan.

It is more than two years since the night of the animal noises. Four months since Tu Aji's death. I am leaving again. This time I plan to be in the U.S. for several months. Amparo has written that everything is fine with my mother, but I want to see her. The driver is picking me up at eight in the morning to go to the airport.

At seven I wander over to the kitchen to make myself a cup of coffee. I am sipping it at the table, mentally checking off all the things I have to do before I leave, when Tu Biang joins me. I can tell immediately that something is up. She is carefully dressed and combed, and when she says that Tu Man has asked her to talk to me, her tone is formal. I am nervous; formality does that to me.

Tu Biang is the first to speak. "Last night Tu Man asked me to speak to you before you leave. He would like me to ask you for Jan's hand in marriage."

I never saw it coming.

"If Tu Man married Jan, you and I would be *besan*. I would like that," says Tu Biang with a big smile.

This is not something they arrived at lightly; it is a considered decision. I must be very careful.

"I am honored that Tu Man would like to marry Jan. And you are right. It would be nice if we were *besan*." I laugh. "But I think it would be very difficult. They don't speak the same language, and they hardly know each other. In the West, young people get to know each other before they decide to marry."

"They could learn to love each other," she says. "That is what happened to Tu Aji and me."

At this point Tu Man joins us. He has waited an appropriate amount of time. Now it is his turn to talk to me, with his mother present.

I speak first. "Tu Man, I am honored that you would like to marry my daughter. I am also surprised. You have talked to me many times about the difficulties of an East-West marriage. Have you changed your mind?"

"I thought about it," he says. "And I realized that it is not the same for everyone. We are all different people. I would give her freedom. If she wanted to live in the United States for six months, that would be all right with me."

"But if she married you, she would want you to be with her."

"Oh, I couldn't do that. I have to be here."

"You know that more than 50 percent of the marriages in the United States end in divorce . . . and usually the woman is given custody of the children."

Tu Man is taken aback by the thought that his children might not belong to him. After a moment of silence, he says, in a voice deep with wisdom, "Well, if divorce happened, she could have one of the children and I would keep the other."

I smile and take his hand. "I am honored by your proposal. I will ask Jan and write you a letter."

I go back to my room and pack my Indonesian dictionary.

The first thing I do when I get to my mother's house is call Jan and tell her that a prince has asked her hand in marriage. Her response is, "Mom, what did you say?"

It takes me two days to write the letter. In very polite Indonesian I explain to Tu Man that I feel very sad because his offer has come when Jan is just beginning a new job and she cannot leave. "It is the American custom that young people get to know each other over a period of many months before they decide to marry. Because Jan and Tu Man (in Indonesian one uses the name of the person rather than "you") are unable to get to know each other first, I cannot give my permission for the marriage."

I hope he understands.

My mother's Parkinson's is getting worse. She needs twenty-four-hour care. Amparo can no longer do the job alone.

I also discover that most of my mother's friends do not come any more. For most of her life, she was a leader in the community and the family member that everyone turned to. But her spirit has dimmed, her body is in the process of giving up, and I suspect it is too difficult for her colleagues and friends to witness her physical deterioration. Americans do not deal well with illnesses. People call and talk to Amparo (or me if I am there), but most of them cannot look at Mom's tiny, weak body, though her mind is still sharp and alert. My mother is a gentle soul; she understands and forgives them.

The Hispanic community, like the Balinese community, comes from a different tradition, one that is loving and attentive to the older generation. My mother's new community is Amparo's family and Gera's and their friends. From time to time I hear Mom greeting someone with *"Buenos días."* I think she's enjoying the attention and the challenge.

Amparo tells me about Claudia, a friend of the family who lives in Colombia. She's in her twenties, dying to come to the U.S., and . . . she's a nurse. Who cares if she can't speak English. She'll learn.

The process of getting Claudia a work visa is long and complicated. It will take four months to get permission to bring her to the States. During those months I have a secret personal plan. I am going to train for the next leg of my journey: trekking in the mountains of Irian Jaya.

Eventually I'll go back to Bali, but not yet. The fire that drew me to the *puri* is no longer burning. My friend, my teacher, my prince is gone.

Indonesia

CHAPTER THIRTEEN

IRIAN JAYA: THE HIGHLANDS

T he day Michael, the German guide, walked into the *puri* was the day I decided to visit Irian Jaya. By the time he left, I had set the date. One dinner and a lot of questions was all it took.

Irian Jaya is the western half of the island of New Guinea. I plan to get myself to the town of Wamena in the Baliem Valley, where, according to the guidebook, there are tons of guides available for treks into the mountains. I am setting aside three weeks for trekking in the highlands.

Then I'm going to meet Michael, and his group of two German men, in Wamena, and we'll go south together. It will be the first tour I've ever taken, but it's a tough trip to do on your own; you need guides and boats and places to stay in remote villages.

I tell no one about my secret plan to work on my body, but I'm very excited about it. I have resolved to diet, exercise, and work out with weights. I can close my eyes and see my new, lean, aerobically fit body, and I love it. For the first time in my life I am going to be one of those people I have read about, who hike at home for weeks, carrying weighted packs on local hills before they go off for their mountain treks. I image my new body and my increased energy, and it feels good. It's a kind of self-blackmail. By choosing to go to the highlands, I am tricking myself into shape.

Except, I don't do any of it. I never join a gym, I don't diet, and I walk four times the week before I leave. That's it.

Sometimes I really don't understand me. I have put on a lot of weight since Mexico and I hate looking in mirrors. Photographs are even worse. Damn. Even when I set up a situation where I *have* to do it, I don't. I have a lot to learn about facing physical challenges. When I board the plane, I am still overweight and out of shape.

The customs man at the airport in Jayapura, the capital of Irian Jaya, is about forty years old, handsome in his khaki uniform, broad shouldered with soft wavy black hair. He is wearing a nametag.

"*Selamat pagi, Pak Sutrisna. Apa kabar?*" Good morning, Mr. Sutrisna. How are you?

He smiles at me. "You speak Indonesian."

"Yes. I've been living in Bali."

"I can hear your Balinese accent. Where are you going?"

"Wamena," I answer.

The line behind me is at least twenty deep. Pak Sutrisna and I continue to chat. The next people in line, an American couple, are directing nasty comments toward me. The customs official doesn't care. This is his territory; he can do what he wants. And what he wants to do is talk to me.

"I'm sorry the airport is such a mess," he says. "When you come back, we'll be in the new terminal." He looks at my feet. "Those are beautiful boots. Will you sell them to me?"

My boots are leather and he's right, they *are* beautiful. I put them on for the first time this morning.

"I can't sell them to you. I bought them for my trek."

"When you come back, then, after your trek, I would like to buy them."

"They are very, very expensive. They are probably the most expensive boots in the world."

"I want them," he says. "How much?"

"I paid 250 U.S. dollars."

"Please come see me when you get back."

I smile. In Indonesia, it isn't polite to say no.

At first, I think that it would be impossible for him to find enough money to buy these boots. A starting government worker makes fifty dollars a month. But then I remember: he's in customs, one of the most lucrative jobs in any developing country. "You must pay an extra twenty dollars to bring in diving equipment," he can tell a tourist, and the tourist will pay. "That will be ten dollars tax for the video camera." "There is a fee if you want to bring in the computer."

If you protest, the customs guys can keep you sitting on a bench for hours. In the end, you'll probably pay. You can't appeal to his boss, because the boss is getting a cut. You don't have any recourse, unless you speak the language. Then you just make a joke out of it and everybody laughs.

Maybe Pak Sutrisna will start his boot account this minute with the angry people behind me. They are carrying big bags filled with wetsuits, regulators, and expensive electronic depth-safety computers. There is no official charge for bringing these things in. But these tourists don't know that. Besides, anger is *never* rewarded in Indonesia.

So, on second thought, I realize it is likely that Pak Sutrisna will have the money for my boots in less than a week. Perhaps by the end of the day.

He gives me his card. "Come see me when you get back."

(I don't. I wonder what he did with the money.)

I check into a motel near the airport. Tomorrow I will take another plane to Wamena. There are more than 250 tribes in Irian Jaya, many in the highlands around Wamena, each with its own customs and language. Many are still living the lives their ancestors lived, still using stone implements, hunting with bows and arrows, growing yams on the sloping hillsides. The western world didn't even know there were people tucked into the mountains until a seaplane landed on a lake in 1938.

Today, with the ill-conceived blessing of the United Nations, the western half of New Guinea is a province of Indonesia, though the people share neither race nor history with the other Indonesians. The natives are black, of Melanesian descent, with curly hair and features similar to those of the aboriginal people of Australia. They share a race and history with the people of Papua New Guinea, the independent country that is the eastern half of the island.

The Indonesians, on the other hand, are light brown with straight hair, and they are thought to be of Polynesian descent. Wherever you go in the towns and cities of Irian Jaya, there are "straight-haired" people. They are the soldiers, sent by the government, many of whom consider the natives savages and animals. They are the police, who are said to beat up the indigenous people for fun. They are the transmigrants, whom the government is bringing over by the thousands from other islands. And the businesspeople, who are nearly all from somewhere else. Irian Jaya feels like an occupied land.

The indigenous people talk of massacres and land theft and destruction of holy places. They are angry. Some talk about amassing guns and infiltrating the police. But logic suggests that the Indonesian government will win. The government is the police and the army; the arsenals are theirs.

My next-door neighbors in the motel are three women. Ursula and Teresia are from Austria, both single and in their thirties. Their friend, Elsa, is a white woman from Namibia. The three of them met in Borneo a couple of years ago. We are all planning to trek in the highlands, and we're booked on the same flight to Wamena.

We arrive at the departure terminal early. So do dozens of other travelers. The room is small and crowded, stuffed with mostly European backpackers. Indonesian is the only language coming over the screeching audio system that squashes the words until they come out an incoherent jumble of sounds. I can't understand a word.

The time for our flight comes and goes. The flight doesn't. No one knows what's happening; all we know is that none of the scheduled flights is taking off.

I climb through the bodies and backpacks that are flopped and strewn all over the floor and find my way to a uniformed man in an office. I lean in, smiling. "*Selamat siang, Pak. Apa kabar?*" Good day, sir. How's it going?

Teri—his name is pinned to his khaki shirt—smiles. "You speak Indonesian. Please sit down. Where are you from?"

"Originally from America," I say. "But I have been living in Bali for a number of years. And you?"

"I'm from Sumatra," Teri answers.

I ask him what his job is, and he tells me that he is the man in charge of flight scheduling. Bingo!

While the noise of chaos spills through the door, we talk about families, lives, and jobs. After about ten minutes of chatting (one never goes straight for the heart), I ask about the flights into Wamena.

"*Pintu tutup,*" he smiles. The door is shut, meaning clouds are covering the gap in the mountains that leads into the valley. There will be no flights today. There had been none the day before. The passengers are accumulating.

"Maybe tomorrow. We never know," he says. "Sometimes the clouds lift for just an hour. We're only half an hour away, but clouds are unpredictable. As soon as we get the call, we take off. Your ring is very beautiful," he adds.

"Thank you," I say and stretch my hand out so he can see it close up.

Two days' worth of people, six flights' worth of passengers will be carried over into a third day. The logistics of getting everyone out is mind boggling. As far as I know, there are no extra planes, and each new day brings three new full flights for possible cancellation. It is going to be chaotic when the "door" finally opens.

Teresia, Ursula, Elsa, and I find a Chinese restaurant for dinner and talk until midnight. The next day we are back in the airport with three days' worth of waiting passengers. I stick my head back into the office. "Good morning, Teri, how are you?"

"*Rita, selamat pagi. Silahkan, duduk.*" Good morning. Please, sit down.

We talk some more . . . about Bali, about America, about my beautiful ring that I bought in Bali for two dollars.

The call comes in while I am sitting there. The clouds have lifted. The first plane in three days will take off immediately. "I have three friends with me," I say as I hand him the ring.

"Go quickly to the desk over there and give them this paper." He writes some numbers down. Please come see me when you get back. Maybe we can have dinner."

"Sure," I say. "We're engaged now."

I don't think he gets it, but we laugh, shake hands, and nod heads. The plane, with the four of us among the passengers, takes off a few minutes later.

When we get to Wamena, we arrange the trek. Like Edmund Hillary before he climbed Mount Everest, we assemble our team: Merinus, the guide; a cook; five porters (one for each of us and one for the cook). Because I speak Indonesian we are able to hire a non-English-speaking guide at half the price of the bilingual guides.

I warn the other women that I am seriously out of shape. I dread the thought that I might hold everyone back, but they are not bothered. Two days after we arrive in Wamena, we begin our trek. Oh, God, I think, remembering that other mountain in Mexico, a mite compared to the monsters I was about to tackle. What am I doing here? Why didn't I train?

I am helpless and irresponsible in the physical fitness department, but I am well prepared in the equipment department. My boots, the ones Pak Sutrisna covets, are the best. I bought them the morning of the day I left

Connecticut, after I got a phone call from a friend of a friend. She had just returned from Irian Jaya, where she and her boyfriend had gone trekking. He'd had the kind of boots I had already bought, Gor-tex and suede, guaranteed waterproof. His feet had been wet, blistered, and sore. She, on the other hand, had bought the finest-waterproof-leather-triple-bladdered-two-hundred-fifty-dollar-boots. And her feet had been dry. Two hours before I left for the airport, I rushed out to the nearest Eastern Mountain Sports store, and I bought the best boots they had.

I had already been talked into the best backpack. "Surely you aren't planning to cut expenses on something so important as your body?" said the salesman. It took us an hour to find the perfect pack for my size.

On the day we begin our trek, my personal porter comes to my hotel room. While I am lacing up my finest-waterproof-leather-triple-bladdered-two-hundred-fifty-dollar boots, he slings my treasured backpack over one shoulder, and we take off for the mountains. He is barefoot.

Our first day's trek is only slightly uphill, and most of it is along a dirt road through cleared areas. I am last in line, but pleased that I'm able to stay more or less within sight of the others.

Along the way we meet giggly shy girls, and boys in bunches. Merinus teaches us a greeting and we call out whenever we see someone. The young people speak Indonesian, so I can communicate with the ones who are brave enough to talk to me.

Most of the women and girls we meet are bare breasted. All of them are carrying a *noken,* a bag that they weave from the bark of trees. Some *noken* are three feet long, and they stretch out more than that from side to side. Some women are carrying two or three. We meet women who are carrying yams in their *noken.* And baby pigs. And babies nested on a pile of leaves. The woven handle of the *noken* goes over the forehead, sort of like a headband with a big bag attached. The bag hangs down the back.

We meet men, some in shorts, others wearing only *horim,* penis gourds. The *horim,* hollow gourds that look like long carrots, some more than a foot long, slip over the penis and are attached at the top by one string that ties around the waist, and at the bottom by another string that loops around the scrotum. The men grow the gourds, shaping them as they grow. There are actually fashions in *horim.* Some men like them narrow and long; others prefer a crooked one. And most men have several for various occasions, or perhaps moods. The gourds point straight up in the air like a permanent erection.

We meet more pigs than people. They're all over, snorting, untethered, and frequently trailed by piglets.

Every once in a while, we come upon someone selling cooked yams or, less often, pineapples. Then we sit and eat and talk and smile as the locals gather around to watch.

Before sundown, we arrive at the village where we are going to sleep. We spread our mats and sleeping bags in the wooden community house while our cook fixes a dinner of rice and vegetables. As we are eating, a group of men waits outside the door, peeking in. When we finish, they take us to a hut where there is a fire in the middle of the room. The men sit on one side of the fire and we sit on the other. They are all a deep chocolate brown color, with curly, dark hair and handsome, chiseled bone structure. They are wearing beads and bones and feathers around their necks. Some of the men are wearing shorts. Others, including the chief, are wearing *horim*.

Our two groups sit looking at each other: the men from the village, about ten of them, and the four of us women. Our guides are behind us. No one is speaking.

I am not sure if they all understand Indonesian, but I know that the chief and the school teacher do; they introduced themselves to us when we first entered the village. I decide to make a little speech telling them how honored we are to be here in their village. I tell them our names and where we are from. Then I turn to my Austrian and Namibian companions and ask them if they know any English songs. They do.

"We would like to sing some songs," I say.

We begin with "You Are My Sunshine" and continue with "Oh, What a Beautiful Morning" and "Home, Home on the Range." After the final "And the skies are not cloudy all day," we stop. The hut is now packed with men and women and children. Our voices have drawn a crowd. Everyone is smiling.

I direct my smile at the village chief. "Now," I say in Indonesian, "it is your turn."

The men huddle. Then they spread out and begin to sing. First they sing a church song. (The missionaries have been here before us.) Then another hymn. Their voices are strong and beautiful. Then they sing a traditional tribal song with percussive sounds and hisses and huffs and humming. There are voices that echo and voices that sing out a beat behind the music. There is a glow in their faces as they sing.

The tribal song is long. It is coming from the depths of their heritage.

I am moved to tears. Here I am in the mountains of Irian Jaya and the local tribesmen are singing to me. And I am singing to them. I ask them to teach us their song.

They laugh to hear us trying to hiss and hum and huff with our voices.

Then we sing "Old MacDonald," and we all laugh as we make cow and pig and duck noises; and then we teach our silly song to them. For more than an hour, we sing and laugh and learn from each other.

The second day, we enter the jungle, with its massive trees, twisting vines, raging brooks, spectacular orchids, and butterflies in iridescent colors. Squawking cockatoos and strange-looking hornbills fly over us. The earth smell mixes with the smells of green bushes, lush moss, and flowering plants in every color. And the harsh song of the cicadas offers the background buzz to birds and insects competing for the airwaves.

The bad news is that I have to jump from stone to stone across brooks, and traverse log bridges that span rocky wet gullies. I do not jump well; and log bridges, without ropes to hold onto, terrify me. When everyone else has crossed, one of the porters steps onto the log, reaches his hand out for me to hold, and I inch my way across, my knees shaking wildly in direct proportion to the distance and danger level of the fall. If I really did lose my balance, there's no way that hand could save me. We'd go down together.

The other part of mountain climbing that I do not like is the climbing. I am not trudging up this vertical monster because "it's there." I am doing it because this is the only way I can meet the people who live in these mountains. I am not a happy climber. I'm always miles behind everyone else, sweating, panting, and hurting. Ursula has volunteered to walk with me. She is a phys. ed. teacher in Austria and very patient. One of the things she does is teach high school students how to climb mountains.

There are near-vertical inclines made of pebbles and rocks, the kind that slide out from under my boots.

"Slowly, slowly," Ursula repeats hundreds of times. "Go very slowly. Watch where you put your foot. Every step you must watch."

"Oh, my God!" I groan, looking up at the incline.

"Don't look up," says Ursula.

I keep apologizing. "Don't worry about it," she says. "If I climb slowly, it gives me more time to look around."

"Don't stop. Take short steps. Walk slowly, slowly."

The slope goes straight up.

"There's no hurry. That's great. You're doing great. Good. Good."

"Very, very small steps. Like an escargot. Don't stop. Don't look up."

After about two hours, I hate her.

When we reach the steepest slope of the day, she says, "Don't look up. You're doing wonderful. When we get to the top, I'm going to give you some Swiss chocolate."

How could I hate her?

On the third day every muscle of my body is aching. I'm in agony just getting in and out of my sleeping bag. And this is the day of the stiles, things I thought existed only in nursery rhymes (the crooked man who found a crooked sixpence upon a crooked stile). Stiles separate property and make it easier for people to climb over fences. You have to climb up crooked posts, throw a leg over the top, and then climb or jump down. In the best of times I don't climb or jump very well. And now, every move hurts. How I wish that I were not wearing my fabulous-two-hundred-fifty-dollar-very-heavy boots (Ursula and Teresia are in sneakers). Though I'm just as sure that if I weren't wearing them, I'd have a twisted ankle.

For the entire six days of our trek, the evening entertainment is the same. We have no choice. Each time we arrive in a village for the night, advance notice of our singing has preceded us. There must be couriers running through the mountains calling out the news of our traveling minstrel show.

Our act gets better and funnier. As we discover other songs we have in common, like "Eentsy Weentsy Spider" and "I'm a Little Teapot," we add to our repertoire. Each evening, soon after I drag myself into a new village, ready to collapse, wanting never to move again, a new crowd assembles, and once again, the four white women from the world beyond the clouds blend our voices, our laughter, our joy, with our gentle dark-skinned hosts of the highlands. And somewhere, wrapped in the music, we become one.

When we get back to Wamena, I still have two weeks before I have to meet Michael for our tour of the south. I ask Merinus to take me, alone, to a small, interesting village, by public transportation. I want to stay in one place for at least four days, long enough to learn some names and play with the kids.

Before we leave, Merinus and I load up on food: a dozen cans of sardines, five packages of crackers, rice, carrots, cabbage, green leaves, string beans, garlic, noodles, soy sauce, tangerines, coffee, condensed milk. And bottles of water. We buy enough food to feed a family for a week. Merinus carries it.

The ride from Wamena at six in the morning is spectacular. Whichever way I look, there are mountain peaks with white fluffy sashes around their middles. I must admit that viewing the landscape out of a van window where I can focus on the scenery instead of on my feet is spiritually and physically very satisfying.

The village consists of four wooden houses, seventeen round thatched huts called *honai,* and a church. The head of the church, whom I call Bapak, which means father and mister, is wearing khaki pants and a blue T-shirt. A local man, not a missionary, he welcomes us and offers us a choice: we can sleep in his wooden house or in a *honai.* I tell him that I would like to know what it is like to sleep in a *honai.*

He offers us a cup of coffee, and I open a package of crackers and a can of sardines to share. Pita, his eight-year-old daughter, comes in carrying her two-and-a-half-year-old sister. The girls are bright-eyed, with loving smiles and runny noses. Mom is sitting outside on a tree stump with her head down.

"Is your mother sick?" I ask Pita.

"Yes," she answers. "Malaria."

A few minutes later, Bapak invites me to go for a walk, just the two of us. The path is level, the giant roots and massive boulders, minimal. I am moving along well until I step into a muddy hole . . . and begin to sink. My weighted feet will not pull out. Soon I am up to my knees in mud. I have visions of sinking deeper and deeper until the tips of my waving fingers go under, but Bapak saves me. He hands me one end of a branch and pulls me out.

Just before the path begins a steep descent, Bapak suggests we sit and talk.

"I was a fighter in the OPM," he begins. Organisasi Papua Merdeka is the organization formed to fight for the freedom of the Papuans, against the Indonesians.

The native people of Irian Jaya call themselves Papuans, like their brothers on the eastern half of the island. Through a complex series of political decisions, this western half of the island of New Guinea was officially given to Indonesia by the United Nations in 1962. Part of the deal was that by 1969, Indonesia had to give the natives a chance to determine if they wanted independence. In a vote that is generally considered to have been a joke, a handpicked group of "elders" unanimously decided to become part of Indonesia.

The OPM fought for independence; they wanted nothing to do with Indonesia. The worst of the battles were in the mid-seventies. Bapak was one of the leaders.

"When we knew we were going to lose, many of my friends ran across the border to Papua New Guinea. But I was afraid that if I ran, the Indonesians would kill my family. We hid in the forest for many months, hunting for our food and frightened for our lives. Today, the retaliation is over, but the Indonesians treat us like animals. We have nothing in common with 'those people with straight hair.' My people want to be a part of Papua New Guinea, not Indonesia. Someday we will fight for and win our freedom."

"But Bapak, Indonesians are the police, the army, the businesses, the government workers, and many of the teachers. The government is filling your island with workers and transmigrants until the Papuans are no longer a majority. How can you win a fight against Indonesia?"

"We have a very strong belief that we are right. No one knows our mountains and valleys the way we do. And we are also building up an arsenal and experience, and we already know where the government stores its weapons. In the last years many Papuans have joined the army and the police."

As we walk back to the village, all I can think of is the power of the Indonesian army, the militias, and the police against the Papuan natives.

At dinnertime, we crawl through the three-by-two-foot door into the *honai*. The wooden floor is covered with grass and there is a fire burning split wood in the middle of the room. It looks as though the fire has been built on a thick layer of ashes that is protecting the wood floor. Above the fire is a four-post structure with horizontal beams, and hanging from the beams, cooking our rice, is a large metal pot.

Ours is the biggest of the seventeen *honai* in the village, with about a fifteen-foot diameter. It used to be the men's house, but now the men go somewhere else, so Bapak's family uses it.

Merinus and I brought the rice and vegetables that we are going to eat; we are nine for dinner. A few more people arrive while we are eating, including the chief of the village, who wears a knitted ski hat and a *horim*, both of which are symbols of his station. All the other men are wearing shorts. And the women are wearing blouses or dresses. The chief sits with us for about half an hour, long enough to eat, talk, and smoke. When he goes home, we all curl up and go to sleep.

Sort of. There are nine of us on the grassy floor: Bapak, three women, three children, Merinus, and I. There are sneezes, snores, coughs, a still-crackly fire, and critters on the thatched roof. At some point in the middle of the night, a little girl, no more than six, climbs in the door, curls up on the floor, and goes to sleep. Where is she coming from in the middle of the night?

I twist, wiggle, change positions, scratch, and dwell on mosquitoes, pig fleas, and malaria. Three of the four adults who are sleeping across from me have had malaria attacks within the last year. Bapak's attack was so bad he had to go to the hospital. Bapak's wife is currently in the middle of an attack. I have never spoken to the fourth person; nor have I asked Merinus if he suffers from it. Nearly everyone does. It will be a miracle if I get off this island malaria-free. (I do.)

All night I am haunted by the image of children with distended stomachs. I can not get their shapes out of my mind. More than half of the young children in this village look as though they are pregnant. The condition, called kwashiorkor, is caused by a diet low in calories, high in starch, and seriously deficient in protein. Some of the other visual symptoms are dry skin, and reddish-orange discoloration of hair. Kwashiorkor can also lead to stunted mental development. In one of the mountain villages during our trek I talked to a teacher who told me that the kids were hard to teach because their brains were affected by malnutrition.

The simple addition of powdered skim milk to the diet could reverse the disease. But who would buy and distribute the milk? And educate the people on how to use it? What about beans and rice? Or chickens and eggs? Or goats? Or cows? Who cares about these people of the clouds, high in the hills of Irian Jaya? Certainly not the Indonesian government.

I have no idea what time it is when the rain starts, but the thatched roof leaks, badly. I wriggle around in my sleeping bag, feeling and looking like a giant worm, until I find a spot where only my feet are being dripped upon. Then I pull my knees up to my chest and fall asleep.

The next day, after we eat boiled yams and corn baked in the fire, I decide to write down some of my thoughts, but there is no place where I can be alone. Every time I sneak off to a quiet spot, I am surrounded by kids. Bapak gives me permission to go into the church, which is on a hill about one hundred meters from his house.

"The children are not permitted to enter unless I am there," he tells me. "If you are in the church, they will leave you alone."

The church is a wooden building, painted white, with a corrugated metal roof, by far the biggest structure in the area. The dimensions of the sanctuary are about thirty by fifty feet with a twenty-foot ceiling. The building is less than a year old. Bapak told me that they raised money to pay for it by having a giant 250-pig feast. People came from all over the island.

I sit in a pew and begin to write. Within seconds I see the bobbing silhouettes of heads and hands in the windows. And I hear giggling. My hideout has been discovered. Before long all the windows have bouncing heads. I ignore my audience. I desperately need these minutes alone to think about the last two weeks. They have been extraordinary. Singing, sharing meals, holding babies. *Horim,* naked breasts, laughing children, malaria, cookfires, river baths, kwashiorkor, pigs, yams, *honai.* The people I have met have been overwhelming and wonderful. We are from opposite ends of the spectrum of human life on earth, but we share a core that makes us human. I have known kindness, generosity, gentleness, and warmth from everyone I have met.

Later that afternoon, I sit down with a group of kids and ask them to sing me some songs. They sing a hymn. Then I teach them, in Indonesian, one of my favorite kids' songs, which I have heard Balinese children singing, "If you're happy and you know it, clap your hands." For nearly an hour we sing to each other, laughing, miming, being silly. When we finish singing, everyone wants to hold my hand as we walk toward home.

I find it hard to say good-bye. Everyone in the village sends me off with hugs and waves and smiles. I am returning to Wamena to say good-bye to Ursula, Teresia, and Elsa, who have been trekking. Tomorrow they leave for Bali.

When I go to the airport to see them off, I decide that since I still have a week before I have to meet Michael, I am going to find another village to live in. But this time I want to go alone. The first time I was with a team. This last time with Merinus. Now I'm ready to go on my own.

Before I leave the airport, I stop off at the MAF (Missionary Aviation Fellowship) terminal. The office is packed with indigenous people signing up to get on flights for immediate takeoff. There are no tourists in the chaos. It's worth a try.

I load up on food, pack a few clothes, and go back to the terminal. I want to go someplace, anyplace, deep in the mountains, where it will be just me and the villagers. I have eight days before my tour with Michael begins.

Sorry, I'm told at the desk, reservations must be made long in advance.

As I'm trying to figure out how to get around the system, I meet Yarit, a man who has been in Wamena for a month with his three-year-old son and a young man from his village. A month ago, the child was watching someone in his village cut brush when the little boy got too close to the knife. His eye was slashed. The missionaries flew him, his father, and a cousin to Wamena, where the injured eye was removed. Now they are on their way home. There is no eye patch, just a hole and what looks like an ooze. I hope it's ointment.

"My first son got sick and died," says Yarit. "And now this." He hugs his little boy. Then he looks at me through the hug. "Why don't you come with us to our village? There is room for you in our plane. It's a Cessna that seats five. We are three, the pilot is four, and you could be five. The plane will take us to Holuwon. From there, we will walk together to my village."

Why not?

I sit in front with the pilot, an American missionary in his early thirties. We fly between mountains, curving as the mountains curve, close to the ground, past waterfalls and rivers, cliffs and thick forests.

After about thirty minutes, a field appears. The pilot puts the wheels down at the bottom of a hill, and he stops the plane by rolling up.

When we are on the ground, I ask about a return flight in six days.

"Today is the eleventh. There's a flight ordered for here on the eighteenth," he tells me.

I am supposed to meet Michael on the nineteenth. It could work.

"But we're only honoring 20 percent of our requests right now. We've got a lot of planes being repaired. And a lot of flights are cancelled because of clouds. If you want to be absolutely certain that you'll be in Wamena on a particular date, you better come back with me right now."

I just got here. I'm not leaving. Within minutes, he is gone.

The whole village of Holuwon has come to meet the plane. Yarit tells them I am going to walk with him to his village.

The teacher of the Holuwon school, Bapak Guru, introduces himself to me. "That walk is very difficult," he says. "There is a six-inch-wide bridge over a river with a rope to hold onto. It sways back and forth as you walk across."

The Indonesian word for "sways back and forth" sounds exactly like the act it describes, *goyong-goyong*. It scares me just to hear the word.

"If I have a hand to hold, I can probably do it."

"It is a one-person bridge," says Bapak Guru. "And there's another place on the walk where you have to put your back against the hill and walk sideways for a long time." He demonstrates, stepping sideways as though the path is no bigger than his feet. "In front of you the mountain drops off; that's why you have to go sideways."

I can feel the panic rising inside me just hearing about it.

"We would be very happy to have you stay with us in Holuwon," says the teacher. "You can stay in my house with me, my wife, and our three children."

Feeling just a little bit suspicious, I ask Yarit if it really is true about the bridge and the drop-off. He confirms it. I'm staying in Holuwon.

The teacher's wife is sweet and young, probably about twenty-three. The kids are seven, four, and one and a half. The youngest was adopted when her mother died in childbirth. I write down and memorize everyone's name. Two of the three children have distended bellies. I have brought enough food, rice, noodles, vegetables, tangerines, and powdered milk to feed all of us for a week. My first night there I cook rice and vegetables. The kids eat as though they are starving.

Bapak Guru is from a distant village and another tribe; he has no land in Holuwon so he cannot grow anything. The family is dependent upon whatever the schoolchildren bring to the teacher. Bapak Guru tells me that he graduated from junior high school, which qualifies him to teach.

The next morning I walk with him to the one-room schoolhouse. There are twenty-two kids in the room from class one to class four. Five girls, probably between twelve and fourteen, fully developed and topless, sit in the back of the room. They are wearing beaded plastic necklaces and grass skirts. Last week there were six; one of them just got married.

The school day begins with Bapak Guru asking if anyone has brought him food. Five children hand him yams; another gives him a bunch of green leaves.

Then come two hymns and a prayer. One of the main jobs of the missionaries in Irian Jaya is to give the people religion in their own tribal languages. Hymns and the Bible and the prayers are translated and taught in the local languages.

Bapak Guru holds a rattan stick in his hand as he calls the roll. Two girls who were absent last week are hit on the legs. Three of the younger students giggle and are hit on their heads.

Time for math.

Bapak Guru opens a book (the students do not have books, only notebooks) and copies onto the blackboard, 125 × 5.

"What is it?" he asks.

No one answers. He writes the answer without comment, and then writes, 12 × 2. Again, no answers.

Twenty-four in Indonesian is *dua puluh empat.* Bapak Guru says, slowly, *"Dua puluh em..."*

"Pat," says the class.

25 × 3. No answers. Seventy-five is *tujuh puluh lima.*

"Tujuh puluh li..."

"Ma," says the class. And so it goes for other examples, each one copied from the book.

There are no explanations of how to do the calculations until he puts on the board, 126 × 7. And he writes the answer, 862, and goes about showing how you can prove that your answer is right. Except he can't because it isn't. He spends ten minutes facing the board, trying to figure out where he made his mistake, and finally he gives up in frustration and puts seventeen new examples (from the book) on the board and tells the class to do the calculations in their notebooks.

"Whoever doesn't do these gets the rattan," he says, and he leaves to go to his house for some coffee.

I stay in the classroom and watch the students write the examples in their notebooks. They can write numbers, but only one girl can do the math.

When Bapak Guru returns, he sends everyone outside to cut grass and go home.

In the afternoon I tell Bapak Guru that I would like to try to arrange for a flight out next week. If I'm going to meet Michael on the nineteenth in Wamena, I have to get a secure flight out of here. Today is only the twelfth, but if I wait for the scheduled flight on the eighteenth, and clouds close the door, I won't make it. So far, all I've seen are clouds. Ideally, I'd like to book a flight for the sixteenth or seventeenth, with the eighteenth as backup.

On the far side of the airstrip is a wooden hut; and inside the hut, a man is sitting in front of a ham radio system. He looks happy to have something to do. He calls the dispatcher, Mr. Naftali, who tells us there is a plane scheduled for tomorrow, the thirteenth, for two villages over. It will be returning to Wamena with two empty seats. If the weather is good, they will come and get me.

I would rather not leave so soon. "Do you have anything the next day?"

He doesn't. And the flight on the eighteenth has been cancelled.

I book for tomorrow, Friday the thirteenth. Now I have to hope the clouds will disappear.

"I will pray for you," says Bapak Guru.

"So will I," says the man operating the radio.

Can't hurt.

That night I cook vegetables and rice again. Earlier I asked Bapak Guru to see if he could find some eggs that I could buy. I am desperate to put some protein into these kids. Just before the rice is ready, a man arrives with three eggs. I scramble them with a fork, make a hole in the middle of the stir-fried vegetables, and add the raw eggs, mixing them in when they're cooked. After dinner, I give everyone a tangerine. Yesterday I saw an orange tree filled with oranges. Bapak Guru said they were sour and no one will eat them; there is no sugar in the village. When we are finished eating, the kids go outside to play. There is laughter and screeching and sounds of joy.

"Listen," says the mother to me, "the children are laughing. Listen," she calls to her husband. "They are laughing."

"It is because they have full stomachs," he says.

Later, as we sit on mats around the fire, the children cuddle in close. There is one child for each adult. As I hold the baby, I sing a lullaby. Ibu (mother) responds with a song of her own. Like an exotic stringed instrument, she "plays" her voice, vibrating it in a repetitive chant, a soft wail that sounds otherworldly, as if it is coming from another dimension. Like everyone else around the fire, I close my eyes and rock to hypnotic sounds that I have never heard before.

In the early morning our mountain is buried in a cloud. After a breakfast of yams, Ibu and I stand outside in the cold. Some neighbors are standing nearby, watching us. I am wearing my fleece jacket. The locals, every one of them, are standing with their arms wrapped around their naked chests, trying to conserve body heat.

I tell Ibu that I thought her song last night was very beautiful and that the sounds she made were amazing. She tells me that she likes to *main mulut,* which means, literally, "play mouth."

Then, as we stand in the cold morning air, Ibu begins to *main mulut* again. She makes gutteral sounds and vibrating sounds, sounds that seem to swish through her throat and out through her teeth, sounds that click somewhere deep inside, and sounds that flap unseen bits of her vocal passage and come out trilling. Our concert ends with a spectacular call that is similar to a Swiss yodel.

"I used to call to my father from one mountain to another with that," she says. "And he would answer me."

My plane is scheduled for late morning. At seven, the fog is dense. Visibility is about ten feet. Then, around ten, the clouds disappear. I pack my bag, which is much lighter without the food, and most of the village follows me down to the airstrip. The sun is shining; the day is clear. It looks good.

It is the job of the man on the ham radio to alert the dispatcher of changes in the weather. While we wait, I sit next to him, listening to conversations that our radio is picking up. There are conversations in English between missionaries, and others in Indonesian between missionaries and Mr. Naftali.

My conversation with Mr. Naftali yesterday was awkward. He made it very clear that it is not his job to arrange flights for tourists and that it makes no difference to him if I miss my tour. His job is to serve the missionaries.

One American woman named Esther seemed to have a relaxed relationship with Mr. Naftali. As I was sitting in the hut yesterday, I overheard two of her conversations with him. He agreed to arrange whatever she requested. Today, as I sit in the hut next to my packed bag, Esther is chatting with a fellow missionary. I am intent on eavesdropping when suddenly I look up and see an ominous white cloud moving toward us. In less than five minutes, the landing strip is totally fogged in. I feel helpless as our radio man tells MAF that we are fogged in. *Pintu tutup.* The door is closed. The flight is cancelled.

We go back on the radio with Mr. Naftali, who informs us that nothing is scheduled for the next week, not for anywhere nearby. Additionally, they are very short of planes and there's no way they can schedule something just for me. When I tell him that I need to be back in Wamena by the eighteenth, he tells me I should have thought of that before I got on a plane to Holuwon.

I am trapped. There is nothing I can do. Then I hear Esther's voice again. She is talking to Mr. Naftali and his tone is warm and chatty.

"Do you think I can talk to Esther?" I ask our radio operator.

A few minutes later, I am explaining my situation to Esther, though I'm sure she has heard my conversations with Mr. Naftali as I have heard hers.

"Are you willing to pay for a charter?" she asks.

I have no choice.

"Let's talk this afternoon," she says. "I'll see what I can do."

That afternoon Esther explains her plan. There is a plane scheduled for somewhere else on Monday; its mission is to pick up two empty oil tanks. The tanks will be taken to Wamena, filled, and returned to the village.

"Tanks and passengers cannot fly on the same plane," she tells me. "So you will not be able to ride with the tanks. But if you are willing to pay for two empty oil tanks, the plane will bring you to Wamena instead of the tanks. You will have to pay 115,000 rupiah for the charter and 65,000 rupiah for each tank." My trip from Wamena to Holuwan cost 17,000. A dollar is worth 2,000 rupiah.

I agree to buy the tanks. It's my only hope.

On Sunday, our three children are washed in water warmed by the fire. At nine-forty, the church bell rings and the whole village walks through heavy morning clouds to the church.

More than sixty people crowd into the room, women on one side, men on the other. Some children are wearing clothes, others are naked except for a string tied around their waists. There are women in dresses and others naked on top. Men in long and short pants, and men in *horim.*

Hymns are sung, the Bible is read, questions about the meaning of the passages are asked and answered. Then the children are taken out for Sunday school. The only kids left are the babies who are tucked inside the women's *noken,* comfortably resting on cushions of leaves.

When the children are gone, we sing and pray and sway some more, and when it is time for the sermon, up steps the ham radio operator, who at this point is my pal. He is apparently the spiritual leader of the church. He delivers his sermon, and when it is finished, he tells everyone about my predicament. He tells them that I will lose a lot of money if I can not get to Wamena tomorrow. And he asks them to pray for me. Then the whole congregation of the Filadelfia Church of Holuwon prays in silence, asking Jesus to clear the clouds so my plane can come in.

After the service I go with the minister and connect with Esther. I tell her, a devout Christian missionary, that all of Holuwon has prayed that my plane will come.

The next morning, around ten-thirty, the clouds lift, the sun warms the village and its people, and dozens of us walk to the airstrip. An hour after that, the plane lands to applause. Two handsome young missionary pilots hop out of the cockpit onto the grass. Dennis is the first to speak.

"I understand they prayed for this," he says, looking around at a crowd whose prayers have been answered.

A month later I send Esther a copy of my book, *Why Can't I Fly?* Her note to me reads:

Thank you so very much for the book you sent as your thank you for helping you to fly! We were so excited to get it, especially since that book has been one of Liselle's and my favorites for a long time!...

We'd love to meet you sometime—maybe in heaven! If you're not sure of heaven, ask God to reveal himself to you, and read the Gospel of John. He wants you to love Him as He loves you! We love you too!

I'm pleased that God and Esther love me, but I must admit that I am even more thrilled that somehow my book found its way to Irian Jaya without my help. Now there are two.

CHAPTER FOURTEEN

IRIAN JAYA: THE ASMAT LANDS

I show up in Wamena on time, thanks to prayer and Esther's creative efforts. Michael is there with two middle-aged German men. Right from the beginning I dislike Hans. His facial lines twist down from a life of negativism, and he can't look me straight in the eyes. The longer I know him, the less I like him. When there's work to be done, Hans feigns helplessness while the rest of us do his share. And in the end, his irresponsibility nearly ruins our trip. Fortunately, he doesn't speak much English, so I don't have to make conversation.

Horst, the other man, doesn't say much, but he doesn't disappear when we have to unload the boat; and he reaches out a hand when he thinks it's needed. I like his manner and smile. Too bad we don't share a language. Over the next nineteen days, we spend most of our time in silence.

A few years ago, I would have felt uncomfortable sitting in silence among people; but the Balinese do it all the time. They rarely talk while they are eating, and often they sit with others without speaking. I have learned that silence is a way of hearing the voices within and of exploring unexpressed and nascent thoughts and feelings. I have come to enjoy sitting in a group where no one is speaking. It is an introspection enhanced by a silent group energy that works its way from the outside to the internal soul. Out of language necessity, and therefore without self-consciousness, my nineteen days with Hans, Horst, and Michael (who speaks English very well) are mostly silent and extremely fulfilling.

Our tour through the Asmat country of the south is in a twenty-foot-long dugout canoe with a forty-horsepower motor. Michael has hired a native, Joseph (in this part of the island the Catholic church is very strong and many natives have Christian names), to pilot the boat. Every morning we load up the canoe with our packs, and Joseph navigates the rivers. We are carrying rice and noodles, cabbage, beans, and carrots, and pots and pans and dishes and cups. And along the way, we buy fish from fishermen and meat from hunters. One day we buy a live ostrichlike cassowary bird that is nearly four feet tall, with vestigial wings, and feet that are bigger than mine. Michael buys it for our dinner and the hunters load it, live and tethered, into the back of our boat. But the poor cassowary can't tolerate the sun. Even though the bird is alive, it begins to stink. I can't even think about eating it; but everyone else says it tastes like steak.

At night we sleep in schools and community houses. To protect us from mosquitoes, Michael sets up individual tents inside the buildings, and the accommodations feel almost luxurious.

In each village, people gather around us, but there is little communication. Our visits are too short. I miss the singing that Ursula, Teresia, Elsa, and I shared with the people in the mountains. None of the three men even whistles for three weeks. I suspect my singing, humming, and whistling in the back of the boat drives them a little crazy, but no one says a word and I try to keep it soft.

We visit carving villages where we watch the men chipping away at exquisite and powerful sculptures, considered to be among the world's finest primitive art. We buy drums and figures and shields and panels, and load and unload them every morning and night.

In many of the villages, the children have the huge stomachs and reddish hair of kwashiorkor, and dry, scaly skin. All because of the lack of proper nutrition. It is difficult to face, so vividly and so often, the inequalities of life.

In one village the chief offers us plump grubs from a sago tree. They are a delicacy, eaten raw and wriggling. I decline with a smile and big eyes. Michael is the only one to chomp them down. Go, Michael.

In that same village, just before we go to sleep, a young woman asks us for medicine for her listless baby. None of us has anything that would be safe for a baby. I make a mental note to bring baby aspirin on my next trip and perhaps some of the packaged oral rehydration powder (made of salt and sugar in specific proportions) that is used throughout the world for dehydration caused by diarrhea. But this baby could be suffering from malaria or cholera or any of the many diseases that make life here so tenuous. Statistics are not easy to collect, but it has been said that infant mortality is as high as 65 percent.

The baby she is holding is barely moving. I tell her that we are going to be passing Senggo, a village where there is a Canadian doctor who has been doing medicine and missionary work in Irian Jaya for more than twenty years. With Michael's permission, I invite her to come with us. It is a day's trip, but perhaps the doctor can save her baby's life.

The next morning, one woman, four children, the village head, and the woman with the sick baby climb into our boat and sit way back. It is early in the morning and cold. I give the mother my purple fleece jacket to wrap around the baby.

The motor is loud, water splashes into the bow, noisy screechy cockatoos fly back and forth across the river. There are eagles and egrets and hornbills. Hundreds, maybe thousands of huge bats burst into the air from one island when our motor wakes them up. They are a scene from a horror film, their giant black wings diving and swooping against the bright blue sky.

I am lost in the glare of the sun, hypnotized by the sound of the motor, the splash of the water, the honking of the cockatoos.

And then comes the wailing of the women.

I turn around. The mother is holding the baby. Both women are rocking and wailing. It is too late for medical help. The baby is dead.

A few minutes later a "water taxi" approaches going in the opposite direction. The two women, the village head, the children, and the dead baby board the taxi to go home. As the mother leaves, she hands me my jacket.

When the taxi is gone, I hang over the side of our boat and wash the jacket in the river. I feel queasy holding the baby's death wrap. It's an old purple fleece jacket that I would have given to the woman if I'd had another.

All day I am dazed and haunted by the baby's death and the sound of wailing women. I do not sleep at night either; visions of the baby, and children with distended stomachs and dull eyes and scaly skin pass in and out of my dreams, and I wake up sweaty and teary and shaking.

For more than a week we have been visiting riverside villages of woodcarvers and motoring along the coastline where in 1961, Michael Rockefeller, Nelson's son, disappeared one day, rumored to have been the victim of fierce tides or cannibals or possibly a shark or a crocodile. One theory is that he was killed by angry tribesmen avenging a murder several years earlier of five of their tribesmen by Dutch police. Joseph, our skipper, pointed out the spot from which Michael swam to shore after his boat overturned. He was never seen again.

But today, we are not in our boat. Instead, we are climbing massive trees. Not the vertical kind. These trees have all been cut down and they're lying on their sides and on each other. Giants have been playing pick-up sticks on several acres of "cleared" space, and they haven't picked up. Some of the trees have diameters of more than five feet.

From a distance, it doesn't look all that difficult, but when I start crossing, I discover that it is almost impossible for me to get up to the top of the logs so I can cross to the next one. And there's no way to go "under." Most of the time, the only way I can get up is by lifting my leg, sometimes by grabbing it and placing it up where it has to go, then reaching out my hand and getting pulled.

We are here, climbing over trees and sloshing through swamps, because I requested it. Wherever I have gone, in both the tribal highlands and the swampy lowlands, missionaries have preceded me. To trek three days into the mountains and arrive at a village that is still living the life their ancestors lived hundreds of years ago, was a privilege. But to discover that beyond the round, thatched huts with cookfires, there is a big, wooden missionary house with a gas stove and a generator, is something of a let down.

"Michael," I said as we passed a church one day, "isn't there somewhere that the people haven't been missionized?"

And that's why we're here in the middle of a swamp, the four of us and Joseph, on our way to Rumah Tinggi. High house. Home of the Korowai.

When we have passed through and over the horizontal trees, we move into the swamp, walking on massive roots, slippery and twisted, on a path that is leading us deeper into the dark forest. Birds are squawking and singing; cicadas are sounding like chainsaws; water is rushing through brooks that we have to cross. I am grateful for my finest-waterproof-leather-triple-bladdered-two-hundred-fifty-dollar-boots. It was for today that I bought them.

Then suddenly, Joseph stops and lets out a Tarzan-like cry. He waits. A cry comes out of the dark and distant forest. Joseph offers no explanation. Before I can ask, he moves on, leaving me to my sloshy steps.

About thirty minutes later, I step into a clearing and I'm face to face with four men with bows and arrows, six-inch white bones through their noses, and body paint on their chests. There are also two women in grass skirts, chests and breasts decorated with scars. And three children. They are lined up, facing our group.

My heart is pounding. We have come upon hunters and gatherers in the forest. Joseph talks to them in a tribal language. He gives them tobacco and candy, which we have brought as a gift. They stand, stiff and formal and beautiful. I can only stare in awe. They are a picture, a dream, a realization of my fantasies.

I smile. A young woman smiles back. For a brief moment we connect in that universal greeting of goodwill.

I feel an urge to go home with these people and share their lives, their songs, their families, their cookfires, until we are not strangers staring at each other across ten feet of space, but friends, learning simultaneously that being human and open is all it takes to connect. If I were not on a tour, I would ask if I could live amongst them, for a month, two months, however long it might take for us to learn to trust each other. I'm sure they would have me.

Then Joseph moves on. I do not want to leave. I want to move closer. To touch them and let them touch me. But that is not our agenda. We go on. But the slippery roots aren't as slippery. I'm practically running. I have an energy that I haven't felt in weeks. I am in the middle of swampland in Irian Jaya and I have just met a group of people who are hunting with bows and arrows.

Several hours later we arrive at our destination. There are two long and high houses sitting more than twenty feet up in the trees. And one longhouse on the ground.

We are invited to enter one of the high houses. Horst, Hans, Michael, and Joseph climb the thin tree trunk that is the only way in. I am sure there are things up there worth seeing. Perhaps skulls from when these people were cannibals. Probably decorated wooden shields that are a part of tribal ceremonies and wars. And certainly there are artifacts of everyday life. These are houses, not museums.

I look up. For a flash of a second, I consider it; I've come a long way not to go in. But the trunk I would have to climb is practically vertical; the foot notches are far apart; and there is nothing to hold onto except the trunk. I think about how my knees go wobbly when I look down from heights. Thank you, no.

I walk toward the longhouse that is on the ground. Huge tree trunks hold up the sides and the thatched roof. The house is about twenty feet wide and nearly two hundred feet long, closed on the sides and open at both ends.

I walk in. Along one side, on a higher level than the dirt floor, there is living space, separated into open family "rooms," each with a place for a fire. I walk down the center aisle. The only person I see is an old man, apparently senile, sitting on the floor of a cage, singing. Joseph tells me later that he is the former chief of his tribe and he is singing the tribal history.

I want to stop, but I don't want to stare, so I keep walking to the back, where there is a young woman probably about twenty years old, and a little boy around five. When the child sees me, he begins screaming hysterically and clutching his mother's legs, putting her between us. The mother backs away as I approach.

I can understand his fear. We are different, his mother and I. Her skin is dark; mine is light. Her eyes are deep brown; mine are light blue. She is bare-breasted and there are scars in a pattern, running from each shoulder down to her nipples; I am wearing a T-shirt. Her bottom is covered by a grass skirt; I am wearing long khaki pants.

The mother and child are huddled together, just inside the back opening. I pass by them and go a few feet beyond the house. They watch me as I sit on a tree trunk and take a small bottle of bubble stuff out of my pack. It's the kind that has a little wand inside that you dip in and blow through, making dozens of bubbles with each blow. Wherever I go, I carry that little plastic bottle of bubbles.

The child stops crying; I am far enough away (about twenty feet) and ignoring them. I dip the wand in the liquid and blow. Bubbles float into the air. I sit there, blowing bubbles and smiling as I follow the bubbles with my eyes. Mother and child watch.

Then a bubble floats inside and close to the child. He reaches out and touches it. It pops. He touches another. And another. He looks up at his mother and smiles. She begins popping bubbles too. They come closer to me. I blow bubbles directly at them. They smile and chase them, laughing. I am laughing too.

After a few minutes, I hold the wand toward the mother and she dips and blows. Too hard. We try again. Another failure. I exaggerate the slow steady blowing and give her another chance. Yes! The bubbles float out of the wand; and as the child chases them, the mother and I exchange smiles. Soon, we are all giggling and chasing bubbles.

When we are finished, the little boy walks over to me and looks up at my chest. Then he reaches up and cups my breast in his hand. The mother comes over and does the same thing with my other breast. Yes, I am the same, I nod. Look. I pull up my shirt and unhook my bra. My breasts pop out and they both smile.

I think about the Zapotec village in Mexico where I was not accepted until I was wearing their clothes, and the Balinese ceremonies I would never have attended in anything but a *kebaya* and a sarong. I smile when I realize that if I were to live here, I would walk around topless. If I weren't with three westerners, I would do it right now.

That night the mother leads me to her cookfire, which is one of many along one side of the longhouse. We are the only ones cooking; most of the people who live here are off hunting and gathering.

The main food in this part of Irian Jaya is sago, a flourlike paste that is collected and filtered with great effort from the pith of the sago palm tree. The mother pats and cooks the yellowish blob in the fire, adding no flavoring to the dough. And then with a look of affection and anticipation, she offers me a taste. It's dry and flavorless.

I smile and indicate that I like it. I take some more. Accepting food is a fundamental part of forming a relationship. She is pleased.

As we sit, legs outstretched and touching, white and dark side by side, I hum a quiet lullaby. She hums with me. And then I put my arm around her and she puts hers around me. The little boy sits between my legs and we sing in the dark. I wish I could stay. If I ever come back to Irian Jaya, this is where I will live.

Several days later, we are about to visit a traditional men's longhouse that stretches for perhaps two hundred feet along the river. When our boat pulls up to the shore, we are greeted by a crowd of men, smiling and waving. But as we are disembarking, Hans bangs his leg and splits open a deep gash. Blood is spurting. Michael stares. Horst climbs out. Joseph looks on in shock. And the blood keeps gushing.

I grab the cleanest shirt I can find and apply pressure to the wound until the bleeding stops. Then I clean it with Betadine, put on some antibiotic ointment, and cover the wound with clean bandages. (Before we left Germany and the U.S., Michael sent us each a list of stuff he wanted us to include in our medical kits. I made sure that mine was complete.)

"Don't stand up," I tell Hans. "It's a deep wound and it will open easily. Just sit there and keep the pressure on." My hands are bloody. "I hope you don't have AIDS," I say, only partly in jest.

"I was tested two weeks before I left. I'm fine," he says, standing up and trying to climb out of the boat. The blood begins to spurt again.

Our onshore greeting committee is horrified. I don't know the cultural significance of spurting blood, but from the looks on their faces, something frightening and perhaps evil has happened. None of us is permitted to go anywhere near the longhouse. We are polluted.

"Hans," I say, when we are en route once more. "Keep your wound clean and don't get it wet in the river."

The next morning I ask him how it feels.

"Oh," he tells me. "It's fine."

"You should probably let me clean it," I say.

"The scab will keep it clean. I don't need you," he announces, sounding hostile. His English is better than I thought. He takes his towel and heads down to the river for a bath.

"Don't get it wet," I call after him.

Then he turns to me and blurts out like a child, "Who do you think you are? A doctor? Leave me alone."

I do. I watch as he bathes in the brown river, but I don't say another word. Neither does he.

Four days later, Hans cannot walk. His leg is swollen and sensitive and he's burning with fever. Michael tells him to take the antibiotics he was told to bring. He didn't bring any.

The other three of us exchange glances. We have all brought antibiotics in our medical kits. But the fact is, we aren't doctors and none of us has any idea about the appropriate antibiotic. Additionally, we are in the middle of nowhere, and we might need them ourselves. Do we give him ours? And what if the medication doesn't work? What if our antibiotics are wrong for him? It's one thing to treat yourself; another to treat someone who is very sick.

Instead, Horst and Michael carry him to the boat and we change our itinerary, going many hours out of our way to get paramedical help. Hans says he has no rupiah to pay for the treatment, so we pool our money and buy him penicillin at the clinic. The next day we take him hours away to Agats and the only hospital on this part of the island. By this time Hans is nearly delerious. The doctor performs some kind of surgery; I don't ask what kind. I care enough to want him to be treated, but not enough to want the details.

Once again, we pool our cash to pay the doctor. Hans claims to have a credit card but no cash.

Our programmed trip is over . . . three days early because of Hans; but we are still far from an airport, and Hans needs to go home. He is too sick to go with us on the ten-hour boat trip that will take us to the big airport at Timika; but we cannot leave him here alone. Poor Michael has to find a way to get him airlifted out.

Turns out there is an American tour that is flying out of nearby Ewer the next day on a chartered plane (they are flying to Timika). Their plane has empty seats. The timing is perfect. It's too good to be true.

The rest of us hang around the town of Agats for two more days, days we would have been touring if Hans hadn't become ill. We walk along the raised planks that are the sidewalks. Because of very high tides, Agats is built on stilts and wooden walkways. We visit an intriguing museum about the local tribes and their art, and a Roman Catholic church. And we watch a boat unload sharks' fins for export to Hong Kong.

When it's time to go to the airport, Joseph, who lives in Agats, tells us that the best time to take the ten-hour boat trip is at night. The water, he says, is calm; and the trip to the north and west along the coastline is less dangerous.

We assemble in the rain and board our canoe. It is already dark. Joseph arrives an hour and a half late, drunk. About an hour after we leave, a dense fog descends and we have zero visibility and no navigational tools. I offer Joseph my compass, but he does not know how to use it. I begin to get nervous when he stands up, puts his hand to his forehead like a cartoon, and looks around. He can see nothing. And if he can't see, he can't navigate. He turns off the motor and announces that we have to wait until morning. In the cold. In the rain. In the dark. He needs to see the coast in order to navigate.

We dig out our sleeping bags and try to stay warm, all of us hoping the sea stays calm. In one direction, no more than a couple of kilometers away, is the coast of Irian Jaya. In the other direction, around a thousand kilometers away, is the coast of Australia. And our captain doesn't know which way is which. I am frightened by the randomness of it all. At least Joseph knows enough to admit he doesn't know. And he doesn't look nervous. He's confident that when it gets light out, our problems will be over. And if it comes down to it, I could find north on my compass.

The night is long and cold, and it's one of the only times in my adult life that I've ever wished I were a man; the guys have no trouble peeing over the side. At least it's dark and foggy.

I use the sleepless hours to think about my Irian Jaya experience. There were ecstatic moments and agonizing ones. Physically, I was a disaster, unfit and achy during the trek, barely able to get out of my sleeping bag a couple of mornings. I'm still angry at myself for being so out of shape. But I made it. And connecting with the people of the highlands through singing was thrilling, unexpected, and worth the pain. It would never have happened if I hadn't met Ursula, Teresia, and Elsa. And we might never have trekked together if I hadn't spoken Indonesian and gotten us seats on that first plane out. I love it when things come together like that.

And I particularly loved Holuwon, that place in the clouds, where I arrived out of the sky and was accepted so comfortably, treated so gently, and literally sent off with a prayer.

The tour with Michael confirmed my feeling that I am best suited to traveling alone, without a plan, moving on instinct and trust. I'm definitely not a tour person. How badly I wanted to stay with the hunters and gatherers and settle in with the people of the high houses (living, of course, in the low one). I think I will return someday. Next time I will just get on a plane and go.

But I also know that I would never, could never, have made that first trip by myself. Meeting Michael in Bali—another of those extraordinary serendipitous events of my journey—brought me to a world I have dreamed about.

One by one, all my nomadic dreams are coming true.

Two days later I fly to Bali.

CHAPTER FIFTEEN

ON TO MAS

Telephones have come to Kerambitan. The mayor has one. The bank has one. And the king has one. I have decided that Tu Biang and I need one too.

A phone would benefit the *puri*. They have no income. If they had a phone, they could work with travel agencies, as well as with individual tourists, in offering a Balinese banquet and a tour of the palace. I would write and produce the brochures, and Tu Biang and I could take them to travel agents and hotels together. She has often done banquets and tours, but never in an organized way. A phone could be the answer to her financial worries.

I also want a phone for personal reasons. My mother is fragile and I want to be in closer touch. I volunteer to pay the astronomical connection fee of five hundred dollars. The monthly fee is also high; but if the brochure brings just one guest a month, the fee would be paid.

Since Tu Man is making the decisions these days (Tu Biang has yielded her authority to him), I sit with him and explain my proposal. He thinks about it and decides that the monthly fee is too much. He rejects the phone plan. As he tells me his decision, I feel myself tighten up. My breathing quickens. How can he do this to his mother, to me? Why did she turn over her authority to her son?

I want to tell him that it is a shortsighted decision, but I don't know how to say "shortsighted" in Indonesian; so I use the word *bodoh*, which means "stupid." I should never have said it. Tu Man is insulted and he refuses to talk to me.

The next morning I stop by Tu Aji's altar with a Cadbury milk chocolate bar offering. It is easy to know what to bring a spirit if you know it well.

"Oh, Tu Aji, I am sorry. I have failed you. I tried to help Tu Biang build her guest business, but all I did was offend your son. I have no right to tell your family how they should live. But I cannot stop myself. The time has come for me to leave Kerambitan. Thank you for your guidance, for your wisdom, for your wonderful family. You have enriched my life forever."

A few days later I hire a driver to take me and my belongings to Ubud, the tourist town an hour and a half away. My plan is to rent a bungalow there. By the time I leave, Tu Man is talking to me again. I apologized for telling him he made a stupid decision and he accepted my apology. Tu Biang is tearful as I climb into the car. Dayu Biang and Jero Made feel abandoned. Dayu Biang tells me that the laughter goes out of the *puri* when I am not there.

I too am filled with emotion. It is nearly four years since I arrived in the *puri* with that piece of paper from Dr. Djelantik, and nearly two years since Tu Aji died. In those four years I have seen courtships and feasted at weddings. I have participated in animal sacrifices and heard the voices of the ancestors. I have cooked and danced with the women, prayed with the *banjar,* and given permission to spirits to go on to the next world. I have loved and learned from these extraordinary people, and wrapped myself in their sarongs and their culture. It's been wonderful.

But I have become too involved. It is not my place to change their lives. I am here to learn from them, not to alter their history.

I have adapted in many ways to the pace and style of living in Bali, but I will never be a Balinese woman, or a Mexican or a Nicaraguan. I can live in other cultures, celebrate their rites, love their children, but I must constantly remind myself that my background will always slant the way I see things. When I am tempted to change who they are or rush what they are becoming, it is time to move on.

I ask the driver to stop at the house of some friends. I want to let them know that I will be living in their part of the island. Ubud is just fifteen minutes from Mas, the wood-carving village where they live.

Dayu Mayuni, her husband (whose sister is married to one of the king's sons), and their daughter are my second family in Bali. Dayu and Jan became good friends when Jan was here; they are nearly the same age. It was Dayu's husband, Ida Bagus, who came to Kerambitan to tell me that my father had had a heart attack. I feel close to them.

Dayu is the youngest sister of Bali's most famous and talented wood sculptor, Ida Bagus Tilem. In a world where copying is an art form, Tilem's work is breathtakingly original. The gallery that bears his name is the finest in Bali.

Dayu is happy that I am moving closer. "But you cannot rent a bungalow in Ubud," she tells me. "You are not a tourist. I will find you a place to live. Come back at six."

I do. Now there is another couple with Dayu and her husband. The two women are dressed exquisitely, in silk sarongs and lace *kebaya*. They have just returned from a ceremony. I have met the other woman before; she is Dayu Mayuni's niece, Ida Bagus Tilem's daughter.

Dayu Raka is small, delicate, and exquisitely beautiful. She is in her mid-thirties, nearly the same age as her niece. Her husband is a Ph.D. economist who teaches in a university in Surabaya on the island of Java. He is closer to my age. We are reintroduced.

Dayu Mayuni speaks first. "Raka has a place where you can stay."

I smile at Dayu Raka and say what a Balinese person would say. "Oh, thank you, but I could not stay with you. I will be here for at least two months."

It is common etiquette to say no at least twice.

"That is no problem," she says in beautiful English.

"Thank you, but I couldn't," I repeat. "I will find a place to rent in Ubud. It is very kind of you to offer to let me stay in your home, but I cannot accept."

"Please," she says. "I would like it very much if you would stay."

I give up the game and accept. I have no idea what she is offering; I assume it is a room in her home.

"Please, come with us," says Dayu Raka. She, her husband, and I climb into a Toyota SUV and travel about a mile along the main road. Then we turn into a driveway and stop in front of a big bamboo gate. Dayu Raka gets out and rings a bell.

A few seconds later a young man named Putu opens the gate and we walk through a garden along a stone path and across a bridge that traverses a lily pond. The frogs stop croaking as we cross the bridge and begin again when we step into the house.

The first room we enter is tiled in marble. There are quiet silk pillows on the couches and spectacular art on the walls. The second room is about twenty by thirty feet, with marble floors and tabletops. Every piece of furniture is handcarved. There are six paintings on the walls, all of them museum quality.

I am overwhelmed by the beauty and the simplicity. We sit and talk.

After about half an hour, Dayu Raka says, "You will probably want to sleep in this room," and she walks me into yet another exquisite space with art on the walls and craftsmanship in the furniture. "And you are welcome to use the upstairs, of course. If you need anything, ask Putu. He will take care of you. I am pleased that you will be here. A house should not be empty; it needs people."

And they leave.

The house, it turns out, is mine. Dayu Raka and her husband built it, furnished it, and continue to fill it with paintings and sculptures and antiques. There are trunks with inlaid abalone shells, lifesize figures made of Chinese coins, corner chests with antique glass, and several sets of beautifully carved chairs, no two exactly the same.

There is also a phone in the living room.

Dayu Raka, daughter and granddaughter of brilliant sculptors, has their artistic genes coursing through her body. But in Bali, women rarely carve. All of Dayu Raka's creative energy has gone into her house. This place of such impeccable taste is her creation. And she does not even live here. She lives in her father's house, next to the gallery, with her mother, her eight-year-old son, her husband (when he is in Bali), and her father's spirit. (Ida Bagus Tilem died just a few months ago.) Dayu Raka and her father were very close when he was alive, and she does not want to be separated from the place that holds his masterpieces, his collections, and his spirit. Someday she expects to move her family into *her* house, but not yet.

When they are gone, Putu introduces me to three young men. They live out back in a separate building attached to the kitchen. (Dayu Raka told me that she thought about putting the kitchen in the house, the way we do in the West, but she didn't want cooking smells permeating the other rooms.)

Two of the men Putu has brought in to meet me are guides in the Njana Tilem Gallery (Njana was Tilem's father, also a fine sculptor); they tell me they are hoping to practice their English with me. The third man is Dayu Raka's driver.

Over the next months the five us talk for hours every night, play cards (the Chinese game of *ceki*), and watch television. Often I add a dish to the meal that the gallery provides for them, and we eat together. I am pleased. Dayu Raka has provided me with a new, instant family. They call me Ibu Rita, or Bu Rita, Mother Rita, a form of address used with older women. Sometimes Wayan, my young friend from Kerambitan joins us. He comes by to say hello and stay in touch. Often Wayan and I go off on his motor-cycle to have dinner in Ubud.

That first night, as I listen to the croaking frogs in the lily pond outside my window, I think about what I can do to reciprocate. I have been given this exquisite place to live in, without even a hint of their wanting any-thing in return. But life has taught me the doctrine of *reciprocity,* and I have found that it is alive and well and operating all over the world. Kind-nesses must be returned.

What I have to offer is English.

The next day I walk to the Tilem gallery, about half a mile down the road, and reintroduce myself to Pak Tut, the manager. I have met him many times over the years because I always bring guests to this extraordi-nary gallery.

The two young guides from my house are working. *"Selamat datang, Bu Rita,"* they say softly, welcoming me. Everything in the Njana Tilem Gallery is gentle, including the staff.

Pak Tut introduces me to the other guides, and he and I chat a while. I tell him I am here to talk to Dayu Raka about how I might use my English to help her and her family. I am thinking about giving English lessons to her eight-year-old son, conducting formal classes for the guides in the gallery (they begin the next week), and perhaps helping Pak Tut with gallery correspondence. But I have to tread lightly. I don't want her or the family to feel obligated to accept my offer. And I don't want Pak Tut to feel judged or hurt if I correct his English. He speaks well and writes well; but English is not his first language.

"If there is anything I can do to help you," I tell him, "Please let me know."

"Oh, there is," he says, and he takes an album from a shelf. The album is filled with plastic slips that hold sheets of information. "When we sell a sculpture of a god or a character from the *Mahabharata* or *Ramayana,* we give the buyer an explanation of the piece. I would like it very much if you would read the stories and correct any mistakes."

"I'd be happy to do it, but I want to warn you before I begin, that as a writer and an editor, I always have corrections. I hope you will not be insulted if I make changes."

"I would be happy to learn from you. Take the album home and read it tonight. Tomorrow we can discuss your comments."

The grammar in the stories is impeccable. The sentences are correct.

But Pak Tut is not a writer. He offers more information than the customer needs, filling the stories with the names of mothers and fathers and sisters and priests instead of telling a good story. And often he rambles, as do the texts of the *Mahabharata* and the *Ramayana* (and the Bible and the Koran). We talk about the idea of telling stories in a more modern style. Pak Tut says he would be happy to rewrite everything with me.

The next day we begin what will take us two months to finish. We take out a sheet and I read it. Then he shows me some sculptures of the characters in the sheet so I know how they are represented. And then we sit down and he tells me the story of the sculpture. I ask him questions. Together, we write a new story on the gallery's computer.

For me, our sessions are fantastic. I feel as though I am taking a class in Balinese folklore and Hindu religion. Pak Tut is a scholar and a fine teacher.

For Pak Tut, our sessions are a revelation. He cannot believe how slow I am, struggling with words, staring into space until I come up with a way of presenting a theme.

"English is your first language," he says to me one day. "And you are a writer. I thought you would just sit down and write." I wish I could.

I love spending time in the gallery, especially in the collection room, which is filled with carvings by Tilem and his father that are not for sale. They are so exquisite that I often find myself in tears simply because I am in their presence. No one has been able to buy an Ida Bagus Tilem sculpture since the early seventies, when Tilem decided that he would not sell any more of his or his father's work. (The gallery sells the sculptures of their students, the master carvers who sit in the courtyard every day, carving.)

Pak Tut tells me that King Hussein from Jordan fell in love with one of Tilem's masterpieces, *The Seven Circles of Life*. After making several offers and being rejected, he finally sat down and wrote a blank check. The carving still belongs to the family.

Pak Tut and I develop a close relationship. So do Raka and I. (She has asked me to call her Raka, without using the *brahmana* label.) She invites me to family ceremonies and offers me her driver if I have errands to do. When we go to the supermarket in Denpasar together, she always insists on buying me lunch or dinner. Raka is not comfortable when I offer to pay; it is far more common that the members of this leading and highly respected family be the givers, not the takers.

I am also teaching English to her eight-year-old son, Gustu. Every day after school he comes to my house with Nyoman, the fourteen-year-old boy who is Gustu's companion when Gustu is not in school. Raka has told me that it is her dream that Gustu be able to speak many languages.

Nyoman, the young man who takes care of Gustu, participates in our classes. But when I bring out the markers and drawing paper, he moves off by himself, creating beautiful flowers and scenes and characters from history. He is clearly talented. His job, when Gustu is in school, is to sweep the grounds of the family gallery compound and wash windows. He works long hours, from early morning until Gustu goes to sleep. And sometimes he does the night security watch. Nyoman is surrounded by art and carvings and brilliant carvers, but the only art he is creating is with magic markers.

One day, after several months in Raka's house, I decide that I would like to travel to the Balinese island of Nusa Penida, where Nyoman is from. I steal Nyoman (with permission) for three days. Wayan from Kerambitan comes too. Together we visit the seaweed farms, sleep at Nyoman's uncle's house, and wander along the beach. As we walk on the sand, Nyoman keeps picking up pieces of coral or driftwood.

"Look," he says, pointing to the twists and turns of a piece of wood. "See the fish. Look at the shrimp." And later, "This one has the head of giant."

I can feel the sculptor in this boy; it is crying out to be developed. I see coral and driftwood; he sees alligators and gods.

When we return to Mas, I tell Nyoman that I want to thank him for being my guide by buying him a set of carving tools. When I hand him the money to buy tools, I tell him there is a string attached to the gift: like an evil witch in a fairy tale, I want his first baby. He agrees. Shortly after that I leave Bali for a trip to the U.S. for five months.

When I return to Bali, Raka again offers me her home. This time I have brought a telephone and wires. Putu connects my extension cord to the main box, and I have a phone in my room. I can hardly believe it. Before I left the U.S., I signed on with Compuserve. Now I can talk and e-mail with my kids, with friends, with my agent and editors.

Staying in touch gives me a foot in both worlds. From the first e-mail I send, I am addicted. Even though I'm a nomad, now and probably forever, I have a permanent cyber-address that will follow me around the world.

When I first arrive at the gallery after my five-month absence, Nyoman rushes over to me. He is excited. "It is finished," he tells me, referring to his firstborn sculpture. I ask him to present it to me formally in the gallery, and I sit on the visitor's couch and wait while he goes to get my gift. I am expecting a fish or a piece of fruit; it is, after all, his first woodcarving. He walks in holding a head about a foot and a half tall.

"It is the giant who ate the moon," he tells me. "See, he is about to eat her."

The monster's mouth is open in a grotesque way and one of his eyes is shut "because he has just seen his own image in the lotus pond and he is horrified at the expression on his face."

The carving is incredible. I am thrilled and feeling a little guilty at being gifted this magnificent sculpture. I think about telling him to sell it, but I'm afraid he'll think I don't want it. And I'm worried that he may be insulted if I offer him money.

Raka shows me another piece he has finished, of fish and shrimp, hiding and intertwined in twists and turns of wood that has become ocean. She paid him nearly one hundred dollars for it. She also tells me that she wanted to buy his giant-head, but he told her it was for Ibu Rita.

Nyoman stops by my house later that day and I ask him where he got the wood for my giant. From the cook's woodpile, he tells me. Too shy to ask the gallery for a hunk of wood, he'd found a piece that was destined to become fire.

I am overwhelmed with his talent. I ask him when he has time to carve. At dawn before he begins his job of sweeping and washing windows, and after dark, when his gallery chores are finished. I cannot help but wonder what he would be creating if he had time.

I am feeling the urge to interfere. I have to stop myself from speaking to Raka about giving Nyoman time to carve. I know it is wrong to step in where I don't belong, but I want so badly for this young man to fulfill his potential. I stay away from the gallery, knowing that I cannot trust myself.

I stay in Bali for only two months. On my last trip to the U.S. I discovered that my mother's health was failing, and I am afraid to be away from her for a long time. I have a sense that these are her final days, and I want to be nearby. Additionally, because of the Nyoman conflict surging inside me, I'm pleased to be leaving.

When I see my mother's condition, I am frightened. She sleeps most of the day, and says little. Her eyes tell me she has had enough, but her heart is strong and her appetite hearty. I decide to put my travels on hold and stay for a while.

I do not want to live in Mom's house and break the routine; it is working well. I am also afraid that if I live with her, I will not be able to write, and I have several children's book projects that I'm working on. So I rent a house at Fairfield Beach (I answer an ad for a "share"), about ten minutes from my mother's house, and I visit her every other day. She says little during our visits. But I have learned to be comfortable in silence. Each time I see my mother, I think she will not make it through the night. I keep wanting to say good-bye, to give her permission to leave, but I cannot.

While I am there, Mitch becomes engaged to Melissa Tarkington, a beautiful young woman who connects with my mother in a very special way. The first time they meet, I watch the two of them together. There is a sincerity and genuine interest in Melissa's eyes and voice as she asks my mother about her Russian ancestry. And my mother, who has barely talked in weeks, sits there telling Melissa stories, with a look of joy on her face.

For nearly a year, I live in Fairfield. Then one day I have a realization. Perhaps my being there is preventing Mom from moving on, encouraging her to fight what must be an agonizing battle, because she doesn't want to abandon me. How much better it would be if she could yield to serenity and peace. I wish I could tell her that it's OK, that there is another world where she will feel no pain; but I sense that she doesn't want to hear it from me.

I believe that people can choose the time when they will die, and I fear that my presence is trapping my mother in her suffering. I decide to return to Bali.

Jan's call comes ten days after I am back in Raka's house; my mother has died. Perhaps she really was waiting for me to go.

Within minutes of the call, my Mas community is there for me. Putu and Raka's driver pack my bags and bring me water (I have an insatiable thirst). Nyoman arrives and packs up my computer and printer. Raka's husband finds me a flight to the United States. Raka brings me lunch. And as the car passes the gallery on the way to the airport, Raka's family and the entire staff of the gallery, more than twenty people, are out in front, waving and wishing me well. I do have a community; and at that moment, I feel and need and appreciate their love and support.

In a way, I have already mourned my mother's passing; her special glow has been fading for several years. But facing the reality that she is no longer here is still painful. The house is empty without her, and there is something missing inside me. Her ability to inspire people to get involved in charitable work will keep her legacy alive forever; and I'm sure that her spirit, like Tu Aji's, will continue to offer the world her wisdom.

It takes my brother and me more than four months to go through the cellar and the attic, to fix up the house, sell it, and settle the estate.

Just before I leave, I take a trip to Vermont, where Mitch and Melissa are going to have their wedding. They are living in Seattle, and I'm geographically much closer. I meet with people like florists and chefs and hotel owners. I like being a traditional mom for a change.

Soon after I get back from Vermont, I leave for Bali.

First I visit the *puri,* and then I move back into Raka's house; but things are different. There are no more classes in the gallery for the guides, Gustu is too busy to study English, and Pak Tut's projects have been completed.

In looking for new and appropriate ways to contribute to the culture, I decide to teach an English class three nights a week to Putu and Nyoman and two young men from the neighboring island of Lombok, Budi and Ogi.

I met Budi when I stopped in at the Lombok craft shop in the center of Ubud that Budi was managing. Business was slow and we talked for more than an hour. Budi was saying how badly he wanted to take an English class, but he couldn't afford the tuition. I told Budi that if he was serious, I would start a class.

"The class is free," I tell Budi when he and his friend Ogi arrive at the house. "But if you sign on and don't show up, you have to pay." (I never held them to it, but I like the concept.)

Our class meets regularly for nearly two months. Budi and Ogi are especially diligent. I enjoy their enthusiasm and I'm pleased with their progress.

Then one day Budi and Ogi tell me they are going home to Lombok, an island four hours away by ferry, to celebrate the end of the Muslim holiday of Ramadan with their families. Budi invites me to join his family for the holiday weekend.

I've been thinking about going to Lombok to take a scuba diving course, and there is just enough time for me to take the course and then visit Budi's family. I make plans to leave the next day for the little island of Gili Trawangan off the coast of Lombok.

Our scuba classes begin in a pool. There are only two students. The first time I go under with the tank on my back, the mask on my face, and the regulator in my mouth, I feel as though I am only half breathing and I am overcome with a claustrophobic sensation. After several more efforts, I can stay under long enough to do the exercises, but I'm not relaxed. I'm glad we're in a pool; there is something reassuring about knowing I can swim a few seconds and stand up.

The next day we go off into the sea, where we go down twelve meters for fifty-two minutes. First we do the class tasks, getting used to the regulator, and then breathing from someone else's regulator, and then filling our masks with water and emptying them. We get acquainted with buoyancy and weightlessness as we move through an underwater forest of coral and dozens of gorgeous tropical fish. And turtles. And anemones and a manta ray with a twelve-foot wingspan about ten feet away. How glorious.

Four dives, several videos, a math class, and a written exam later, I am presented with my Padi Open Water card. Yippee! I'm a scuba diver.

As soon as the class is finished I take off for Budi and Ogi's village, which is about five hours' worth of boats, buses, more buses, and finally, a horse and carriage away. As we clomp the final few miles into the village, a motorcycle pulls up behind the carriage and two girls call to me.

"Who are you going to visit?" asks one of them.

"Budi and Ogi," I say.

"Budi is my brother," she smiles. And they speed off to tell Budi that I am arriving.

Toward evening, one of Budi's teenage girl-cousins asks me if I would like to join her and the women of the village tonight out on the street. At least that's what I think she says.

"Oh, yes," I answer. "I would like that very much."

"You will have to dress in traditional clothing. I will help you." And off she goes.

The white hooded blouse is like a tent. The head part of it nearly covers my face, and the rest hangs down past my hips. Neatly ironed and much whiter than the whites in my wardrobe, it slips on easily. She also brings me a sarong, white with black squares, similar to the one I just brought to Budi's mother; Budi had helped me pick it out. "No colors," he'd said when I brought him into a shop in Bali.

By the time we are ready, it is dark out. "Come with me," says my guide and we go outside and begin walking. As we walk, my young friend teaches me a chant praising Allah. I am wearing rubber flip-flops with very worn thin soles and I can feel the tiny rocks in the dirt alleyway that leads to the main road. Once again, I am following someone somewhere, but I have no idea where.

I am pleased when we finally arrive among a group of her friends, most of them in their late teens, like her. They are standing around a ten-foot-high, twelve-foot-wide model of a mosque. It is exquisite in its details, with columns and entryways and a tower at the top from which the call to prayer is given. The girls explain to me that there is a contest every year to see which of the three mosque congregations in the village can make the best model mosque. They are speaking quickly and I am able to understand most of what they are telling me. Unfortunately, I miss the point of this gathering, which is to organize a procession of the three mosques.

Soon after we get together, one of the young women in the group tells everyone to line up, and suddenly I am third in from the side and fifth from the front, and I am part of the procession. And then we begin walking and chanting the prayer I was just taught.

At the end of the first block I see Budi and his family. They see me and wave and point me out to the people around them, all of whom crane their necks to spot the tourist in the middle of this holy procession. My face is nearly covered and my shape is well hidden under the white tent I am wearing. And . . . it is dark.

As we walk, I hear voices in the crowd on my left, the side where Budi was standing. *"Turis." "Turis." "Turis."* The news moves through the spectators like a giant wave. I hear the voices before we pass and the cries of discovery as we go by. *"Di mana?" "Di mana turis?"* Where? Where is the tourist? The game moves just ahead of the procession. The point of it all is to find the *turis* . . . me!! I have become Waldo!

The procession does not stop when we reach the end of our village. It passes through two more villages before we reverse the route. On the return route, word has spread and both sides are looking for the *turis,* but on the return trip I am easier to find. My feet are touching the ground through the holy soles of my flip-flops, and I am walking with a limp on my multiple blisters.

All weekend I participate in the festivities with Budi's family and I tour the island on the back of Budi's motorcycle. When I get back to Bali, I'm restless and eager to return to Lombok to take the advanced diving class. I am in Bali for less than a week.

My first morning back on Gili Trawangan, I am drinking coffee on the deck of my thatched-roof bungalow when a great-looking blond guy walks by. He's tall, blue-eyed and in his mid-thirties.

"Good morning," I smile, and he stops. An hour later, after we have breakfasted together, his partner passes our way and joins us.

Lars is a chef from Sweden; Nirin is a doctor, the exquisite combination of a Danish mother and a father from Madagascar. They live in Nantes, France, and are staying two cabins away from me. The bonus is that they speak perfect English. Whenever I am not in class, at the bottom of the ocean, or studying, I hang out with them. We walk and talk and laugh a lot. We share life stories, travel stories, books, recipes, and dinners.

Lars and Nirin are foodies . . . and we never run out of food talk. One day we preorder a grilled fish at a restaurant. When we arrive, the owner shows us the barracuda they are about to put on the grill. It's gorgeous, about two feet long, and it's been out of the water for two hours. It is served unadorned, moist and sweet, with a touch of soy sauce and lemon and ginger. The three of us sit, moaning in pleasure as we bite into the succulent fish.

My scuba classes are not going well. There are eight in the class and no one else is over twenty-five. A fireman from Australia adopts me and helps me carry my tank. We become buddies in the water.

The first sign that this is not going to be easy is when I completely forget how to use my regulator to achieve buoyancy, which is the essence of diving. Then, after a deep dive, I forget to do the safety stop at the ten-meter depth to prevent the bends. Fortunately, we were not so deep that they have to rush me off to a decompression chamber.

The next day we learn to navigate with compasses. Our instructions are to go out to a spot about forty feet from the boat, then, using our snorkels, swim in a square until we end up back where we started. When I come up, I am nowhere near where I should be.

I have never been very good at navigation. I try again and do no better. Everyone is a little amazed at how totally inept I am at reading the compass. The thing is that you have to hold the compass level or it won't work. I can't seem to get mine to stay level. I swim back to the boat and promise that if they pass me, I will never do anything in my entire life that requires compass navigation.

"Night diving is wonderful," says the scuba teacher the third day. "You're going to love it. All the nocturnal creatures are out."

The thought of going down into the black depths with a tank on my back and a regulator in my mouth terrifies me; but I have to do it if I want the advanced certification. Besides, I don't want to quit. All those under-twenty-fives in my class are rooting for me. I'm the senior mascot. How can I let them down?

As we motor out to the dive spot, my heart is pounding. I cannot remember ever being so frightened. Our teacher informs us that the combination of the full moon and the hour might make the current too strong for us to dive safely. He will send his assistant down first to assess the safety of the current. Please let it be cancelled. Oh, how I do not want to go.

The assistant comes up with his assessment. We can do it.

Now I don't know how it happens that I go down first, but once we do our over-the-side-backward-into-the-water entry, I am told to descend along the rope and wait for everyone else down there. I do not remember if we have been told at what depth to wait, but I go down into the black water and I keep going down. When I level off, I look around me for the next person and I see nothing but the beam of my flashlight in the water. Where is my buddy? He should have followed me down. There is a strong current and I can feel it pulling me. Why did I let go of the rope?

For what feels like a very long time, I try to stay in one place, moving my flashlight around, hoping someone will see it, but no one arrives, so I swim around searching for another light. I can feel myself floating in the current, my head is light and empty, and I suddenly feel giddy. I know that I am experiencing nitrogen narcosis, but one of the characteristics of this condition is that you don't care. I don't. I should be looking at my regulator to see how deep I am, but I'm not. I have no idea how long I have been alone when the teacher's assistant finds me and pulls me up. I am many meters below where I should be. This is a deep dive (twenty-four meters) and I am well below that.

Once I am at the level of the rest of the class, I look around for my partner, but all I can see are flashlight beams. Everyone looks alike in the dark. I try to stay still and wait for my partner to find me, but the current is pulling me. Don't panic! This is all about remaining calm. Finally, my partner taps me on the shoulder and we move on together. I cannot bring myself to search for night creatures. I keep my flashlight focused on my partner. We are down for a total of five minutes when we go up. It feels like an hour.

As we ascend, slowly, I repeat over and over, don't forget the safety stop. I am afraid that I will whiz by and end up at the surface with the bends. But I do it right.

When I am finally on board, I am both relieved and disoriented. It was worse than I imagined. I vow that if he passes me on this dive, I will never, not ever, do another night dive.

I don't have to. But the teacher, with an apology, informs me the next day that I am not ready to be issued an advanced certification. I agree.

Over the next two days, I do four fun dives, playing, exploring, and enjoying the underwater world. My confidence is restored and when I finally go down for an assessment dive, it's perfect. We float past a shark on the bottom, giant clams, hundreds of spectacular fish of every possible color, two massive manta rays, and several of the gorgeous tiny sea slugs called nudibranchs, the most beautiful creatures I have ever seen, decorated in ruffles and paisley prints and iridescent colors.

That night Lars, Nirin, and I celebrate my hard-won Advanced Diver card. The next day I return to Bali.

When I am back in Mas, I decide that it is time for me to move on. I have been in Bali, on and off, for eight years. During those years, I have meditated on the beach, prayed in the temples, feted and released the spirits of the dead, and deepened my belief that there are other levels of existence. In Bali I have felt a warm smooth flow inside of me, an ethereal sensation of well-being. Now I feel it is time for me to reconnect with my family for a while.

I say good-bye to my friends in Mas. Then I go to the *puri* for my last night.

I am sitting at the dining table, which is set for one. All through dinner I can sense Tu Aji's spirit. He is sitting across the table in the chair where he always sat when we talked into the night. There are tears in his eyes as there are tears in mine. After eight years, I am about to leave him, perhaps never to return. How can I leave this man who was closer to me than my father, who taught me more than any teacher, who told me his secrets and helped me through pain. I'm sorry, Tu Aji. Please forgive me for leaving. He does.

I am still sitting at the table, surrounded by the kindness of Tu Aji and filled with his spirit, when Wayan greets me. *"Selamat malam, Bu Rita."*

"Hi," I say. Wayan senses my sadness.

I don't want to say good-bye to him either. We have shared so many conversations, so many motorcycle trips and dinners and lunches. It is from the back of Wayan's motorcycle that I have seen the villages and hills and vistas of the island, done my shopping, visited computer repair people, toured rice fields to see how rice grows, and gone to the cool mountains when the heat of the lower lands got to me.

I remember in the beginning, when he used to come over in the evenings after dinner; as we talked, I would give him wonderful words, the kind you don't learn in school, like *serendipity* and *silhouette*. And when he came back the next night, he would somehow manage to slip his newest word into our conversation.

Wayan has remained a good friend. He's followed me to my various homes in Bali. And even when I'm in the U.S., he stays in touch by e-mail. He's become a certified guide, and everyone I send to him loves him.

"So what do you want to do on your last night?" he asks.

"Let's go eeling," I say.

"Eeling?" He laughs. It's an odd request.

The first time I saw eeling was one midnight, about a year after I first arrived on the island. I was staying in Ubud, alone, in a thatched-roof bungalow in the middle of rice fields. The air was heavy, the night was dark, and I couldn't sleep. I walked out onto the small deck that stretched across the second story of the bungalow. There were two balls of fire dancing in the pitch-black fields.

Leyak? I had read that *these* evil spirits sometimes take the form of fireballs. Several friends had related stories about the terrifying black nights when they'd encountered them. Now I was staring at a strange fire-ballet in the midnight *sawah* (rice fields).

Turned out that *my* balls of fire were not *leyak* but people with lanterns who were out catching eels. Now, eight years later, I am saying good-bye to Bali, and I realize that I've never seen eeling up close.

"I don't know when I'm going to come back again and I've never caught an eel. Will you take me?"

"Sure," said Wayan. "But we can't go until after the moon sets. The eels only come up out of the mud if there's no moon in the sky."

At about 10:30 Wayan picks me up and we go to his family's house to get the eeling tools: a pail, a plierlike gadget for gripping the prey, and a lantern, the kind that pumps and throws out blinding light. Wayan's father and mother and some neighbors are waiting for us. Like everything else in a Balinese village, our activity is no secret.

"We'll bring you dinner," I joke as we leave.

Wayan carries the lantern and I carry the pail. The paths between the terraced fields are raised, sometimes three or four feet higher than the cultivated part. As we walk, Wayan explains to me that we are headed toward a group of fields where the seedlings are still tiny.

"If the rice plants are big," he explains, "You can't see the eels lying on top of the mud."

There is no rice season in Bali as there is a corn season or an apple season or a summer growing season in other parts of the world. At all times you can find rice at every stage of development. The folklore says that there was once a giant who came to the island and threatened to eat all the children. "Wait," said the parents. "We need the children to help in the harvest. You can have them when the harvesting is done." The giant agreed, but the farmers staggered their planting and the giant never got his feast. And so it is even today. Wayan and I walk through nearly ripe rice on our way to an area with tiny seedlings.

The paths through the *sawah* are narrow. Wet and narrow. I place one foot in front of the other. Mud oozes into my flip-flops. Now my foot is sliding in the sandals and the sandals are sliding in the mud. From time to time, we have to step wide, from one path across a dip to another path. My legs are short, my feet are slipping, and I am afraid to take the long step.

"Wayan, hold my hand over this part," I say every time we get to a difficult step, a muddy stretch, or a particularly narrow path. Fortunately this is a culture where young people are very solicitous of their elders. Wayan stays close.

Finally we get to the fields that are newly cultivated. We walk the paths, barefoot, holding the lantern down so we can spot the eels. Every few feet I slip. Every couple of minutes I call out, "Wayan, give me your hand."

Besides holding my hand, Wayan's job is to spot the curvy shape of an eel lying on top of the mud, slip down from the relatively solid path into the six-inch-deep mud, nab the eel with the pliers, and put it into the pail with our flip-flops.

"Where are the eels?"

"There's one." He points. I don't see it. Leaning over for a better look, I slip, slide down the two-foot drop, and end up lying in six inches of mud on top of a bunch of unfortunate seedlings. The eel has slithered away.

"Show me another," I say, laughing, as he puts down the lantern, lifts the pail out of the mud, and pulls me back up to the path.

Finally I see an eel. It's a little darker than the mud. A shadowy dark "S" on top of the brown bottom. Wayan slips down and grasps the wiggly creature with the pliers and we have an eel in our pail, along with two pair of flip-flops and a muddy straw coinpurse that was in my pocket.

Wayan continues to help me along the paths. He keeps pointing to eels that I can't see. Only once do I try to snag my own eel and I get squeamish at the last minute and slip again in the mud.

"So how many eels do you usually get?" I ask an hour later as we start back.

"Oh, a hundred, a hundred fifty. Depends on the night." We have eleven.

Wayan walks me back to the *puri*. He has been quiet on the way home; it's always hard for him when I leave. We are standing just off the little patio outside my room, the same room that Tu Aji showed me eight years ago, on my first day in Bali. Wayan cannot see the tears in my eyes.

The sky is black and filled with stars. There are squeaky bats eating the fruit of the *sabah* tree. The *sabah* fruit is brown and figlike, and every night when the fruit is ripe the bats squeak and streak around the garden. The buzzing of the cicadas is harsh and endless. The family is sleeping, each room dotted with a light that is keeping away the evil spirits.

Wayan and I are surrounded by the sweet perfume of night-blooming jasmine. He is quiet. Then, after I give him a hug and he turns to go home, he finally speaks.

"You're not very well balanced are you?"

The next morning I leave for the airport. Tu Biang, Tu Man, Dayu Biang, Jero Made, Wayan, and an assortment of neighbors all accompany me to the car. As soon as the driver starts the engine, everyone begins to wave. As we drive down the street, I stick my head out the window and wave back until they are out of sight. There are tears in my eyes. It is the end of an extraordinary chapter in my life. But Bali will always be with me.

In Bali I have learned to listen to the spirits, the inner one that is a part of me and the ones from the other, invisible, world, who have been such an important part of everyday of my life on this magical island. In Bali I have experienced a serenity deeper than I have ever known.

Canada/
United States

CHAPTER SIXTEEN

VANCOUVER AND
SEATTLE

I t is 1997 when I leave Bali. I first arrived in December of 1988. A lot has happened during those years. My mother, my father, and Tu Aji died. Mitch got married. Jan, Mitch, and Melissa all moved from New York to Seattle to work in Internet journalism. And I've gone through a significant spiritual development. Right now I feel that I'd like to be near the kids for a while.

I am still uncomfortable with the idea of moving in on top of them. Ideally I'd like to rent a place for a few months within two or three hours of Seattle, a place that they could come to whenever they wanted, for weekends or vacations. Years ago, when we were a young family living in Manhattan, we had a country house that was three hours away. We all enjoyed the drive and we did it every weekend and all the school holidays. I'd like to offer them a country house again, this time outside of Seattle.

A few days before I leave Bali, I am talking to a friend from Taiwan. Innovette mentions that she is planning to visit a friend of hers in Vancouver.

Vancouver. It's perfect. Three hours from Seattle. A great place for a country retreat. I've never been there, so it'll be an adventure for me. And I love the idea that there's a huge ethnic Chinese and other Asian population there. And I even have two Canadian friends in Vancouver that I met in Bali.

When I mention that I might rent in Vancouver for a few months, Innovette says, "Call my friend Sue. I'm sure she'll be able to help you."

A new destination is created and a friend is born. When I call Sue from Seattle, she invites me to stay with her while I look.

I ring the doorbell of a suburban Vancouver house and a beautiful Chinese woman welcomes me. Sue is tiny with long shiny black hair and a warm matter-of-fact smile. She makes me feel as though there is nothing special about the fact that she is welcoming a perfect stranger into her home and giving me bed and board. Sue, her partner, Stephen, a Canadian, and her teenage daughters, Vicky and Waylin, take me into their family. For nearly a week I eat Sue's great Chinese cooking, meet her friends, and tour around Vancouver with her, looking at different neighborhoods and houses. I also take everybody out for dinner several times. Sue picks the restaurants—all of them Chinese—and orders the meals. We eat magnificently.

Each morning I pour through the *Vancouver Sun*. I want something wonderful, with land and a view, something the kids will love, something big enough for everyone—them, their friends, my friends. It's a good time for this. My investments are doing well and I'm ready to break my rule: I'm going to sell some stock and splurge.

I call on an ad for a house outside of Vancouver in a community called Belcarra. According to the ad, the house is modern and it has a view, a brook, trees, and wooded land. And dogs, says the ad, are welcome. Mitch and Melissa have two of them; sounds like a place Riley and Abby and all the rest of us will like.

I find Belcarra on a map. It sits at the end of a peninsula, forty minutes from downtown Vancouver. To get to it, you have to drive through a national park. Sounds intriguing.

The house is spectacular. I step inside and feel as though I am still outside. Only glass walls separate me from the trees and the sky. The house, natural wood inside and out, sits on a hill with a view of water and islands and pine trees and sky. From the kitchen and the patio, you can hear the brook that runs through the property. The massive bathroom Jacuzzi looks out at water and tall pines, through a tub-to-ceiling window. The view from nearly every window is breathtaking. And the house is elegantly but simply furnished.

There are four bedrooms, four bathrooms, and a deck. The owners tell me that the house has been empty for several months. I offer sixteen hundred U.S. dollars, which is about a third less than they are asking. It's a deal! For three months. As an added perk, the owner is paying for a cleaning crew every other week.

Now I need a car. Jan is driving a battered old Honda that used to belong to Mitch, and she's been mumbling about wanting a new car. A three-month car rental would cost me fifteen hundred dollars.

"How would you like fifteen hundred dollars toward a new car?" I propose. "I'll take the Honda." Done. I have a car and a spectacular house. Now for the guests.

Sue and family are the first to see my new home. I invite them to spend the day at my little resort; the invitation includes a hike, dinner, and a Jacuzzi. Together we go through the kitchen cabinets. I told the owner that it was fine with me if she left baking ingredients and spices in the cabinets.

Waylin, who is fourteen, decides to bake cookies. She is nearly finished with the dough when she discovers that we have no baking soda. "Let's see if your neighbors have any," says Waylin, and off we go. I haven't even met them yet.

Maria answers the doorbell. Waylin and I introduce ourselves and explain our mission. We meet Maria's daughters, Atlanta and Natasha, and their father, Walter. And we leave with a tiny plastic cup of baking soda. Later that afternoon, we bring over a plate of cookies.

There is also a neighbor on the other side, though we cannot see each other through the thick lot of trees. The owner of my house has said that if I am ever in trouble, I should call John, and she gave me his number. He's a policeman.

Two nights later I am leaving to meet Mitch and Melissa in a supermarket parking lot about twenty minutes away (there is not even a mom-and-pop grocery in Belcarra). They are arriving from Seattle between eleven-thirty and midnight, and I told them I would lead them to the house rather than have them try to read signs in the dark.

At eleven-fifteen, as I am backing out of the hill, which is my driveway, my rear wheel goes over a curb and into the pansy patch. I can't move forward and I can't move back. I spend ten minutes trying to get out, but I just dig deeper in. The car won't move.

I decide to call John the policeman. It is late, but I'm in trouble. Mitch and Melissa will arrive to an empty parking lot and no directions. John's wife answers the phone. I explain who I am and tell her my problem.

"I'm so sorry," she tells me, "John isn't home. But you could borrow my car if you like. Then John could come by in the morning and help you with your car."

How kind. I have never even met this woman. I thank her and say that I will first try Walter on the other side; there are lights on in his house.

Walter and Maria both come over to have a look. Walter tries to drive out, but he can't do it either; so he goes home for their car and a rope, and he pulls me out.

I like my new neighborhood.

Belcarra turns out to be great for hiking, crab fishing, lying in my hammock by the brook, and having lots of guests. Jan, Mitch, Melissa, and Jan's friends Craig, his dog Jasper, and Robin. Sue, Stephen, Waylin and Vicky, and even Innovette, my Taiwanese friend from Bali, who visits Sue while I'm in Vancouver. And Don, a university professor, and Dan, both of whom I also met in Bali. And many more.

A couple of weeks after I arrive, Don takes me to a children's festival where there are people painting people, others playing guitars and drums, others singing and dancing. There are balloons, plays, food stands, and even literary characters running around. We have been there for ten minutes when the Mad Hatter from Alice in Wonderland rushes toward me shouting, "Rita, what are you doing here?" It's Dan Vie. I met him when he was studying masked dancing and comedy in Bali. I love it.

My favorite Vancouver activity is going to T & T supermarkets. I can't stay away from them. They're a chain of mammoth Asian supermarkets where you can get stuff for any Asian recipe anywhere. Sometimes I drive forty minutes into downtown Vancouver just to spend a couple of hours in this Asian foodie paradise. The exploding Hong Kong/Taiwanese population of Vancouver has brought not only brilliant and talented students, a wonderful mix of people, bilingual street signs, and fabulous restaurants but also this chain of spectacular supermarkets. You can buy duck's tongues and shark's fins, and Indonesian bird's nests (at $250 an ounce). There are sixty different brands of soy sauce and forty varieties of frozen fish, including whole eels and cuttlefish and dace and sandgoby and keo fish. And there's a wall full of thousands of frozen dim sum, and fresh mangosteens (the fruit the dying Tu Nini requested) in the produce department.

And another wall of fish tanks with carp and tilapia and rockfish, crabs and shrimp and lobsters and clams and mussels and cockles, swimming and crawling and hanging out. My favorite live animals in the tank section are the geoducks, pronounced "gooeyducks" after the Nisqually Indian word *gweduc,* which means "dig deep." They live around a meter down in the sand on the ocean bottom, sometimes fairly close to shore. They are the giant clams of sushi, chewy and sweet, and they can weigh up to seven pounds. The ones in the markets are usually between four and five pounds. The round, clammy part is as big as a man's hand, but it's the neck, or siphon, that makes these guys memorable. It looks like a huge brown phallus, it can be as wide as five inches and as long as three or four feet, and it expands and contracts.

"I want one," I tell Sue. "Do you know what to do with it?"

"Yes, of course," she tells me. And then she shows me how to squoosh the siphon before I weigh it so the water will squirt out. The siphon is the part that is sliced up raw for sushi. The part inside the shell can be fried or boiled.

Sue does the cooking and I eat the neck part raw, like sashimi, and I am buried in fifteen by four inches of thinly sliced heaven.

I spend a lot of time in my hammock by the brook, the water trickling down the hill toward the salty bay, the leaves rustling in the wind. I sit for hours in my Jacuzzi, reading, thinking, dreaming.

Jan, Mitch, Melissa, Riley, and Abby come up often.

My college friend Debby from Maryland arrives with her friend Pat. The three of us talk nonstop for three days, close, intimate, personal woman-stuff.

June, our childhood friendship having been renewed at a high school reunion a few years ago, comes up from L.A. to work with me on a collaborative writing project.

Marianne from the Sunshine Coast arrives to work on a joint book-project on nudibranchs, those gorgeous little sea slugs that I met when I was diving in Lombok.

Kathy, an artist and friend from L.A. who now spends half the year in a wonderful old farmhouse on the Sunshine Coast (it's through Kathy that I met Marianne), comes with her dog en route to L.A. I like being in the hosting mode.

And Don, the university professor; Dan, the Mad Hatter; my neighbors Walter and Maria, who pulled me out of a ditch; and Bonnie and Brian, who live a couple of houses away, all become better friends as we exchange invitations.

While I'm in Vancouver, the kids suggest that when my three months are up, I should rent for a while in Seattle. They want me closer. I'm flattered.

Jan and Melissa and Mitch live within walking distance of each other, and they want me to try to find something nearby. After a couple of weeks of searching, we're all getting impatient. Everything I see is a box. The only place that intrigues me is down the street from Jan.

Nearly every day, en route to Pert's deli for coffee, I walk by a "For Rent" sign on a ground-floor apartment that has Lake Washington in its back-yard. The rent is fifteen hundred dollars a month, which is high for Seattle . . . and for me. To avoid temptation, I don't even write down the owner's number.

Then one day, while Mitch and I are passing by the sign on our way to look at what we know will be yet another box down the street, we impulsively ring the upstairs doorbell. John introduces himself and tells us he and his wife are tenants; the owner doesn't live here. John offers to walk with us around the back so we can see the view and peek in the windows.

I like what I see. There's a glass-walled living room that looks out on the lake. And a backyard with a boat dock. I do not own a boat, but I like the idea of having a slip, just in case a boat comes into my life. Who knows? If I live here, maybe I'll buy a kayak.

The apartment is unfurnished and I don't own any furniture, but I can live with very little, and I love the location, the view, the picture window, the charcoal grill, the umbrella table, the benches, the dock, and the lake. And I like the second bedroom. If I'm going to settle in for a while, I want a guestroom. John says the owner is flexible and would probably give me a six-month lease if I ask for one. I give in and write down the owner's name and number.

I have plans to fly to New York the next morning, so Melissa meets Bron, the owner, at the apartment, with my check in hand. I call Melissa from the airport. She reports that the apartment is great.

Then I call Bron. She and I talk until the plane begins boarding. Melissa has told her that I write children's books. Bron tells me that she grew up with books; her father is a literary agent in New Zealand.

As soon as I return from New York, I move in, with a futon and bed linens from Jan's apartment, a table and three chairs from Mitch and Melissa's house, one towel, one toothbrush, a bag of clothes, my computer, and a book. That's it. No couches, dishes, glasses, silverware, pots, or lamps . . . not yet. I feel as though I'm still on the road, which makes the transition easier.

The day I move in, I phone John, my upstairs neighbor. A woman answers. I introduce myself and invite her to stop in and say hello. I apologize in advance for the fact that I have no dishes and I won't even be able to offer her a cup of tea, but I'd like very much to meet her. She tells me that John will be home in a few hours and they will come down together.

It is already dark when the doorbell rings. I open the door and find John and his wife, Jip, holding a pot of tea, three cups, and a plate of cookies.

The three of us sit facing the lake, at the lone table and chairs, in the dark unfurnished living room. It takes less than a minute to know that I am going to like them. John is a librarian in an elementary school and Jip is from Thailand. They met in a Cambodian refugee camp in northern Thailand, where John was a volunteer and Jip was a nurse. Three and a half years later, after they both finished graduate school, they married, with weddings and receptions in Seattle, Washington; Chicago, Illinois (where John is from); and Ban Krud, Thailand.

I furnish the apartment from Goodwill, my kids' closets, and a care package of kitchen utensils from John and Jip that they had packed up to go to Goodwill. (This is only a brief detour, since everything will eventually find its way to Goodwill.) Mitch and Melissa have extra glasses and dishes, a colander, and a few pillows and sheets. Jan has some pots and pans and towels. Jan's friend Christine delivers a combination TV/VCR that she isn't using. And Jan has a closet full of my mother's paintings, which turn the place from a space into a home.

I buy a twenty-dollar open-up couch from Goodwill and another for thirty-four dollars. I also buy four Goodwill lamps, a bunch of serving dishes, a small cast-iron frying pan, and a few low tables, one of which I put at the foot end of my futon, and two sets of placemats.

Jan has also given me a good, firm double bed that she doesn't want. I put the bed in the guestroom and opt to sleep on the futon on the floor.

I finish my decorating with a couple of cotton throw rugs from Goodwill. The only new things I buy are a wok and a grapefruit knife with two close-together blades that straddle the sections; I've never seen such a thing before, and I can't resist buying it.

For the first time since I started my new life, I am living on my own in the United States. Over the years I've stayed with my mother for long stretches, with my kids and friends and family, each for no more than a week at a time. And I've had brief stints house-sitting and house-sharing. Now, I am about to live the life I decided, thirteen years ago, that I never wanted to live. My kids are here with their own lives and jobs and friends. I'm sure we'll see each other a lot, but I don't ever want them saying to each other, "Oh, God, we better do something with Mom on Sunday." It's not the doing I worry about. It's the "Oh, God."

So, as I begin my six months in Seattle, I set about building my own community. John and Jip are my first friends. They're responsive, close by, and spontaneous. Jip and I do yoga three mornings a week, we plant a vegetable garden together, take walks, have dinners. And twice we go to a Buddhist center for all-day meditation. I visit John's school and talk to the kids about books and writing. And one day, early on, when I mention to John that it's a terrible waste for me to have a boat slip and no boat, he tells me he has a friend with a boat and no slip. And that's how I meet Tom.

Within days there's an eighteen-foot sailboat in my backyard, and Tom and I are sailing mates. Tom, who is in his thirties, single, and a child advocate in Seattle's Department of Health and Social Services, is happy to have a pal to sail with. And I'm thrilled to be seeing Seattle from the waters of Lake Washington. Tom loves pointing out lakeside attractions such as Bill Gates's mansion and hidden coves filled with spectacular homes. From time to time we tie up somewhere and go off for lunch or a walk.

Tom is part of John and Jip's extended Seattle family. Tom's mother, Libby, welcomed Jip from the first moment Jip landed on U.S. shores. Now Libby is welcoming me, another stranger, at her potluck dinners. It feels good.

Bron Richards, my landlady, also becomes a friend. Until I entered my nomadic life, I thought of "friendship" as a relationship that needs years to develop. To truly call each other friends, I thought, two people need a history together in which they share and celebrate and mourn the events in each other's lives over many years. But my lifestyle doesn't give me the luxury of a shared history, and I need friends.

So, like other long-term travelers I've met (all women), I have learned how to compress time through introducing, early in my conversation, intimate details of my life. My "homelessness" is always a good way to begin. And I openly talk about my divorce, my discovery of a nomadic alternative to a traditional life, and the joy and occasional loneliness that goes along with it. Once I've opened the conversation with intimate details of my life, the usual superficialities of an initial conversation have been bypassed.

Bron and I click immediately. She is recently divorced and still struggling with the trauma. The first time we talk (she has come by to cut the grass in the communal backyard), our conversation lasts through dinner. At some point I mention that I'm in the market for friends. The next day I get a phone call from a friend of Bron's, inviting me to join a writers' group, and a new set of friends is born.

Being near the kids is fun. We get to spend a lot of lost time together. It feels very comfortable. I thought I was going to learn how to be alone in the U.S.; I never have to.

Then one day, Jan calls me.

"I just picked up a message on my answering machine from Lars," she says. "Call him."

Lars is the chef I met in Lombok. I visited him and Nirin last year, in Nantes, France.

He and Nirin are desperately looking for me. It's 5:00 P.M. in Nantes and they just got a call from their travel agent, who has found them a cheap ticket to Seattle. They have to pick up the ticket in the next two hours and be on the plane in Paris tomorrow. They need to know immediately if they can come stay with me. If so, they'll be here at five tomorrow afternoon. I call France.

Lars and Nirin will arrive half an hour before Don from Vancouver, who booked in for the weekend two weeks ago. (I'm glad I bought the open-up couch.) First I'll meet the plane, then the three of us will meet Don's bus.

As I am planning dinner, I remember my week of gourmet eating in Nantes, when Lars cooked fois gras, vegetable puff pastry appetizers, fabulous shrimp, lemony desserts, homemade bread, and quiche. We breakfasted on personally preserved jams and snacked on home-cooked chutneys.

How do you cook for a great chef? I decide the only direction I can go is Asian. As far as I know, Lars doesn't cook Asian dishes; but I have no doubt that he and Nirin like them. A foodie is a foodie in any cuisine.

Seattle is a great place for buying Asian ingredients. As Lars and Nirin are winging their way across the Atlantic, I shop in Asian markets and spend the day chopping. For our first dinner, I grill Vietnamese shrimp balls and chicken *sate*. I cook mu shu pork (I buy the pancakes), chicken and broccoli with hoisin sauce, beef with snow peas, eggplant with garlic sauce, and pork lo mein. Bron happens to stop by, and she joins us. When dinner is over, we sit outside and enjoy the lake and the moon.

It must have been Jan who told Lars that I had a birthday coming up. He and Nirin decide to throw me a dinner party. The invited guests are Jan, Melissa, Mitch, John, Jip, Bron, Jan's friend Craig, and Lars, Nirin, and I. My pots are OK for the cooking, but my Goodwill placemats do not satisfy Lars's vision of elegance. So, while the gravlax is curing in the refrigerator, and I am vegetating in my hammock by the lake reading *A Year in*

Provence, they raid Jan's cabinets for tablecloths, linen napkins, crystal wineglasses, dishes, serving platters, and candleholders. And then they go off shopping in my car.

By the time the guests arrive, my Goodwill room is transformed into a romantic paradise, with candles flickering, wineglasses sparkling, and escargots, brought from France, waiting to be dipped in melted garlic butter.

The gravlax (made from a whole fresh Seattle salmon, boned and cured in the refrigerator for three days with equal parts coarse salt and sugar and lots of fresh dill stuffed into the middle) is served with a traditional Swedish sauce: three tablespoons French mustard, two tablespoons sugar, one-half cup vegetable oil, and chopped fresh dill, ground pepper, and salt.

Nirin, who is a doctor, cooks the main course, which hails from Réunion, an island next to Madagascar where his father is from. It's a spicy chicken stew.

And Lars whips up a chocolate mousse for dessert, struggling with American ingredients and measurements and having to add more and more cream until we have mousse for fifty.

Good people. Great birthday. Makes up for all the birthdays I've spent alone and feeling lonely.

On a Saturday several weeks later, I find myself alone. Jan's in New York, Mitch and Melissa are off for the weekend, John and Jip are down in Oregon, and Bron is taking a weekend class. I don't feel like being alone, but I can't think of anyone to call. I decide to take a public bus down to REI, the recreational equipment store. My mission: buy a rain parka. I need one and they're having a big sale. I do have an umbrella, but hardly anybody in this rainy city uses one. They just pull up their hoods and go about their business. I've been wanting to see REI ever since I got here. There's an outdoor mountain bike track and I've been eager to see the giant pinnacle for climbing inside the store. And it'll be fun to look at the kayaks and tents and exotic equipment.

I've never used the buses in Seattle; I still have the old Honda. But I like taking public buses. I call Metro and get the bus route. Then I throw on some sweatpants, a turtleneck shirt, and my worn purple fleece jacket. I take $1.25 in change out of my wallet and put it in my pocket. I toss my empty book bag (I'll put the parka in it later) over one shoulder and I'm off.

About five stops after I get on the bus, a withered woman in her eighties sits behind me and announces to everyone on the bus that she lost her husband last year and she's been sick ever since. The doctors are too dumb to figure out what's wrong with her. She can't afford the medicine they've told her to buy. And she hurts all the time.

"This country doesn't care about its old people," she screams. Everyone is avoiding her glance.

I turn around and say to her, "I'm so sorry you're hurting. You are absolutely right about medicines. These days no one can afford to buy them."

"You know," she says, softer but still loud enough for everyone to hear, "all over the world countries provide health care for their people. And here we are, the richest country in the world, and our government doesn't care what happens to people when they get old and sick. Remember when Hillary Clinton had a plan for universal health care? Now there's a smart lady. She cares. Where is the conscience of our Congress?"

The woman is astonishingly articulate and her argument is lucid. I wonder when she lost touch and began ranting. Who was she forty years ago? Or even three? How did she get to this place? She gets off before I do. I say good-bye and wish her luck.

REI is fun. I wander for about two hours, picking out a blue Gore-Tex parka and a pair of Teva sandals. (I've been here only five months and already I'm buying labels!) When I'm ready to go, I stand in the cashier's line and put my purchases on the counter.

She smiles sweetly as I reach into my book bag for my wallet. It isn't there.

At first I suspect it's been stolen; but when I think about it, I realize that the book bag has never left my sight. The more I think, the clearer it becomes. My wallet is sitting on the counter at home. I took it out of the book bag to get the bus change and I never put it back in. And then it hits me. I don't have the bus fare to get home.

Jan is an REI member and I have her number. I ask the cashier if she can charge $1.25 to Jan's membership number and give me bus fare.

"Oh, I'm so sorry, ma'am," she says. "I can't do that."

I ask where the customer relations desk is and I take my purchases to put on hold. My head is spinning. I don't even have a quarter to make a phone call, but it doesn't matter because there's no one I can call. And it's too far to walk.

I'm going to have to beg for this money. But from whom? Maybe the other customers, who can certainly afford to give me $1.25. Then I realize that they will probably try to avoid my eyes, like the people on the bus avoided that other woman. I look at my appearance and realize I could easily pass for a homeless person. I am wearing sweatpants and a worn purple jacket, the one we wrapped that dying baby in more than a year ago.

Maybe I should go outside and find a cop. I wonder how many hard-up middle-aged women approach cops every day for money. Maybe I should just get on a bus and plead with the driver.

I think again about the old woman on the bus. She was just ranting. I'm going to be begging!

I get to the customer relations desk and stand in line. First I give the young woman my purchases and ask her to hold them for me. Then I tell her my story and ask if she can charge $1.25 to Jan's membership number and give me the money.

"I'm sorry," she says, sweetly. "I can't do that."

Oh, God. This is really happening; I'm not imagining it! I look around at all the people and I feel so alone, so alienated. Here in Seattle, in the U.S., in this upscale sporting goods store, I am the outsider.

I'm going to give it one last shot. I ask for the manager of the department. She points to José, a young man two lines over. When I get to the front of his line, I tell him my story and make the same request.

"I'm so sorry," he says. Then he reaches in his pocket and takes out $1.25.

An hour and a half later, I return to REI with his money, a credit card, and a note to the store manager about the kindness of José. I wonder if he has any idea how much that meant to me.

While I'm in Seattle, the news of the economic disaster sweeping Southeast Asia breaks. Indonesia is one of the hardest-hit countries. When I left more than a year ago, one U.S. dollar was worth 2,500 rupiah. In June of 1998, the paper reports that the dollar is now worth 16,950 rupiah. It hurts. Indonesia is not a country and a government to me. It is Wayan and Tu Biang and Putu and Dayu Raka. It is Pak Tut in the gallery and Nyoman and the guides. What is happening to them? I make plans to go back.

Bali has never left me. There are moments when I stare out my living room window at Lake Washington, and instead of seeing the lake with

Mount Rainier looming in the distance, I see terraced rice fields with dragonflies fluttering in the sun.

Sometimes I hear Tu Aji's voice when I am telling a story, "And then? And then?" he says, impatient, as always, to hear the rest. And I often think of that invisible world, filled with spirits both good and bad. If it exists in Bali, it must be in Seattle too. But I feel so distant from spirituality here in the land of Microsoft. And I miss it. Does Tu Aji hear me when I "talk" to him from Seattle? How about my parents? I find it easier to "talk" to all of them when I'm in Bali.

I especially think of Bali during my yoga and meditation sessions with Jip. I feel a peacefulness in my soul that reminds me of the serenity I felt in Bali. In spite of the caste system, in spite of women's second-class status, in spite of the feudalistic society, I yearn to be back.

New Zealand

NEW ZEALAND
VIA BALI

'm going back to Bali. The Southeast Asian economies have collapsed and the news out of Indonesia is scary: the country is exploding with violence. I need to see firsthand what is happening.

In July of 1998, Wayan writes that there has been no violence in Bali, but tourism is dead and many people have no work. Businesses are closing and banks are failing.

I need to know that my friends can feed their families. Most of them are not losing money in the failing banks; they live from one day to the next without savings, hoping that they will be able to make the monthly payments on their motorcycles. Their money problems are much more basic than banks: food, clothing, gas for the motorcycle, and money to pay for the ceremonies that are the essence of Balinese life. If they are in trouble, I want to be there for them.

For me, financially, the time to help has never been better. The volatile rupiah has strengthened a little in the last two months, but its value is still dramatically diminished. By August, a dollar converts to 12,000 rupiah. When I left, it was worth 2,500.

My plan is to stay in Bali for a month. Before I leave Seattle, I have to decide where to go when the month is over. My destination has to fit with my plan to work on a proposal for a book about my life as a nomad. That means I have to settle in somewhere for about six months. I'll need English-language libraries, not too many distractions, and a relative degree of comfort.

It would be logical to work in the U.S., but I can't afford it. I've been in Seattle now for nearly seven months, in an apartment that is costing me fifteen hundred dollars a month. My annual income last year was in the vicinity of twenty thousand dollars, and I don't want to dip into my savings again.

Like most of my destination decisions, this one comes about serendipitously. Bron, my landlady in Seattle, who has become a good friend, is from New Zealand. I've looked through her books and pictures; the country is exquisite. Not only that, her parents live in Auckland, run a literary agency, and they already know about me from Bron. And the best part, if I settle in New Zealand for a while, Jan, Mitch, and Melissa say they'll come visit.

Additionally, Servas is strong in New Zealand. Even though I don't plan to stay with Servas people (I will look for something to rent), if I need friends, I can always call and meet them.

My month in Bali is both happy and sad. I love seeing everyone, but life is hard. The first thing people say, after telling me how fat I've gotten, is that the price of rice has nearly doubled. There is an uncharacteristic fear of the future, rare in a community that usually lives in the present.

I am angry at the injustices of the world economy. For the western tourist with dollars, everything is ridiculously cheap. I can buy sarongs for a dollar-fifty, meals in the best restaurants for two dollars, and antiques and jewelry and artwork for five times less than the same things cost a year ago. It's wrong and I am overwhelmed by the urge to give away dollars on street corners.

Except in emergencies, I have never gotten into the habit of giving people money. I feel strongly that accepting charity robs people of their dignity and usually puts them in the uncomfortable position of being unable to reciprocate.

Reciprocity is an on-the-ground, real concept in Bali. When you bring a wedding gift, you bring it on a tray or in a basket with rice and sugar. Your tray is "checked" when you arrive, as you might check a coat in a restaurant. When you retrieve your tray, it is filled with cakes or fruit or some other food item for you to take home.

In 1990, when I was giving the king's wives English lessons, I grew very close to them. When it was time for me to leave Bali for a three-month visit to the United States, I decided to give each of them, and their unmarried daughters, a small gift. Hoping to bypass the reciprocity ethic, I distributed the gifts one hour before I was to leave for the airport; too late, I thought, for them to bring me anything.

I was wrong. As my bags were being loaded into the car, a procession of princesses arrived bearing rings and gold flowers and sashes and fans.

What the Balinese do not understand is that I have already received my gifts from them. Their inviting me to share their ceremonies, eat at their tables, and learn their skills is more valuable to me than the gifts I bring to them. But I cannot convince them; so usually I do not bring gifts.

Mostly my contributions to the cultures and the people I am visiting take the form of teaching English, visiting schools, and just letting people know they have as much to give me as I have to give them. I ask them to help me with language and to teach me their customs. I always accept food and drink when they are offered. On occasion, though I do not smoke, I will ask for a cigarette, just to lower my pedestal and give someone a sense of giving to me.

When I bring clothes from the U.S. (for Tu Biang to give away), they are always secondhand. Most of my Balinese friends think I collect them from acquaintances and that they cost me nothing, which takes the clothes out of the gift category. But actually, I fill up my giant duffel bag with dozens of T-shirts and dresses and pants and toys that I have bought in Goodwill and the Salvation Army. If there is a label on a T-shirt, which would indicate that the item is new, I remove it. In the past, the only time I have given people money has been for emergencies, for my annual contribution to the neighborhood organization (the *banjar*) or for a family ceremony where all family members are expected to help out.

This visit is different. My friends do not need English lessons; they need food. For many of them, a five-dollar gift is the equivalent of a week's salary. It seems unfair that I should have become so rich and they so poor.

Everyone knows what has happened to my dollar and they are not as uncomfortable as they once were about accepting my gifts. So I tile a bathroom floor for one friend, which will allow the family to have paying guests in their home. And I help other friends to paint some rooms and put in furniture so they can become a "homestay," if and when the tourists return. And I am uncharacteristically generous to other friends. I hope I am not causing them shame.

The day before I leave Bali to go to New Zealand, I begin to feel the anxiety that always sweeps over me when I'm going to a new place. I haven't done any research on New Zealand; I haven't even bought a guidebook. I have no idea where I will go from the airport. I need the name of a bed and breakfast or a backpacker place.

I always get annoyed at myself for not planning ahead, but I almost never do. Plans and beginnings are hard for me; but that doesn't stop me from going. I guess I know, deep down, that the anxiety is worth the payoff of yet another adventure.

On the way to the airport in Bali, I ask my driver to stop at the Telecom center, and I call Bron's parents in Auckland. Barbara, Bron's mother, answers the phone. I introduce myself. Her response to my request for a B&B recommendation is, "What flight are you on? I'll pick you up and you will stay with us."

I'm excited. Barbara tells me she has white hair. I tell her I'm wearing a purple jacket and carrying a yellow book. We will meet in about twenty hours.

My flight goes from Bali to Kuala Lumpur, three hours in the wrong direction (it was the cheapest flight), and then on to Auckland. When I get to the airport in K.L., I discover that my departure gate is right next to the transit hotel. I have four hours until my New Zealand flight boards.

I love transit hotels. I used to stay at the one in Singapore when I was en route to Bali (I made the reservations when I bought my plane ticket). As a transit passenger, I didn't have to get my checked bags. I'd shower after the twenty-hour flight and sleep for six hours. When I got to Bali (it's a two-and-a-half-hour flight), I was alive.

The transit hotel in Kuala Lumpur is new, open only a month. I don't want to sleep; but it's been four weeks since my last hot shower. I pay six dollars and I'm handed a towel. The shower room is immaculate and private, the towels are fluffy, the water is hot, the showerhead is powerful. Too bad they don't have tubs; I could happily soak for two and a half hours (which is probably why they don't have tubs).

When I emerge, I am clean and wonderfully soggy. And since I paid for my shower, I figure I'm entitled to sit on a comfortable couch and have some coffee in the hotel lounge. Beats the plastic airport seats. There's even a rack of newspapers.

After an hour in the lounge, I decide to have dinner at the Thai restaurant in the main concourse; I need about ten dollars worth of ringgit from the money changer. When I get there, there's a woman grumbling at the man in the booth.

"In the whole airport, there's no place that I can get money with my Visa card?"

"Sorry."

"I can't believe it," she says to me. "A newly renovated airport and I can't get money."

I hear her New Zealand accent. I figure the money changer doesn't want her New Zealand money.

"I'm on my way to New Zealand," I say. "If you have New Zealand dollars, I'll get you ringgit with my travelers' checks."

"I don't have cash. That's the problem. All I have is my Visa, and in this whole airport, there's no money machine! All I want to do is call a friend in K.L. and say hello."

Meanwhile, I have changed a ten-dollar bill. "Here," I say, handing her a bunch of coins, probably about a dollar's worth.

"Oh, no. I couldn't. I won't be able to pay you back."

"Don't worry about it. Just take it."

"Oh, no, really, I can't."

We go around again. Finally she says, "Well, maybe. What flight are you on? My husband is meeting me. He'll have money and I can pay you back."

"Please, just take it. Don't worry about paying me back. Help somebody else someday." Finally, she accepts.

She has obviously never been introduced to the "Favor Bank" concept, which asserts that the whole world is one giant "Favor Bank." We go through life making deposits whenever we do favors for people, and that means that whenever we need a favor, we're entitled to a withdrawal. It's just as important to take out as it is to put in, because each time we accept a favor, we are allowing someone to make a deposit. I like introducing this idea to people who have trouble "taking."

I have dinner and then I stop in the stationery store to spend my left-over coins. I pick out a newspaper and a magazine and go to the cashier. I have two ringgit. The purchases come to two-eighty.

"Oops," I tell the cashier, starting back to the magazine rack. "I'll find something cheaper."

"No, no, no," says a young, well-dressed Malaysian woman who is standing next to me, waiting her turn. "Here." She hands the cashier the missing change.

"Thanks," I accept with a smile.

Half an hour later, I squiggle into my window seat on the plane. The man wearing wire-rimmed glasses on his Teddy Bear face and eyeing the aisle seat is tall and big. He puts his bag into the overhead compartment and sits. I smile and nod. He does the same.

When the passengers are free to wander, several come over to talk to him. The subject is always the same: rugby.

"We're all coming from the Commonwealth Games in Kuala Lumpur," he explains without being asked.

During the ten-hour trip, I discover that my seatmate is Keith Quinn, *the* rugby broadcaster of New Zealand. Rugby is a national passion; they worship their All Blacks, the national team. (I am in New Zealand a year later when the All Blacks play France for the World Cup rugby title. Nearly everyone I know sets the alarm for some middle-of-the-night hour so they can watch. When New Zealand loses, the country goes into mourning. A few months later, when all those millennium polls are printed in the newspapers, the loss is voted a place on the list of worst twentieth-century disasters!) Keith Quinn, my seatmate, is the voice of the All Blacks. Nearly every Kiwi on the plane greets him by name.

When I mention that I'm a writer, Keith tells me that he's written a few books as well . . . all of them about rugby. So now I know three people in New Zealand: one is a famous sportscaster and writer and the other two, Bron's parents, the Richards, run the top literary agency in the country.

"Do you know Ray Richards?" I ask.

Keith tells me that it was Ray who turned him into a writer. Keith was still in bed one morning, years ago, when the phone rang. It was Ray Richards. They'd never met. "Keith," said Ray, "have you ever thought about writing a book?" Keith had never written anything before, but by the time the conversation was over, Ray had convinced him to try. Keith tells me that Ray walked him through every page of that first book. Keith would send Ray yellow, handwritten sheets and Ray would call with his comments and his encouragement.

So Keith Quinn, national icon, and I talk and eat and sleep and finally exchange e-mail addresses. "If you get down to Wellington, call me," he offers.

When the plane lands, we stand by the baggage rack and watch a lively little beagle sniffing the incoming baggage for "risk goods" like apples, meat, honey. Every year New Zealand's Biosecurity Authority intercepts around 4,500 organisms and 86,000 "risk goods." Island ecosystems are fragile. An official of the Ministry of Agriculture is quoted in the paper as saying, "In my personal view, a biosecurity defense system may be more important than traditional defenses such as an army or airforce." I'm going to like this country.

I am a little concerned that I might not recognize Barbara; all I know about her is that she has white hair. And all she knows about me is that I'm wearing a purple jacket and carrying a yellow book. Then I remember the connection.

"Keith," I ask. "Do you know Barbara?"

"Of course," he says.

"Good. Will you find her for me?"

Later on Barbara tells me that she was out there focusing on jackets and books when she suddenly saw Keith walking toward her. *Oh, dear,* she was thinking. *If I talk to Keith, I might miss Rita.* Nonetheless, she greeted her friend warmly.

"Hello, Barbara, how are you?" he said. "Rita will be out in a minute."

After dinner that night, Barbara sits at the piano, and as she plays, Ray and I sing Cole Porter and George Gershwin songs. We are eons away from the mountains of Irian Jaya, an ocean away from the *salsa* of Nicaragua, and yet, once again, I am connecting with new friends through music.

The next morning I tell Barbara that I have to buy a car.

"Just yesterday, we traded in a wonderful car," she says. "There's not a thing wrong with her. Ray bought Old Blue in 1985; he loves that little car. Maybe we can get her back. The dealer is a friend of my son-in-law."

We do get her back. She's a 1985 Mazda who has never had another owner. She's perfect. I pay Barbara and Ray what the dealer paid them, five hundred U.S. dollars, and Barbara takes me to get insurance and to register Old Blue in my name. As we drive, she tells me that Old Blue was named after a little black robin with a blue band on her leg who was singularly responsible for saving her entire species from extinction. Old Blue, the car, will serve me well for more than a year, and when I am finished with her, she too will make a significant contribution to her community. (More on that later.)

So, after only twenty-four hours, I'm all set, except for one problem: I'm terrified to drive. New Zealand drives on the left.

The next morning at 7:30, Barbara takes me to a supermarket parking lot. By 8:30 I have parked about twenty times, pulled over to a curb dozens of times, and only once, on the way home, do I nearly get us killed when I try to turn right into oncoming traffic.

Later that day and the next, Barbara takes me to look at neighborhoods for possible house rentals. A beach community, Warkworth, an hour north of Auckland, and Devonport, a charming suburb, are both too middle class and homogeneous for me. Ray suggests I look in Rotorua, a community three hours away that has a considerable Maori population.

So, on the third morning, I'm ready to seek my fortune. Anticipating that I will probably rent an unfurnished house or apartment, Barbara packs my trunk (the "boot" in New Zealand) with things from her garage (they have just sold and moved out of a beach house): towels and blankets and pillows and sheets, pots, an iron, a kettle, placemats, a picnic basket filled with plates and cutlery, and a gorgeous, fluffy white sheepskin.

Nikki, Barbara and Ray's daughter, Bron's younger sister, comes over to say good-bye. We are all worried about my driving. The thing that worries me most is, if there's an emergency and I have to rely on my instinct, it's going to be wrong.

We're about to leave when Nikki says, "Wait! I'm going to put an 'L' for 'Learner' on your rear window. It's what they do in driving schools."

She runs inside, makes me a big red "L" on a white background, tapes it to Old Blue's rear window, and we take off.

Barbara drives Old Blue for more than an hour. Ray follows. It's a week-day morning. They both take more than two hours out of their workday to get me out of city traffic for my maiden voyage.

We wave good-bye as I take off for Rotorua, knowing that with my scar-let letter, the world will be wary around me.

The city of Rotorua, with its sizable Maori population, its bubbling sul-fur baths, and a friendly bookstore, where they look me up on the com-puter when I introduce myself and drop Ray's name, is an interesting place. When I first arrive in town, I meet a woman, Lee, and her daughter, Erica. Lee, originally from the Philippines, immigrated here about ten years ago. When I tell her I am looking for a place to rent for six months, she gets excited. She has just arrived from Auckland to get her weekend house ready to rent. I am certain this is another of my serendipities until I see the house, a tiny trailer with no yard, no view, and very close neigh-bors. We say good-bye and I check into a B&B.

Later in the day I am walking down the street when I hear people call-ing my name. It's Lee and Erica. How fabulous to be newly arrived in a strange city and have someone calling to me in the street. We tour a bit, wander around among the steamy sulfur hot spots, and visit the Maori craft center. At the end of the day we stop in a supermarket and buy bread and cheese for dinner. That's when I notice the poster announcing a concert in a Maori meeting house at seven o'clock. *Powhiri* at six. Lee explains that a *powhiri* is the welcoming of visitors.

"Let's go," I say, buoyed by having someone to go with.

We take a taxi and walk together through a carved wooden gate. There are people gathered outside a wooden building with dark beams crossed in an *A* above the entrance.

A handsome man in his thirties approaches. He has dark skin and deep eyes, and his facial features remind me of the Balinese, who, like the Maori, are thought to be of Polynesian descent. I recognize the man from the poster; he is the singer.

"Welcome," he says, smiling and introducing himself. Then he explains that the purpose of this concert is to keep the young people involved and active in the Maori culture. "Most of the songs I sing are in the Maori language, but they're original, not traditional."

Like indigenous people all over the world, the Maori are struggling to maintain their cultural identity.

A young couple come over and introduce themselves. He's a brother of the performer. We talk. Then, after observing the circulation patterns, I walk from group to group, as they are doing, and introduce myself. There are children and elders, men and women. I am the only *pakeha*, light-skinned westerner. I spend considerable time talking to an elderly man who has eight children, all of whom are running around on the grass. He is very heavy and dark, with long hair, high cheekbones, and a ministerial voice. His wife tells me he is an elder of his tribe.

"I arrived in New Zealand three days ago from the U.S.," I tell him. "I am honored to be here."

We enter the building, which is decorated with carved wood and geometrically patterned designs, typical of Maori art. Lee sits in front of me; Erica sits onstage with the other children. Raewyn, one of the women I talked to outside, sits next to me and explains the significance of the opening chorus of singers, which includes women and children. And she translates parts of the welcoming speech given by the elder I had been talking to.

Finally, the concert begins. Most of the songs are about Maori pride and about anger at the way they've been treated historically by the colonizing *pakeha.* From time to time Raewyn translates a song for me. For one stretch, I hold one of Raewyn's kids on my lap. Dozens of children are sitting on the stage, both listening and talking to each other. No one reprimands them. They are an integral part of it all.

About halfway through the concert, Lee turns around and says she is leaving. I'm not ready to go. I probably wouldn't have come if I had been alone, but I have no problem staying. Five minutes after she walks out the door I realize that I don't have the address, name, or phone number of my B&B. I do, however, have the phone number of the taxi. At the very least I can ask the driver to take me to the park in the center of town. I can probably find the B&B from there.

Toward the end of the concert, the singer invites friends and family to perform. And finally, to close the entertainment, the elder returns to the stage and gives another speech in the Maori language. Then, as I am drifting, I hear my name. "Rita from the United States has been our guest tonight. We hope she enjoys her visit in New Zealand." I acknowledge his welcome.

I approach the elder when he steps down. "Thank you for letting me share the evening."

"I hope you will join us in the school for the reception," he says.

Then he leans over and takes my head in his hands. "This is our greeting," he tells me, pressing his nose and forehead into mine. "It is called a *hongi.*"

A year and a half later I will watch on television as President Clinton is welcomed to New Zealand with a *hongi;* but here, on my fourth night in the country, I am startled by the intimacy. After an initial millisecond of surprise, I realize that I am being honored, and I smile, nod, and thank him.

Raewyn shepherds me across the green and into the school. It is what they call an intensive school. All the subjects are taught in Maori. The pictures on the walls are labeled in Maori. There are Maori words on the blackboard. Maori sentences on posters. And Maori legends depicted in the art that is hanging on the wall.

It was only a few generations ago that the Maori language was prohibited in schools, and children and adults were taught to be ashamed of their heritage. Today most Maori between twenty-five and sixty-five years old cannot speak the language. But with the enlightened seventies, Maori pride was reawakened and the New Zealand *pakeha* government was forced to admit it had made a mistake when it attempted to "disappear" a heritage. Today the Maori language is taught in all schools; and the "intensive" schools, like this one, teach everything in Maori.

Everyone gathers in one of the classrooms, where women are serving tea and coffee, until they run out of clean cups. Low tables, designed for six-year-old children, are filled with snacks: little sandwiches, dozens of different kinds of cakes, stuffed hard-boiled eggs, and squares of homemade pizza topped with spaghetti from a can. It is the first of dozens of "potluck" receptions I attend in New Zealand.

I bite into a small square of spaghetti pizza. It's a new experience, canned spaghetti on bread. I take a second piece, mashing the spaghetti against the roof of my mouth and remembering lunches I ate as a child.

Then, uninvited but welcomed, I help wash cups.

"Raewyn," I ask my protectress half an hour later. "Is there a phone here? I have to call a cab."

The phone is locked up.

"Let me see if I can get you a ride," she says. "Where are you staying?"

I laugh and tell her I've forgotten both the name and the address of my B&B, and I vaguely describe the neighborhood. I do remember that it is across from a park in this city full of parks.

"You'll find it," she says, unconcerned, and walks away. She returns with two men. "This is my brother and his friend. They will take you home."

"Hey, if we have to, we'll drive around until you see the place. Don't worry," says the brother. I don't.

Once again, I am trusting strangers. There is not even a flicker of fear . . . as there wasn't on that first night in Mexico when I dined with the Englishmen. Or in the Zapotec village when I asked if I could stay. Or when I arrived in Kerambitan with a bunch of words on a piece of paper. Or when I got on that missionary plane with the man from the mountains.

People often ask me how I have managed to have so many interesting people-experiences in my nomadic wanderings. It's because I trust; I always have. It's not something that has developed with experience, though perhaps with constant reinforcement I do it more often. I've never been disappointed, though I've sometimes been surprised. I know there's a risk, but it's one I'm willing to take. My life is constantly enriched because I trust people.

So, five minutes after I meet them, I go off with these two Maori guys in their twenties. I describe everything I remember about the B&B, the view from my window, the bright pink color of the house next door, even the place I'd had lunch. Half an hour later we are there.

I'm excited. I already have friends in the Maori community here; Raewyn has given me her phone number, and so have two other women. And the elder has invited me to visit him and his family in a nearby town. The next day I go to my first real estate agent.

Two days later, I've run out of agents and places to look at. I haven't seen anything I want to live in for six months. I'm actually pleased that there is nothing in the central part of the city. It smells of bubbling and steaming sulfur. As a soak, hot sulfur baths are hedonistically delicious; as a smell, they stink.

I also look in the mountains and around the lakes that surround Rotorua, but I can't find anything that's right. Where now? New Zealand is a small country, but at the moment, it feels huge.

That afternoon, I am sipping tea in the B&B and consoling myself with scones just out of the oven. Pulling a scone apart, I slather butter onto the inside surface and watch it drip around the little peaks and sink into the crevices. Neville, the owner of the B&B, is a sympathetic ear. Like most people here in New Zealand, he feels personally responsible for my experience of his country.

I bite into another scone and breathe deeply. It is like a meditation on butter.

"Where else should I look?" I ask him.

"Have you looked in Coromandel? There are a lot of writers and artists up there," he says. "I think you'd like it."

Happy to have something to pursue, I open my Servas New Zealand book. There is one listing in Coromandel: Judy and Arnold Piesse. Judy, says the book, is a part-time journalist. Good. She won't be thrown by a challenge.

"Please, use the phone," says Neville. "Don't worry about it."

Judy answers and I introduce myself as an American Servas member. "But I'm not looking for a place to spend tonight," I explain. "I'd like to rent something in Coromandel for six months. I'm hoping you can help me."

I take another bite of scone.

Judy gives me Lisa's name and number. She's a real estate agent. Then Judy adds, "Please be sure to call me when you're in the area. I'd love to meet you."

I call Lisa and tell her my quest.

"Six months?" says Lisa. "When would you like to begin?"

"Tomorrow," I say.

"I'll call you right back."

Before I finish the scone in my hand, Lisa calls back. One of her neighbors, Marian, is looking to rent her house.

The drive from Rotorua should take two and a half hours. I leave at nine for our twelve o'clock appointment. Two hours north of Rotorua, the road begins to wind like a double helix up the west coast of the Coromandel Peninsula. For more than an hour and a half, it twists with the whims of the rocky shoreline. With every sharp curve I worry that my right side is too far over the center, so I move to the left, worried then that my left side is going to go off the road, rolling me into the water. From time to time the road is so close to the water that waves, crashing into the rocks, spray my windshield. This is the New Zealand I've read about. It's spectacular.

I am happy to discover that every few miles there's a place for slow cars to pull over and let others pass. I do it whenever there is a car on my tail. I wonder what the drivers think when they see me driving this treacherous road with a red learner's "L" on my rear window.

I arrive at Marian's half an hour late. The house sits about a hundred yards up a gravel (the Kiwis say "metal") road, and it looks out on a gentle bay surrounded by islands and hills and mountains. There's a dock within view, where pleasure boats launch and mussel barges unload their harvest. The view is spectacular.

Marian and Lisa are sitting on the deck, waiting for me to share lunch—another spaghetti pizza!

Canned spaghetti was a part of my growing up (and my kids' as well, I am embarrassed to admit), and I secretly crave that mushy, overcooked, tomato-soup-flavored pasta, devouring whole cans when no one is looking. My open passion for pasta has nothing to do with canned spaghetti; they are different species. It has been probably ten years since I've had spaghetti out of a can. I am happy to be in a land where I will not have to hide my bizarre craving.

Marian's house has pine-board walls, three small bedrooms, a kitchen, and a deck with that fabulous view. It is a house that feels loved: there are interesting paintings on the walls and beautiful pottery on the kitchen shelves.

"It's wonderful. I definitely want to rent it," I say within one minute of my arrival. "Tell me about the community. Is it friendly?"

"Well," says Lisa, "I live around the corner, and Judy, the woman from Servas, lives up the hill. We're friendly."

Marian says that she will be around for a couple of weeks while she sorts things out. There's a small room attached to the garage where she's planning to sleep. It feels a little weird kicking her out.

"We can share the house until you're ready to go," I say.

"It's no problem," she says. "The room is there for just these circumstances."

"OK," I say, "But let's have breakfast and dinner together." She agrees.

I've done it. I'm renting a spectacular view and a house that fits me. I already know three people in the neighborhood and I haven't even tapped into the alternative community that Neville spoke about. All this for four hundred U.S. dollars per month, a lot more than Bali, but a lot less than most of the places I saw in Rotorua and Auckland.

When Lisa leaves, Marian and I have a chance to talk. She's around my age with a strong, square body that has been tramping (that's Kiwi for trekking) in the surrounding mountains on a regular basis, even though she has a bad hip. Her dyed red short hair is half grown out, the white roots considerably longer than my white roots. She tells me she's growing it in; I'm just lazy.

Turns out that both Marian and Lisa were relieved when I stepped out of the car. They'd been afraid that I would arrive, young and svelte in heels and makeup. Instead, I arrived in sweatpants, sandals, and white roots.

For Marian, renting helps with the expenses of running the house. Just that week she had mentioned to Lisa that the place was available if anyone came along. She was thinking weekends or Christmas, but a six-month rental will give her a long visit with her daughter on the South Island, and money for the winter.

During the first week, before Marian takes off for the South Island, I discover that I have rented more than a house. I have rented—for the next six months—Marian's life.

- "The book club meets on the first Monday of every month," she says. "Here's the book for next Monday." She hands me *Heart of the Country* by New Zealand author, Fay Weldon.
- There is the cat, Blackie, whom I have offered to take care of (Marian is taking Nick, the dog).
- There's the vegetable garden (I plant tomatoes and basil and dill to

add to Marian's New Zealand spinach, silverbeet (Swiss chard), parsley, green onions, rhubarb, and mint.

- And the Forest and Bird Society. I have a list of the lectures.
- And Judy and Lisa, who are both accustomed to stopping by Marian's for tea or a chat. They continue to do it, even after Marian is gone.

Only the name, shape, and accent of the occupant have changed.

When I stand on the deck of my house, I can watch the mussel barges en route to their mussel farms. The barges are small, gray boats about fifty feet long; the mussels are the succulent, sweet, juicy greenshell variety that New Zealand exports all over the world. Before I am settled in, I rush off to a little white shack about a mile away with a metal corrugated roof and a big sign: OYSTERS AND MUSSELS.

"Hi," I say, standing in front of a table stacked with craggy gray oysters. "My name is Rita, and I've just rented Marian Williams's house for the next six months. I can't wait to taste your mussels and oysters."

"Welcome, Rita," says the young man in jeans and white, rubber "gum-boots." "My wife and I stayed in a caravan on Marian's property when we first got here. I'm Greg. Where are you from?"

He is being polite by asking. Three words are more than enough to tell anyone that I'm a Yankee. Greg gets his oysters from his own oyster farm just a few hundred meters around the bay. I buy a big bag of mussels and two dozen oysters.

"But I don't know how to open the oysters," I say.

"Then why don't you take a tube?" He holds up a plastic container about the size of an olive jar.

I watch him insert the knife, twist it, and pop the oysters into the tube. Rushing home with a bag of mussels and a tube of oysters, I ecstatically devour them all, cooking the mussels in about a quarter inch of water, some white wine, garlic, and a sprinkle of herbs. Even if the people weren't terrific, even if the geography weren't spectacular, even if the town weren't so charming, I could live forever in Coromandel, ecstatically consuming its seafood.

The next time I buy oysters and mussels, about five days later, Barbara and Ray are with me. They've come over on the ferry from Auckland for the weekend. I suspect they want to be sure that this foreigner they have taken under their wing is settling in OK. We pull up to Greg's shack and get out of the car. Ray is driving, happy to be renewing his relationship with Old Blue; it is obvious that he still has an emotional attachment to her. We walk inside.

"Hi, Rita, how are you?" says Greg.

Barbara and Ray smile like proud parents when they hear him greet me by name.

That night, Judy, Arn (Judy's husband), and Marian (she hasn't left yet) join us for dinner. I feel as though I've been here forever. When English is the spoken language, things move more quickly, especially when everyone is as warm and welcoming as these Kiwis.

Over dinner, I mention that while I'm in New Zealand, I'd like to visit some schools and talk to kids about writing, words, my life. I'm thinking that I will visit a different school each week.

"Why different schools?" says Ray. "Why not develop a relationship with one school. You could sort of adopt them."

"Is there a predominately Maori school in the area?" I ask.

"There's a Maori community just over the hill in Manaia," says Judy. "It's ten minutes away. The principal of the school is a friend of mine."

The school is a complex of white buildings with bright red roofs, sitting in the middle of bright green fields (called paddocks). There are sixty kids, ages six to thirteen, three teachers, and a pile of parents and paraprofessionals. I visit all three of the classrooms. The kids are beautiful, natural and relaxed, even in front of a strange-accented foreigner. Most of them have dark hair, bronze skin, and big curious eyes.

I talk about where I'm from and where I've been, and I pass around a pile of my books, which I leave with Vicki, the principal. I tell the kids that I will be coming in once a week. I'll talk about writing, play games with words, fool around with poetry, and I'll tell some interesting stories about the places I've been.

"You can ask me anything you want," I say. "And I also want to learn about you."

Before I leave each classroom, I share with them the fact that I've only been here for a little more than a week and I don't have very many friends.

"One of the reasons I visit schools is to make friends. So I'm hoping that whenever you see me in town, you'll shout, 'Hi, Rita,' even if you're across the street. Can you do that now?" Everyone shouts out my name.

"I feel less lonely already. See you next week."

I live in Coromandel, on and off, for twelve months; and nearly every time I go into town (ten minutes from my house) some little voice shouts at me from somewhere, "Hi, Rita."

I make as many inroads into the community as I can. My plan while I'm here is to write a book proposal, but I don't intend to be compulsive about it. I also want to become as much of a local as I can. I get a library card and I chat with the librarian; I subscribe to the *New Zealand Herald* and introduce myself to Jan, the mail and paper delivery person (who also will deliver stamps, milk, or emergency shopping items). Whenever I go into a store (the small supermarket, the butcher, the pharmacy, the stationery store, the craft stores, even the post office), I introduce myself and try to remember the faces and names of the people who take care of me. And I go religiously to the book club meetings and the Forest and Bird lectures.

Forest and Bird is a national organization devoted to protecting the delicate ecosystem of New Zealand. Introduced plants and animals are the enemy. Up to twenty thousand kiwi chicks are eaten by predators each year. Rats, mice, stoats, all introduced animals, are decimating the native birds. It has been estimated that seven out of nine hatchlings are killed by stoats (a kind of weasel).

The possum is another introduced animal that is causing trouble. The first ones arrived from Australia a century ago. Today there are 70 million of the pests eating twenty thousand tons of foliage every night. There are so many of these nocturnal creatures that "possum trapper" is a respectable occupation.

Every Friday morning I make an appearance at the Bizarre, formerly called the Bazaar, a secondhand store ("op shop") that benefits the community. It's run by a group of women who are nearly all past seventy. They sell plants and vegetables, clothes and knick-knacks. The locals show up before nine, which is when I run into my Forest and Bird friends, fellow book clubbers, and neighbors.

Coromandel is a real community. I like the people and the size and the mix. I have met descendants of old pioneering families and newly retired city folk, fishermen and marine farmers, businesspeople and weekenders, sheep farmers and orchid growers, ministers and yachties. And the Maori community of Manaia.

I still haven't met the "alternative" segment of Coromandel, the artists and writers and potters that drew me here in the beginning. But I'm just going to live. It'll happen.

And it does. I'm having trouble with my computer. Not too long ago I saw an ad for "Cyberplace" in the local newsletter. It's time for a visit.

Early one morning Old Blue and I drive into town, past hills dotted with cows and sheep (there are more than 47 million sheep and around 3¹/₂ million people in New Zealand). We drive between fields filled with white daisies, yellow thorny gorse (the curse of farmers), and Queen Anne's lace. I stop for a family of pukeko, big black birds with long red legs, that are ambling across the road. En route I count four dead possums, flattened by tires while on their nocturnal eating frenzies. And in the water on the left, just beyond the mangrove trees, are hundreds of sticks coming out of the water . . . Greg's oyster farm. At low tide, you can walk out and see the oysters clinging to the wooden frames, waiting to be harvested.

When I park Old Blue outside the post office, a woman is getting into the car in front of me. There is a big CYBERPLACE sign on the side window.

Christine and I talk on the street for the next twenty minutes. She's a writer and a computer whiz. We make an appointment for the next morning. When our conversation is over, she says, "Come to my birthday party tomorrow night."

I do, and another part of the Coromandel world opens up to me. Christine and her partner, Henry, are building an earth house, brick by clay brick. The party is on a dirt-floor living room with a roof but only one wall. There is singing by a bonfire (several of the guests play guitar) and a potluck dinner. And writers and artists and actors and potters and musicians.

Gradually I slip into a rhythm, writing, teaching, going to meetings. One Wednesday, after I spend the morning talking with the three classes in Manaia School about Borneo, orangutans, and books, Vicki, the principal, invites me to come to "Pit Day" on Friday. I have no idea what "Pit Day" is, but I tell her I'll be there. I am fairly certain it must be what the Maori call a *"hangi,"* where they dig a pit and cook meat and vegetables over hot rocks. I've been wanting to try a *hangi* meal ever since I heard about them.

On Friday, I arrive to discover a playground filled with calves, lambs, dogs, horses, birds, rabbits, and even a spider in a cage; not a pit in sight. "Pit Day" turns out to be "Pet Day." The short Kiwi *e* is pronounced like the American short *i*. Pet is *pit*. Seven is *sivin*. Kevin is *Kivin*. The next week I tell the kids my mistake and we discuss the different ways languages and pronunciation develop.

There are "heaps of" Kiwi words and expressions that we don't have in the U.S. "Good on ya" instead of "Good for you." "Buggered" means exhausted. "Chuffed" means pleased, and "dodgy" means bad, unreliable, spoiled. "Bickies" are biscuits. "Rellies" are relatives. "Presies" are presents. And a "bach" is a weekend/holiday home.

A "cobber" is a close friend. A "chook" is a chicken. You buy a "punnet" of strawberries at the market. "In the nick" means naked, but "in good nick" means in good shape. "Shit ay" means fancy that, bit of bad luck, reckon. And a "fly cemetery" is a sliced cake filled with raisins.

If you're invited for a "cuppa," it's usually tea in the afternoon. But if you're invited for "tea," it could be dinner.

There are also a heap of Maori words that have crept into people's everyday speech. Newscasters and telephone operators say hello with *"Kia ora"* and good-bye with *"Haere ra."* Your *mokopuna* are your grandchildren, your *whanau* (*wh* is pronounced like an *f*) is your extended family group. Your *whakapapa* is your family geneology. A *waiata* is a song. A *paua* is an abalone; a *pipi* is a kind of clam.

And then there are the "blokes," as in, "He's a good bloke." The *Oxford New Zealand Dictionary,* quoting *Review of 1959,* says a bloke is a "practical, unimaginative, adaptable, prejudiced, smug, kindly, resilent, casual, slangy, independent, open-hearted she'll be right New Zealander."

One week I ask everyone I meet what defines a "bloke." Some of the answers are: Blokes drink beer, not wine. They wear black wool singlets (sleeveless shirts) and dark green shirt-jackets, gum boots, and rugby jerseys with sleeves cut off. They eat stews made with carrots and onions and potatoes and dumplings. At a "barbie" they favor the grilled sausages over the salads. They'll eat cold mutton sandwiches for lunch and maybe fried eggs, sausages, and bacon. Meat pies. Fish and chips. Things like asparagus, cauliflower, peppers (called "capsicums") are suspicious. So are foreign foods, like quiche and even pasta. If you can hunt it, like wild duck or rabbit or pigs; catch it, like fish; or pick it, like watercress, it's OK.

I have fun playing with the differences in our languages. And I am shamelessly stopping people in midsentence with "What was that word? What does it mean?"

As a word-person, I love listening to and discovering the differences in our speech. I find myself saying "Good on ya," and "tomahto." And asking whether the "chooks are laying."

I'm feeling very much like a local when I get an e-mail from the kids. Mitch, Jan, and Melissa are coming in February. I can't wait to see them. We've been e-mailing practically every day since I got here three months ago. I feel as though they're very much a part of my life. Also, calls between New Zealand and the United States are easy and not that expensive, so we talk often. But even daily e-mail contact isn't the same as face to face.

The kids begin their visit in Auckland with lunch at Barbara and Ray's house and a drive around the city. I feel as though I am introducing family to family. They are all fascinating individuals in their own right. Mitch, and Melissa are hyphenates: each is a journalist-writer-editor. Jan is an executive producer for a new media company, having recently shifted from the editorial to the business side. They are all teaming with technical crews to break new ground in an industry that changes by the minute. I find it incredibly exciting to talk to them about their on-line jobs, where there is no past and a limitless future.

Ray and Barbara are fascinating as well; they have been an integral part of the literary history of New Zealand, guiding, encouraging, and discovering literary talents. My greatest pleasure for the past months has been reading the novels and stories of New Zealand authors, many of whom Ray has represented or published.

While the kids are in Coromandel, Mitch plays golf on a course that is built over old gold mines where, today, hundreds of sheep graze on the greens; and Jan goes scuba diving and comes home with forty scallops for dinner, doubling the twenty-scallop limit when her dive partner contributes his catch to us. I sauté the scallops, both the white part and the succulent sweet pink roe, in butter with a little garlic, a touch of parsley, chopped green onion from the garden, and a few squirts of lemon from our neighbor's tree. We begin the meal, of course, with mussels and oysters (which I can now open by myself).

One afternoon I have a chance to relax with Melissa, which is always great; she's so easy to talk to. There's something about my daughter-in-law that is so much more than just a single addition to a family. She adds a depth and a dimension that makes everyone bigger and better and more relaxed.

After a week, we take off for the South Island in Old Blue. En route we soak in the sulfur baths of Rotorua and bike along the Marlborough Sounds. In the magnificent Abel Tasman National Park, we tramp, swim, and go kayaking. What a beautiful country.

The kids fly to Auckland for their flight home, and I drive to meet Christine (my writer and computer friend from Coromandel), who is taking me to see D'Urville Island (20 miles long and 6 miles wide), where she grew up, one of five children of a sheep farmer and a nurse. She and her parents left long ago, but friends of hers, Percy and Gill, are still there. They own 1,700 acres of land, rolling hills, sandy bays, rocky cliffs, and about three thousand sheep. They've invited us to stay with them.

Our timing is perfect. Tomorrow, the sheep are going to be mustered and brought to the barns for crutching (shearing their rears) and drenching (giving them medicine). The day after we arrive, Percy piles us and two dogs, a black-and-white one and a brown one, into the pickup. We start out on a dirt road and turn off into the paddocks, bouncing and rocking up hills, across fields, down slopes. Then he stops, opens a gate, and lets the dogs out, shouting directions to them as they bark and eye and run the sheep through a complex series of gates that open up and close off paddocks. The dogs direct the flock along paths, across and up and down hills, until they all end up, miles away, at the barns.

The whole farm is a brilliant series of spaces that move into other spaces through strategically placed gates that eventually lead to the barns. When one paddock has been cleared, Percy gets back in the truck or runs up the hills to open or close gates.

The whole farm is a fabulous maze that is constantly changing by a flip of a board and a shouted order to a dog. And the water and rocks and hills that these sheep look down upon are postcard-perfect scenes. By the end of the day, most of the sheep are down by the barn.

The shearing gang arrives the next morning for the crutching and drenching. The shearing sheds are as well planned as the paddock paths. There are two floors with ramps and doors and pens and fencing. When the sheep are crutched, they are slid down a slide to another area, where they line up for medicine. There are four men and two women, well-practiced teams, delivering the sheep, shearing the rumps, sweeping the wool, shoving the sheep down the slide. It's hard work and they barely stop all day. Tomorrow they'll be at it again. A shearing gang eats and sleeps on the farm until the job is done.

Yesterday, Gill, Percy's wife, complained that she hated cooking for the gang. I volunteered. Now, a couple of hours before dinner, the potatoes are boiling in salted water, enough for two nights' worth of mashed potatoes, and I'm sautéing onions and beef (from home-grown cattle), and tossing in carrots and celery and tomatoes. I have decided on stew because my bloke research said that blokes like stews, and these guys are definitely blokes.

The only way on or off this island is by boat. When our visit is over, Percy rows Christine and me out to the mail boat, which will drop us on the mainland. People get their mail by rowing out to meet the boat. There are lots of sheep on D'Urville Island, but not many people. Most of the children who live here are home schooled.

We make a stop at another island, where Charlie, a small man with a beard, meets us in a rowboat and Peter, the mailman, passes him a box with a new television set inside. Charlie lives alone on the island, with fifty sheep. He used to have five hundred, but now he keeps just enough for food. Charlie sometimes goes for two years without leaving. Peter tells us that Charlie watches rugby (powering the TV with a generator) and reads books.

I find myself wondering what it would be like to live alone for two years, with nothing but books, a TV, and sheep. I don't think I'd do well as a hermit.

After six months in New Zealand, I pay a visit to the U.S. When I return to New Zealand, I have a contract, a check, and a deadline for my nomad book. I'm ready to write seriously.

Marian is back from the South Island and we're sharing the house. I like living with her. She's generous, respectful, and stone solid. And she understands that while I'm here, I need to feel that this is my house as well as hers. She has given me two of the three bedrooms so I can set up an office. And she and I have rearranged the kitchen the way she knows I like it . . . putting the spices out in the open and burying the decorative pieces. And she has no objection to my spreading a few Balinese sarongs around for color and familiarity.

The most interesting part of our shared life revolves around food. We cook and eat together. I learn to like her oats and bran and various seeds and oils at breakfast, and we chop together in the preparation of my Asian and Mexican dinner dishes.

Between breakfast and dinner, I write, nonstop, all day every day. My only break comes one cool spring morning in October, when, for the first time, I go out on a mussel barge. My Uncle Bob and Aunt Elaine are visiting from the States, and Marian has helped me set up the trip.

Ever since I first arrived more than a year ago, I have been cooking and eating the greenshell New Zealand mussels. I have had steamed mussels, fried mussels, mussel fritters, marinated mussels, mussel chowder, mussels with pasta, mussels on rice, mussel salad, and avocado stuffed with mussels. There's a cookbook in Marian's kitchen that was put out in 1988 by the local school to raise funds. It has twenty-two mussel recipes, including mussel quiche, creamed mussels, curried mussels, bacon-wrapped mussels, mussel turnovers, mussel munchies, and mussels in fresh tomato sauce.

I'm actually kind of a purist about my mussels. I like them steamed with garlic, wine, and a little bit of water. When the mussles open up, they provide plenty of liquid for the steaming, and a nice base for a chowder.

They're big and sweet and juicy, these greenshell mollusks. I try to always have some uncooked ones in the refrigerator so I can pop one into the microwave (for less than a minute) when I'm in the mood for a snack. Today I'm finally going to see where they come from.

It is just light out when we take off at 6:15. There is still one star in the sky and the moon is about to set. We ride for less than fifteen minutes and stop just a few coves away, about a half mile from the shore.

On the surface, a mussel farm is hundreds of huge black floats (each about one and a half meters long) neatly lined up in rows. The rows are anchored at the ends, and the floats are held together by a thick rope. That's all you see from the surface.

We stop at the beginning of a row and the action begins. A hydraulic crane lowers a hook into the water, and when it comes up, it's holding an endless rope covered with thick bunches of mussels in clusters of ten, twenty, thirty. There is also an assortment of slimy hangers-on. Our crew tells us that the hangers-on are orange fudge, dogs' balls, and sea slugs. There are also heaps of little crabs, tiny fish, goo that squirts, goo that looks like white and orange eggs, grassy stuff, seaweed, and a few oysters that got into the wrong farm.

The end of the rope is threaded through a hole in an onboard machine, and as the rope is mechanically pulled through the hole, the mussels and their slimy friends are scraped off into a spinning barrel, where they get washed. Then they spin some more and all the extra stuff goes one way and the mussels go onto a conveyer belt, up, over, and in front of Beany, the crew member in charge of tossing away what's left of the orange fudge, dogs' balls, and other slimy things. Nearly clean, the mussels are then dumped into white bags, until the bags weigh in at thirty-three kilos.

The whole operation is a bit like a dance. From time to time the other crew member speeds up the rope and conveyer belt and Beany moves like Charlie Chaplin, his hands rapidly grabbing and tossing before the conveyer belt dumps the dogs' balls into the bag.

Mussel farms are good places to fish. Most people who are lucky enough to be guests on a mussel barge bring their rods. It's the smashed mussels that attract the fish. Uncle Bob catches a snapper and two other fish that Beany says are no good. I ask if I can buy a bag of mussels, thinking six kilos but not being specific. I end up with a thirty-three kilo bag, more than I, my guests, and my neighbors can eat.

The next day Bob and Elaine leave for the South Island and I go back to being a sedentary writer. But not for long. I'm getting restless.

Thailand

CHAPTER EIGHTEEN

IN THAILAND
SPEAKING FOOD

I've been in New Zealand on and off for nine months. It's feeling like home. I have a gym, a library card, a house, two pets, and six potted plants. The garden tomatoes are hearty, the lettuce is ripe, and when I walk down the street in town, I always meet people I know. I'm much too comfortable.

Tomorrow I leave for a vacation in Thailand. My spirit gets nourished in faraway places. Sometimes I wonder if it's a biological need, perhaps a biological flaw, that compels me to seek the excitement and challenge that comes of being in a place where nobody knows me.

Other times I think that my compulsion to settle into communities that are different from the ones I know is related to my passion for experiential learning. I learn best and most happily by doing, touching, sharing, tasting. When I'm somewhere I've never been before, learning goes on all day, every day. In Thailand, I plan to specialize in tasting.

Thai cuisine is one of the most playful and exciting eating experiences in the world; it tickles, taunts, challenges, and teases the palate. I've decided that I want to watch and cook with Thai women in their kitchens.

I also want to remind myself what it's like to be in a setting where I don't speak the language. For the next three weeks I'm going to cook, eat, and write in Ban Krud, a small village tucked into the waistline of Thailand, four hours by car south of Bangkok, where hardly anyone speaks English.

Jip, my friend from Seattle, grew up in Ban Krud; and when I first decided to visit her village, she was expecting to be there. I was hoping she would introduce me to the best cooks in the village so I could become an observer in their kitchens. But Jip had to cancel. I'm going anyway. Without Jip as my translator, I plan to communicate through "food."

I'll be staying in Rim Haad, a small bungalow resort for Thai tourists that Jip has recommended. "If you call Fon," Jip e-mailed to New Zealand, "she will pick you up at the station. Rim Haad is her family's business." Before I board the train in Bangkok, I find someone to make the call.

Fon is at the station in a white pickup. She's a pretty woman in her thirties with a take-charge manner. I tell her my name and mention that I'm a friend of Jip's. When John and Jip got married in Ban Krud several years ago, about twenty of their foreign guests stayed in Fon's "resort," a complex of bungalows and a patio restaurant that looks across the street at the beach.

When we arrive at Rim Haad, I am greeted by a friend of Fon's who speaks English. This is the first and last time I see him; but I am glad he's there. I tell him I'm planning to stay for three weeks, and that I'm hoping Fon's family will let me learn about Thai cooking in their kitchen. He passes the message on to Fon. She is pleased. Most of her guests come for a weekend.

We negotiate a price of five hundred baht (about thirteen U.S. dollars a day) for an air-conditioned cabin. The room is white and clean; the floor tiles, shiny. And there's a television, a table and chair, a small refrigerator, and a bathroom with a cold-water shower and a drain in the floor.

I tell Fon's friend that if it is possible, I would very much like to see the village tomorrow. I'd like to get a sense of where I am.

He discusses my request with Fon and answers, "Willage no tomollow. Fon busy. Gobamen. Clouds." I have no idea what he's saying.

"Is there a bicycle I can use?" I ask. I do not need to bother Fon.

Fon smiles and gets a bike. "No money," she says.

I thank her and we all go to sleep. It's after eleven.

I wake up starving and wander over to the dining area, which is a big covered patio about twenty by thirty feet, with tables and chairs for forty. There are three women standing near the kitchen; I'm the only guest.

I mime that I want to eat. Ei, the eighteen-year-old maid, points to a picture of scrambled eggs and toast, but I shake my head. I'm in Thailand; I want a Thai breakfast. But I have no idea what that might be.

I look at Ei. "What do you eat?" She does not understand me.

Finally a small woman wearing sunglasses, whom I later learn is Manit, Fon's mother, says something about rice and soup. I nod and smile.

A few minutes later I get a tasty breakfast soup with celery, green onion, rice, and fish; and cilantro sprinkled on top. As I eat, I look across a small road at the sea. It's calm and quiet, but the motorcycles shooting by in both directions are not. They are nearly all family occupied . . . two, three, four, and five people; no one is wearing a helmet.

When I finish the soup, I decide to go into the village to see if I can figure out what the young man was talking about when he said the English words "Gobamen. Clouds." I climb on the small red bike and the seat rolls back, almost dumping me. I straighten the seat to a horizontal position and discover that the handlebars have a life of their own that has nothing to do with the front wheel. And the chain keeps slipping.

Fon's father, Somkit, a handsome man wearing a sarong and sandals and a T-shirt, brings out the tools and goes to work tightening bolts and attaching chains. While he is working, Fon's mother, Manit, beckons to me. She is getting into a car and gestures for me to join her. I do.

A smart-looking western-dressed man in his fifties is sitting at the wheel; his wife is sitting next to him. I later find out that the man is Fon's uncle, Nark, who is down for the weekend from a town an hour north of here. I sit silently in the backseat.

Nark drives to the main road, which is lined with small, one-story shops selling pots and woks, clothes and paper goods, furniture and cleaning supplies. Then he turns down a small alleyway and stops. I look around and suddenly last night's conversation becomes clear. We have arrived at a polling place. "Gobamen" meant "government"; it was the word Fon's friend had used when he didn't know the word *election*. "Clouds" meant there would be crowds of people waiting to vote; not a good day to see the village.

I walk with Manit as she signs the book and enters a large room where three-sided wooden screens are perched on tables to assure privacy while people check off their paper ballots. Manit checks her ballot, folds the paper, and drops it into a box. Then she walks me over to a poster hanging on the wall outside and points to the picture of the number ten candidate. It is her husband, Somkit. He is running for local office. I shake my fist in the air, smile broadly, and say, "Yay!"

At our next stop, another election district, a much bigger crowd is milling around. There are carts selling grilled chicken, meatballs on skewers, fruit on sticks. And inside, where the voting is taking place, is Fon. Working.

"Willage. No tomollow. Fon busy. Gobamen. Clouds." It all makes sense.

It's been a long time since I've been in a country where I don't speak the language. I feel stupid sitting in silence. I don't like it. And I certainly don't expect them to speak my language; I am in their country. I resolve to learn some basic words, so I can at least be polite in the Thai language.

On the way home, Nark stops off at a roadside stand, where we all have a bowl of soup with noodles, pork balls, celery, and scallions.

"Lawn," says Nark, holding a bowl of red sauce and adding some to his bowl. Then, in English, he says, "Hot. Thai like hot."

"I do too," I respond, spooning about the same amount into my soup along with marinated chilies and assorted leaves. I feel the heat on my lips, my throat, and all the way down. It is hotter than anything they serve in the U.S., but I'm determined to eat Thai food the Thai way. I only choke a little. Manit hands me a glass of water. As I eat, I remind myself to always carry a tissue. I love spicy hot foods, but they make my nose run.

Everyone watches to see how I react. *"Aloi,"* I say. *"Aloi mak mak."* Delicious. Very delicious. I learned it from Ei at breakfast. Everyone smiles.

My hosts will not let me pay.

It turns out that Nark knows more English than anyone else in the family. He spends the rest of the day teaching me basic Thai words, which I write in my notebook. Words like "thank you," "no problem," "I like Thai food," and "I am sixty-two years old." (Everyone wants to know.)

I try to memorize the words, but Thai is a tonal language. Even when I am staring at the words in my notebook, I have trouble saying them correctly. My voice doesn't go up and down at the appropriate times.

Late in the day, Nark takes me to see a spectacular temple that is still in the process of being built, and a massive golden Buddha who sits high on a hill looking out at the water. The Buddha must be forty feet high.

At the temple there are men on scaffolding, gilding the spires, and both women and men delicately painting in the garments of outlined figures on the walls. There are people cutting and fitting marble floor tiles, and still others working on intricate carvings in alcoves. This is my kind of sightseeing.

I'd much rather see something in process than visit the finished product. I like workshops more than museums, rehearsals more than concerts. I would rather watch an artist painting or a sculptor chipping away at a piece of wood than view their finished works in a gallery.

We climb over scaffolding, on stairs that have no rails yet, to the top of the temple where there is a 180-degree view of the area, miles of sandy beaches and sea on one side, acres of coconut groves on the other.

When we get back to the bungalows, I go to my room. Two hours later, about seven o'clock, Fon knocks on my door calling, "Lita, Lita!" (The English *r* is almost impossible for the Thai speaker.) She charades the fact that there is cooking happening in the kitchen. I rush after her.

The kitchen is filled with people, six women and Nark, all standing around the stainless island in the middle of the room, cleaning and cutting and dicing and slicing and chopping and pounding. As with Chinese food, the ingredients must be prepared before the cooking begins.

Cherry tomatoes are popped in water to clean them, and then they're cut in half. Onions are cut in half vertically and sliced into thin vertical strips; tiny celery with stems like toothpicks and thin green onions are washed and cut up into one-inch pieces. People are peeling and slicing cucumbers, and cutting off the top leaves of tiny eggplants the size of cherry tomatoes. Squids (which were cleaned in the afternoon) are scored and then cut into rings.

Manit, still in sunglasses even though it is dark out, is pounding tiny red chili peppers and garlic in a six-inch-high mortar. (Two weeks later I will discover that Manit lost an eye in an accident many years ago.) Fon is peeling and grating two unripe mangos, and her brothers' wives are squeezing limes and peeling garlics.

Nark is in charge. He takes a huge hunk of pork out of the refrigerator and cuts it into small chunks. Then he cleaves the chunks into minced pork. No grinder, just a cleaver.

Two giant stainless steel bowls, around two feet in diameter and filled with uncooked white noodles, sit, untouched, on the table.

I love communal projects. Everyone in this big family is helping to prepare dinner. I figure with spouses and kids there will probably be about twenty people eating. As I cut the little tops off of tiny eggplants, I study the ingredients and decide that we are going to have a squid dish, a noodle dish, and a pork dish . . . at the very least. Maybe a Thai soup as well.

Finally the cooking begins. Along the back and side walls are tiled counters with four wok-size holes. Each hole has gas piped in from a tank. The gas is ignited and woks are placed on the holes.

Squid and sausages boil.

Eggplants cook.

Onions fry.

Pork sizzles.

Noodles soften when a wokful of boiling water is poured over them.

Then, one by one, *all* the ingredients are added to the noodles. The squid, the sausages, the pork, the onions, the tomatoes, the leaves, the egg-plants, the chili paste, and a lime-juice-based liquid with fish sauce, water, sugar, and MSG. *Everything* goes into the noodles and gets mixed around. There went my squid dish, my pork dish, and my soup. It has become one big noodle dish. Not a problem. I love noodles.

Nark is the one assembling it all. Soon he begins to taste and add and mix. He is wearing plastic bags on his hands as he lifts the slippery noo-dles from the bottom and brings them to the top, distributing the squid and meat and vegetables, and mixing in the flavorings. He makes more lime liquid and adds it. Mixes. Tastes again. Adds more fish sauce. Mixes and tastes again. The mixing and tasting and adjusting go on for ten min-utes. Nark is reveling in the preparation of this dinner. I can't wait to eat it!

Then, just when I think we are about to sit down to eat, the two giant stainless bowls of noodles are carried out of the kitchen and into a car. And four of our cooks climb in behind them. The fabulous, cooperative dinner, it turns out, is going to the night market to be sold!

I sit with the family at one of the tables. I'm the only guest (tonight and for most of the three weeks that I'm here). Nark has saved one plate of the noodles for the family, enough so that we all get a tiny taste. It's good, but it's one forkful. Dinner is rice and some red pork and vegetables . . . hot and good, but not what I was expecting. All I can think about is the squid and sausage and chopped pork, the eggplant, the noodles . . .

It is 9:30 P.M. of my first full day and I am struggling to stay awake. Before I go to my bungalow for the night, Fon's brother asks me if I would give his daughter English lessons. Nek is a beautiful, bright fifteen-year-old. I'm delighted that I'll have a chance to give back.

The next morning, Manit and I board a motorcycle-driven transport that takes us to the open-air market in the center of the village. The sellers, mostly women, are wearing hats of every shape and size. Some are squat-ting; some are sitting on blankets; others are sitting on little stools, eight inches off the ground, surrounded by their vegetables. A truck is blaring soft rock and Thai ballads.

I walk and smell and look and touch and taste. There are basil leaves, celery, green onions, kaffir lime leaves, mint, lemon grass, and lots of other leafy things. I taste them all, touching a leaf and looking at the seller as I put my fingers to my mouth. Some leaves are strong. Some are barely flavored. Some taste just like, well . . . leaves.

And there are roots: tumeric, galangal, ginger. The ginger is younger than the ginger I know, not as brown or strong. Some sellers are selling it shaved in plastic bags.

There are also rows of mounded pastes as in the markets in Mexico, but the smells are different. Brown and fishy. Fiery red and garlicky. Lemon grassy.

And trays of tiny eggplants, mounds of red chilies about two inches long and a half inch wide, and squashes and mangos and pineapples, bananas, tomatoes, cucumbers, onions, shallots, cabbages.

Meat is hanging on hooks and languishing on tables. And fish of every size are flopping on tables, some of them gasping their final breaths. I feel a twinge of sadness when I see a magnificently colored parrotfish, whose relatives I admired in Lombok on the bottom of the sea.

There are also tons of ready-cooked things to eat: soups from steaming pots with add-your-own garnishes, noodles with sauces on the side, cakes in pink and green and white. Chicken and pork on skewers. Stuff wrapped in banana leaves.

I sit down and eat a bowl of noodles. They're good, but Nark's were better.

Later that morning, I am in my bungalow writing about the market when there's a knock on the door. It's Nark. Time to cook again. This time we get to eat it: a Thai vegetable soup with baby corn (fresh), squash, pumpkin, two kinds of leaves, celery, and a shade too much fish paste for my palate.

A few minutes later, Nark and his wife go home. He tells me he will not see me again. They live more than an hour away. I wave good-bye to the only member of the family I can converse with, and an unexpected anxiety sweeps over me. I remind myself that I'm here because I want to experience life in a Thai village that is not geared to serve western tourists. The anxiety remains but I am not worried. I know these moments of fear pass. It's only been two days. I go to my cabin for an afternoon nap.

I wake up around three and work on a plan for Nek's English lesson. She is coming at five for her first class. I know I can make a difference in her language skills, especially in pronunciation. I also need to work on her confidence. Even though she is studying English in school, she has not spoken to me. The fear of sounding foolish is the insidious enemy of learning a foreign language.

Last night, Nek read two of my books out loud to her cousins. I noticed four pronunciation problems dictated by sounds that don't exist in the Thai language: *th, r, l,* and *v.*

I make a list of thirty words that use *th.* And a list of *r* and *l* and *v*-words. I plan to begin every class with pronunciation practice until the feeling of the tongue sticking out between the teeth is not a weird sensation, and until the upper teeth and bottom lip connect naturally when they see a *v.* I can't show a physical thing for the *r* and *l,* but careful listening will do it.

Next I write some sentences about life in Ban Krud. I will ask Nek to memorize them. Learning whole sentences by heart is a good way to develop confidence. When I am trying to learn a language, I hate having to go through the grammar and structure every time I try to say something. If I have a base of sentences that I know are correct, I can plug in different words and I'm confident that what comes out of my mouth will be correct.

Nek arrives at five. Nek's sister Nan and their cousin Nun join us. They giggle over having to stick their tongues out to make the *th* sound, but I know that after a few days, and hundreds of repetitions, the strange thing that their tongue is doing will not feel so strange. Same with the *v* and the *r.* "Seven, eleven, very hot, very cold, TV, television, village," etc. We do the list over and over again. It gets easier each time.

When the class is over, I go back to my bungalow and study Thai. I am sound asleep by nine.

The first thing I do after I brush my teeth in the morning is reach into my cosmetic bag for my hormone replacement medicine. When I take out the Prempro, I discover that the circular plastic pill case is filled with tiny ants. The shiny pink hormone pills, with black writing on them, come in the kind of container that moves around from slot Monday to slot Tuesday and Wednesday and Thursday. Well, sometime since yesterday morning, dozens of ants have entered through the empty Monday slot and they've been ravenously eating away at the pink frosting. Most of the shiny pink pills are white. I have not seen an ant anywhere in my room. Only inside my Prempro case, running up and down the plastic hills between the pills. How do they know there is this little yummy cache of pills in my cosmetic bag?

The next day, Fon tells me that we are going somewhere at 12:30. She mimes that we are going to eat. I assume she's taking me to lunch.

At 12:25 I emerge from my room. Fon and four other women are sitting on mats in the middle of the dining area, looking and sounding a lot like Balinese women before a ceremony. They are cutting banana leaves into circles and stapling them, with metal staples, into little baskets, open at the top. The women are talking nonstop as women do all over the world when they get together in their shared work efforts.

Hmmmm. If there are party baskets, there must be a party.

"No now. Later," says Fon. "Two."

"Mai mi peng haaaa." I say. No problem. There is a murmur and approval from the crowd at my attempt to speak the language. How I wish I could converse.

I join the women on the mat. They nod and smile and say things I don't understand. One of the women puts a bag of leafy basil stems in front of me. Fon removes a stem and shows me how to strip the leaves off and put them in a bowl.

It's been fourteen years since I was in that Zapotec village in Oaxaca stripping oregano leaves from their stems. I have been all over the world, learned two languages, cooked and slept and celebrated and wept on mountains, in palaces, in cities and in swamps . . . and I'm still stripping leaves off of stems. And I still love feeling included.

The woman sitting next to me is uncharacteristically fat for a Thai. She points to me and then herself and says something in Thai.

"Same big," translates Fon. I smile at the dubious bonding and reach out to shake the woman's hand. We all laugh.

At around two, Fon puts the banana-leaf baskets into a big plastic garbage bag. I put the basil leaves into a small one. We are ready to go. I have no idea where.

We ride along the empty beach on Fon's motorcycle. Clearly visible in his gilded dress is the Buddha on the hill, gazing benevolently at the pristine blue bay. All is well.

Less than a mile from the bungalows, Fon turns onto a muddy path, bouncing and splashing through clay-colored mud. To our left, on a grassy spot about twenty yards from the road, there is a crowd of about twenty-five women sitting and standing on six large mats, orange and green and yellow and red. Other women are setting up pots on burners.

Most of the activity is among the mat women who are preparing the ingredients: washing, chopping, slicing, pounding, grinding, peeling. Talking, shouting, chattering, conferring, and calling out orders.

On the perimeter of the mats are dozens of stainless and aluminum pots and giant blackened woks. There are stands attached to gas tanks waiting for the pots, tubs of ice storing fish and uncooked meats, pails of water for washing, and bottles of water and tubs of soda for drinking. There are dishes and glasses and cutlery for hundreds of people. And dozens of people, mostly women, sharing the work. The scene is my dream come true.

There are about nine dishes being prepared at once, and each of those dishes has someone in charge and a team of workers. In addition, there are general helpers who chop when they see something that needs chopping and slice when faced with a pile of meat or a mound of bamboo shoots. The excitement builds as piles of food become pot-ready ingredients.

Everyone is eager for me to taste the things I'm not familiar with, so I walk around on the mats, barefoot, catching eyes, motioning for permission to taste. *"Chan yak lien ahan Thai,"* I say. I want to learn to cook Thai food. They nod and smile and let me taste whatever they have in front of them. I'm not at all sure they understand my awkward Thai; I have learned the words, but not the music of the language.

One woman is squooshing a brown liquid filled with seeds and strings. It is the sour tamarind, a pod with pulpy seeds inside, that is being squeezed into a liquid.

Another woman is stirring a huge bowl of cut-up fish and coconut milk. Stirring and stirring with an energy that seems tireless. She's been doing it since we arrived. Coconut milk and fish. Why all this stirring? I watch and discover that as she stirs, the mixture gets thicker. Then she calls to someone who dumps a huge bagful of hot red paste into the bowl. She continues stirring. Then more coconut milk is poured in and the stirring continues.

"Ho mok," says the woman, naming the dish. I smile.

"Aloi," says Fon. Delicious.

I notice that my basil and our baskets are next to this woman.

As the preparations conclude, the background music changes from chopping noises to the hiss of gas burners. The cooking begins.

Fon calls me to a briskly boiling pot filled with an orange liquid. They have already put in the chili paste and the chicken chopped into bite-size pieces and the bags of coconut milk. A woman is stirring as her team adds more chili paste and tiny eggplants and basil leaves. And fish sauce. The stirring continues. I taste, encouraged by Fon and the cook. It is what Thai restaurants in the U.S. call "red chicken curry." It's hot and delicious. I have forgotten to bring a tissue for my runny nose.

Very quickly the piles of prepared vegetables, chopped meats, bags of paste and sugar and sauces disappear into pots. Most of the action has moved to the fires, but the woman making *ho mok* is still stirring the fish and coconut milk. The mixture now has the consistency of soft mashed potatoes. Then finally, after she has been stirring for more than forty minutes, she adds strips of kaffir lime leaves, stirs a little more, and begins to spoon the mixture into our banana-leaf baskets. First five or six of *my* basil leaves are placed in the bottom of each basket; and then the fish-coconut mixture is scooped in. Each basket is topped off with a tiny strip of red chili.

The baskets are then placed side by side in two huge aluminum steamer trays, until there are dozens of little green baskets crowded up next to each other. And finally, both racks are placed above boiling water and covered.

Fon and I wander from pot to pot, watching the cooks stirring and calling out to their teams for the various ingredients. Fon tells me the names of each dish and I write them down along with the ingredients.

The chicken curry dish is finished and carried over to a wooden platform that is piling up with cooked food. Already there are little fried squids, a plate of raw, cut-up cucumbers and string beans, and a platter of fried fish. The *kang som,* a sour curry with bamboo and tamarind arrives. So does the *pad mie,* noodles with shallots, bean sprouts, tiny garlicky scallions, and a tamarind-sugar mixture.

The pork dishes are still cooking when Fon says, *"Ho mok, ho mok. Ma."* Come.

The first batch of steamed fish in banana-leaf baskets has come out of the steamer and they are brought to the platform. Fon rushes over and gets one for each of us. I spoon out a bit of the spicy *ho mok,* laced with kaffir lime leaf strips and sitting in basil. It is pure heaven. The fish and the coconut milk have blended into a thick, firm, mousse. I have never tasted anything so wonderful in my life.

One by one the pots of cooked food are placed on the platform. The different cooks pull me over to their creations and watch proudly as I taste each one. We are speaking without words in the language of food. They can see the pleasure in my eyes, the satisfaction in my smile, the look of joy on my face.

"Aloi mak mak," I keep repeating. And it's true. Everything is wonderful. Each dish is different in taste and texture from the others. What an incredible experience. I am more than ever convinced that Thai food is the most complex and spectacular cuisine in the world.

Soon, the community arrives to eat. Up until now, it's been just the cooks. After the eating, there is a ceremony at a small temple nearby. This whole event is to honor and pay homage to a particular deity whose statue is in a nearby cave. (At the time I didn't have a clue; three months later, when I am back in Seattle, Jip explains it to me.) For many hours after the meal, women dance, music blares, people pray.

The women who did the cooking pull me into the dancing and I circle with them, moving my feet in the simple step. But I am not interested in the dancing or the ceremony or the music. It is the *ho mok* I am thinking about; I must learn how to make it. Suddenly I know that *ho mok* is the reason I have come to Thailand. It is the dish I am going to take with me around the world, shouting its brilliance and cooking it for people I love.

A few mornings later, I am riding with Fon on her motorcycle when we pass through a coconut grove.

"Monkeys?" I ask. Jip has told me about the monkeys who harvest coconuts.

Fon nods. Before long we are standing with a group of farmers watching coconuts drop from a tree that must be seventy feet tall. One of the men is holding a long string that ends at the top of the tree.

Then the coconuts stop dropping and a little brown monkey scurries down. It has a white forehead, dark eyes, furry jowls, and a curly black tail. The monkey joins the man holding the string. As we stand there, a motorcycle comes out of a driveway. The driver is wrapped in monkeys, two sitting in front of him and another behind, the way families often sit when they go for rides.

Fon and I return home and I discover there's another guest. He's a young Thai man who speaks English quite well. I am full of language questions, and when I discover he's a friend of the family, I ask him about the meetings I've seen in the evenings. Two nights this week four or five people have gathered around a table with paper and notebooks and folders. One night Fon pointed out that one of the group was talking on the phone to a radio station. She was listening in the kitchen.

The guest, Patom, tells me that Somkit (Fon's father) is the leader of a group of citizens who are protesting the building of a power plant just north of the village. He has carried their fight onto television and in the newspapers and is a well-known figure in Thailand. Several years ago the government built a similar plant in a valley up north. The fish died and the blue water turned black, says Patom.

"The builders are the government in partnership with a huge Japanese company. The protesters have delayed the building for two years, but the fight is not over."

"Is it dangerous for Somkit to be the leader of this group?" I ask.

"Maybe," says Patom, "but the people protect him. Everybody loves him."

On Friday of my second week, Manit calls me into the kitchen and tells me that we are going to cook *ho mok*. The ingredients are on the table. So are a stack of banana-leaf baskets. While Ei makes the hot orange paste in the mortar, I am given my first job: picking off the leaves from basil stems.

While I am doing the basil, Manit takes a big white bass out of the refrigerator; it's two feet long and fat. She removes the center bone and cuts the meat off of the skin into bite-size pieces. She ends up with a huge pile of fish about the size of a giant coconut.

The last bit of preparation is slivering the kaffir lime leaves into needle-size strips. I can do that too.

And then comes the miracle of *ho mok*. The fish meat is put into a big aluminum pot with two liters of coconut milk. I am given a short stool, six inches off the ground, and a thick spine from the center of a palm leaf that is more than two feet long. I hold the pot between my feet on the floor in front of me and I begin to stir, briskly, mimicking the woman at the "big cook," holding the top of the spine more or less in one position with one hand while moving the bottom of the mixer with the other hand, around and around. After five minutes, the mixture begins to thicken. A few minutes later, Manit comes over and decides it is time for more coconut milk. I continue to stir. From time to time Manit checks the consistency.

When the mixture is about the thickness of thin mashed potatoes, Manit adds a large bag of orange paste, about two cups of it. Then Manit takes over the stirring with new energy, thoroughly combining the fish with the paste. Toward the end she adds some very thin coconut milk, maybe a half cup . . . and a few minutes later, another half cup, until she is pleased with the consistency.

The final addition is a handful of the slivered kaffir lime leaves, which are thoroughly mixed in. Then we begin to fill the baskets.

Manit puts a handful of basil leaves into each basket and the mixture is spooned on top of the basil. Then the baskets are placed next to each other in an aluminum steamer tray and the whole thing is placed on top of briskly boiling water in the steamer pot. And covered. After about fifteen minutes, Manit lifts the top, pokes one of the fillings and lets it cook a few minutes more before she lifts the steamer tray off the pot. A second tray filled with baskets is placed over the water.

I am the first to taste the treasure. It is exquisite. The bits of fish have become that sensational coconut-milk fish mousse. The texture is amazing. *Ho mok,* a gastronomical miracle. Where does it get its custardy texture, its mousse-y lightness? There are no eggs in here. No flour. No cornstarch or baking powder. Apparently it's all in the stirring. That's the secret, endless stirring.

I hope I can make it when I'm no longer in Thailand, when banana-leaf baskets are aluminum foil, and coconut milk comes from cans. When the basil has a different flavor. And kaffir lime leaves are hard to find.

If I can't eat *ho mok* in the West, I may have to spend the rest of my life in Thailand. *Ho mok* is that good.

A few days later, I spend the morning with Fon's five-year-old son, Boat. We have sung "Do, re, mi, fa, so, la, ti, do" about twenty times, backwards and forwards. We have named—in English—the colors in a striped umbrella. We have played the "pile the hands on the table" game, and snuggled, and sung songs.

We've also viewed all the screen savers in Windows 98 (we both like the fish the best, though the mystery house comes in a close second for him). We've written his name and the names of all his cousins in every size and font we could find. And we've played dozens of games of one-card-at-a-time solitaire. He likes that gush of cards when you win. So do I.

Now we are playing a sound game that we've played before. He says *"saparot,"* which is the Thai word for pineapple. I repeat it. Then he changes the last syllable, *"sapalit"* and I say *"sapanit"* and he says *"sapame"* and I say *"sapaboo"* and on and on until it gets wild and we end the game.

Boat used to try to have conversations with me but he has given up. I can't respond. I'm not sure he understands that I speak a different language. More likely he thinks I'm just dumb, literally and figuratively. I do a lot of grunting and *mmm*'ing. But even so, we manage to have fun.

A few days later, the cool comes. As I walk along the water, a fierce wind blows my three-inch hair strands as though they were flowing locks.

Overnight the weather has changed from oppressively hot to breezy and cool.

The same day, a group of men check in. They are dressed casually, but they are obviously businessmen, a mix of ages and statuses. They are eating at the next table, peeking at Nek and me as we work on her English in front of the computer. I wonder who they are and what they do. The next morning, I find out.

It is before eight when I see one of them across the street, standing on the sand, staring out into the sun-blazed sea. I take some coffee and cross over. He is thin and wearing light-rimmed glasses that are fiery with the reflection of the sun. He speaks first. In English.

"I saw that you were teaching English last night. Are you a teacher?"

"I'm a writer," I say. "And you?"

He tells me he is an engineer who works for the government department of power. He and his colleagues are working on the power plant project that Somkit and his committee are protesting.

"Do you know that Somkit, the owner of Rim Haad, is the leader of the protest group?" I ask.

"Yes, I have seen him on television."

"Are you here to meet with him?"

"No. In fact, I was worried when my boss told me we were staying here, but last night I talked to Somkit and he said it is no problem."

I am amazed and skeptical. They are adversaries, these two men. Could it really be as innocent as all this or is there some devious thing going on here?

I have been told that the government is planning to use low-grade coal in the plant, which is a serious air pollutant; and that the hot water that will pour into the sea from the plant will kill the fish and the coral in the water. There is a similar plant in the north that has ruined the air and destroyed the marine life.

He tells me that the plant in the north is in a valley where the bad air gets trapped. The new plant will be in an open space and the pollutants will disperse. He also says that they will try to cool the water before it enters the sea.

"We have shown Somkit our proposal. He told me last night that he has read it and he doesn't trust the words."

I don't either.

That same night, the people in Ban Krud are preparing for Loy Gathong, a full-moon festival that contrasts poignantly with the massive power plant that is certain to pollute the water. The festival honors the goddess of the river. On the night of the full moon, people thank her for providing the water that sustains them and ask the goddess for forgiveness if they have misused her gift.

It is after dark when Fon, eight kids, and I begin making our boats by wrapping slices of a porous banana-tree trunk with strips of banana leaves, and then decorating the green boats with flowers and colorful buds and petals. When our creations are finished, Fon adds a candle and three sticks of incense to each one and we go off to the river.

We carry our offerings through the crowd, across a bridge, and down a little hill to the edge of the water. Then we light the candles and the incense, hold the boat between our hands, and kneel. I pray silently to the river goddess that she will continue to provide us with water, I ask for her forgiveness if I have misused her gift. And finally, I implore her to help Somkit win his fight against the power plant. Then I place my boat with the hundreds of others in the river.

Even with the full moon, the night is dark. The flowered boats, their flames flickering, float down the river to the sea, in grateful thanks for the gift of water. How beautiful.

I am packing to go back to New Zealand when Fon comes to get me. A couple from Austria have checked in for the night and they've ordered lunch. The chopped pork dish they were served was supposed to have been a tomato salad. It's right there on the menu . . . tomato salad. That's what they ordered. But no one has ever ordered a tomato salad before. The cooks didn't know how to make it, so they made this pork dish. The woman is a vegetarian.

I talk to the woman and tell Fon that I will make the woman's lunch. I put together a salad with tomatoes, cucumbers, scallions, celery, onions, and cabbage. I flavor it with vinegar, oil, lime juice, salt, sugar, and lightly chopped chilies. The woman loves it. The next day I make her a western breakfast.

"Lita no go New Zealand," says Fon. "Stay Lim Haad. Cook Amelican."

The next night Fon and Manit make me a good-bye party. The kids are wonderfully solicitous, filling my Pepsi glass, giving me bits of meat that is cooking at the table, serving me every time a new dish comes out. Obviously, they are sorry to see me go. We didn't have a language in common, but there was plenty of communication ... through cooking, English classes, my computer, and hugs.

The next morning, five kids and Fon are up at 6:30 to get me to the bus. We arrive a few minutes early and Fon hands me a gift-wrapped package.

"Should I open it?" I charade. She nods.

It's a box with five beautiful pens.

"Write book," says Fon.

I kiss her, I hug the kids, and I tell them I'm going to miss them. I doubt that they know the words, but I'm sure they understand.

United States

CHAPTER NINETEEN

A JOURNEY
STILL IN PROCESS

It's a cool day in December and I have just returned to New Zealand from Thailand. Judy stopped by two hours ago to say that some of the neighbors were getting together for a beach cleanup.

It's a funny little beach, just down the hill from Marian's house, probably twenty-five by fifteen feet, set off from the water by a stone wall and a hill. Every spring the town council fills the area with sand for the summer, and every winter heavy tides surge over the stone wall and wash away the sand, leaving a tangled mess of debris, a gift from the ocean.

Summer is coming and it's time to clean up. Marian and I are raking leaves and grass into piles with heavy, short-toothed rakes, separating the rocks from the driftwood and vines that will go into the fire. Judy and Arn are pulling weeds. Several other neighbors are tossing rocks and tending the fire, which is spiking yellow smoke from the wet grasses and salty driftwood. This is a community that cares. I feel lucky to be a part of it.

For the next month, I write, play, go to the gym, and welcome in the millennium with fireworks, friends, and food. I am leaving soon; I have no choice. My visa is up in mid-February.

Packing is easy. I don't have very much. But I have to decide what to do with Old Blue. I paid five hundred U.S. dollars for her and I've gotten more than my money's worth.

I call up Ray and ask him if he'd like her back.

"No, thank you," he says. "Give her to someone who can't afford to buy a car."

I'm still thinking when Ray calls back. "Let's both give the car to Manaia School. They can auction it and use the money for whatever they want."

"Great idea," I say. "But I don't want the money to go for desks or furniture or stuff like that. I think there should be strings, Ray. You're a literary agent and I'm a writer. Why don't we ask that the money go for books."

I can hear his smile through the phone.

Vicki, the principal, and I work it out. On the day I leave, Marian follows me to Manaia School. The door to the playground has been left open so Old Blue can enter. I drive her in slowly and stop on the play area right outside the office.

"Hi, Rita," call the kids when I get out of the car, the same as they do when they see me in town.

I go into the office and sign the transfer papers. Meanwhile, the kids assemble outside. They sing me a song in the Maori language, present me with a pair of carved bone earrings (a Maori craft) and a silver fern pin (the symbol of New Zealand). I say goodbye to Vicki, to the teachers, to the kids, and to Old Blue, who served me well. I am thrilled that she will be turned into books. Like Old Blue, the robin, she too will make her contribution to the community.

The kids follow us out of the playground, waving and calling as Marian and I drive away in her car toward the airport.

And soon, I'm off. To Seattle to visit Jan. To Atlanta, where Mitch and Melissa have recently moved. And finally, to New York, where I have sublet a furnished apartment for a year while I work on my book.

And when the book is finished? Then what? I have no idea. I'm not thinking about the future. While I'm here, wherever that may be (at the moment, it's the library in New York), I want to be 100 percent here. One of the most important things I have learned during the last fifteen years is how to enjoy and savor the present. When I am writing, I am inside the sound and meaning of the words, playing with them, curving them around each other. When I am eating, I luxuriate in the taste and texture of every bite. When I am alone, I listen to and communicate with the silence within me and the noises and messages of the world around me.

And when I am with people, I am really with them. After fifteen years of moving through the world, people are still my passion. I love the constantly budding and blossoming friendships that define my life. Like the rice plants in Bali that are always in all stages of growth (to keep the giant from eating the children "after the harvest"), my friendships with people all over the world are also in all stages of development. I have old friends, new friends, evolving friends, serial friends.

I use the word *friend* loosely, to refer to people I connect with. Wherever I am and whatever the length of our relationship, connection is what I seek. Whether we share a language or simply a shape, I reach out to each individual with love and trust, with a smile, and 100 percent of my attention. Communication is not difficult because we all share the sensations of human emotions, the need to affirm our sameness, and the universal capacity to laugh.

As I reflect on the last fifteen years, I am sitting in the autumn sun a few feet from the lions in front of the New York Public Library. I have been a hermit in Manhattan for the last eight months, living alone, writing in the Allen Room (a wonderful room for writers in the library), and rarely seeing or talking to anyone.

I have intentionally stayed away from friends and family, knowing that I needed to reenter the places I was writing about and interact once again with the people who were such an important part of my nomadic life. And I did. I laughed again at my ragged tortillas and wailed with the woman who was holding her dead baby. I sang in the mountains, fell in the mud, and blew bubbles with a little boy and his mother in the middle of New Guinea. I ate green mussels and gloried in *ho mok* and whizzed through Bali on the back of Wayan's motorcycle. And I communed with Tu Aji's spirit.

When the final words are written, I will think about my next destination. I have no idea where it will be. Probably someplace where they speak Spanish or Indonesian...or English. Maybe I will buy a van and fill it with books and zigzag my way around the United States, a national nomad, staying with families, talking to clubs, visiting bookstores and schools, reading from and signing my book. Hopefully I will find homes to stay in and people to connect with.

I will make myself alert once more to the kinds of chance encounters that are always out there. I turned them off when I began writing; soon I will pay attention to them again and see where they lead me.

I am already taking notes for a web page (www.ritagoldengelman.com) where I will fill in gaps (like a list of my kids' books) and a couple of useful addresses. I'm hoping to keep an ongoing account on the site of where I am and what I'm doing. I'll put in a section of anecdotes that were cut from the book and another of countries that didn't make it. I'll also offer some practicalities of my kind of travel, such as, be sure to take itch cream and plastic bags and arrange automatic payment plans for your bills.

I have already set up an e-mail address (femalenomad@ritagoldengelman.com) so my readers can reach me and I can connect with them. My editor is worried. Suppose I get millions of e-mails? I'll deal with it when it happens. If there are millions of e-mails, I'll have enough money to hire a helper.

It's exciting to think that all over the world, new and old friends will be reading my book and "talking" to me via e-mail.

I can't wait to hear from you.

ACKNOWLEDGMENTS

The paradox of my independent, liberated life is that I could not live it without the help and support of many, many people. I am, in fact, extremely dependent on the generosity of others. During the past fifteen years, people all over the world have opened their homes and their hearts; they have shared their families, their meals, their fires, their ceremonies. They are too numerous to list. Thank you all.

Special thanks to Bob and Elaine Friedman, Susan Lechner, Debby Barr, Susan and Joel Buxbaum, Mickie Friedman, Irv Golden, Nancy and Morris Zaslavsky, June and Jay Zorn, Marianne Vecsey, Judy Sanders, Barbara and Ray Richards, Bron Richards, John Henderson, Jip Chitnarong, Judy and Arn Piesse, Jean Wells, Christine Leov-Leland, Jocelyn Davey, Vicki Sephton, Tu Biang, Dayu Biang, Jero Made, Ida Ayu Mayuni, Ida Ayu Raka, Wayan Sukerta, Scott Drinkwater, Gera and Andres Todeschini, Edith and Leo Quiroga, Carmen Natale, Asunta Natale, Amparo Jaramillo, Lisa Kramer, Lars Johansson, Nirina Rakoto, Yafa Kfir, Batsheva and Gabi Barshi, Claudia Joenck, Diana Estrin, María Esther de la Rosa Duque, Lily You, Lisa Rifkin, Michael Franzblau, Chou Chou Grant, Howard Lefkowitz, Nancy Lamb, Mary Anne Stewart, Sue Yung, and Stephen Selder.

I feel very fortunate to have fallen into the able hands and sharp mind of my editor, Emily Loose, my amazingly talented and available agent, Elaine Markson, and their assistants who never said no, Caroline Sincerbeaux and Gary Johnson.

Without the security of knowing that my brother Dick, and his family, Margaret, Danielle, and Michelle (Kelly) were there for my parents, I could never have disappeared for such long stretches of time. My thanks to them.

And to Melissa, who came into our family and made it better.

And finally, my deepest thanks and gratitude to Jan and Mitch, who took care of my mail, my bills, my books; who always welcomed me, dirty laundry and all; and who gave up their mom so I could live this extraordinary life. I love you.

A FINAL NOTE TO THE READER:

The people, places, events, and adventures that I write about are all real. But for many different reasons, I have changed quite a few of the names. Occasionally I have avoided identifying places as well. And from time to time I have taken liberty with the chronology, sometimes for narrative reasons, sometimes so that I could compress several trips into one, and sometimes because I can't remember the exact order of the various ceremonies, events, or meals.

There are passages in the Nicaragua chapter that have previously appeared in my book *Inside Nicaragua: Young People's Dreams and Fears* (which is out of print).

INDEX

(A GEOGRAPHICAL NOTE FROM THE AUTHOR: Bear in mind as you look through the Indonesia citations that Irian Jaya is the western half of the island of New Guinea. Kalimantan is on the island of Borneo. Bali is its own island. And Yogyakarta is a city on the island of Java. They are all part of the country of Indonesia.)

INDEX